THE LOCALES FRAMEWORK

The Kluwer International series on Computer Supported Cooperative Work

Volume 1

The Locales Framework

Understanding and Designing for Wicked Problems

by

Geraldine Fitzpatrick
Sapient Ltd,
London, United Kingdom

Springer-Science+Business Media, B.V.

A C.I.P. Catalogue record for this book is available from the Library of Congress.

ISBN 978-90-481-6253-6 ISBN 978-94-017-0363-5 (eBook)
DOI 10.1007/978-94-017-0363-5

Printed on acid-free paper

Originally published by Kluwer Academic Publishers in 2003.
Softcover reprint of the hardcover 1st edition 2003

Contents

Preface ix

Part I Introduction

1. THE WICKED PROBLEM OF DESIGN 3
   - 1.1 Systems Design as a Wicked Problem 4
   - 1.2 A Research Narrative 7
2. THE CSCW DESIGN CHALLENGE 15
   - 2.1 Understanding Cooperative Work 15
   - 2.2 Designing Systems 28
   - 2.3 The Understanding - Designing Dialogue 36
   - 2.4 Summary 42

Part II Evolution to the Locales Framework

3. THE WORLDS SYSTEM 49
   - 3.1 A Brief wOrlds Tour 51
   - 3.2 Summary 53
4. SYSTEMS ENGINEERS AT WORK 55
   - 4.1 Appearance of Work in Isolation 56
   - 4.2 Breakdowns in Work 59
   - 4.3 Summary 62
5. HOW SYSTEMS ENGINEERS ACCOMPLISH WORK 63
   - 5.1 Making Sense of an Unknowable Environment 64
   - 5.2 Working with Workspace Characteristics 66

5.3 Work Around Strategies 71
5.4 Summary 74

6. MOVING FROM SPACE TO PLACE 77
6.1 Ethnography to Design 78
6.2 wOrlds Away From the Systems Engineers' World 78
6.3 From Space to Place in Systems Design 84
6.4 Summary 86

Part III The Locales Framework

7. INTRODUCTION TO THE LOCALES FRAMEWORK 89
7.1 Locale as Unit of Analysis 90
7.2 Overview of Framework Aspects 92
7.3 Centres and Perspectives 93
7.4 Summary 95

8. LOCALES FRAMEWORK ASPECTS 97
8.1 Locale Foundations 98
8.2 Civic Structure 108
8.3 Individual Views 115
8.4 Interaction Trajectory 120
8.5 Mutuality 130
8.6 Summary 140

9. LOCALES FRAMEWORK APPROACH 143
9.1 Related Approaches 143
9.2 Using the Locales Framework 148
9.3 Summary 151

Part IV Working with the Locales Framework

10. DISTRIBUTED RESEARCH WORK: A TALE OF TWO GROUPS 155
10.1 Introducing the Internet Exploration Unit (IEU) 156
10.2 Introducing the Romany Initiative 160
10.3 Key Features of Collaboration 162
10.4 Conclusions and Reflections 168

11. DESIGNING FOR TELEHEALTH 171
11.1 Current Intra-ICU Practice 172
11.2 Current Remote Consultation Practice 174
11.3 Evolving a Telehealth System in Practice 183
11.4 Conclusions and Reflections 186

12. CSCW ENVIRONMENT DESIGN: ORBIT AND TICKERTAPE 189
12.1 Evolving Orbit 189
12.2 The Coincidental Tickertape Lesson 196
12.3 Summary 199

13. CONCLUSIONS, REFLECTIONS AND FUTURE WORK 203
13.1 Review of the Locales Framework 204
13.2 Reflections on Using the Framework 205
13.3 Moving Forward — Future Work 211
13.4 Postscript: Reflections from a Distance 214
13.5 Conclusion 221

References 223

Index 239

Preface

So much technology works, not by good design or by being a good fit to purpose, but because people make it work because they have to for some reason. We humans are incredibly creative and resourceful when it comes to getting something done. There are numerous stories we could all tell of the ingenious work-arounds we've developed to make something do what we want it to; or the enormous amount of time we've spent trying to find out how to make some technology work as we want, e.g., trying to find out how to turn off auto-editing commands in a word processing package when all we want is for it to 'do what we tell it'.

A good example of this principle was what motivated me to switch from neural networks to the area of Computer Supported Cooperative Work (CSCW) for my PhD research. I had undertaken a case study looking at the deployment of a multi-million dollar health information system throughout a hospital network. I could not believe that so much money had been spent to support the accounting and management functions of the hospitals with so little support provided to the nurses, doctors and allied staff on the ground who had to feed the system with information. Not only was this huge investment not supportive of clinical staff, it negatively impacted their practice by demanding extra time and effort to enter duplicate information into the system, time they would have much preferred to give to patient care. The clinicians still managed somehow to deliver quality care *and* to feed the system but how much better accounting and management information could have been captured if the core of support was for clinical health care delivery not the retrospective accounting of the outcomes of such care.

My fundamental concern became the creation of technologies that fitted with people and that actually helped not hindered what it is they wanted to do. Maybe it was because I came to my computer science degree having had another career in the messy event-drive world of healthcare that I couldn't quite buy the neat abstractions and conceptualisations that underpinned a lot of systems development, no matter how seductive they were nor how much they simplified the task of design by having everything nicely bound up and organised. I didn't believe the messiness of the real world could be dealt with like that. By chance, my husband Mark came across an article that mentioned CSCW and he said it sounded like me (or at least sounded like it was concerned with the sorts of issues I had been chewing his ear about). With little more information than that, I switched at the last minute to CSCW for my research area.

From the very early days, there has been much written in CSCW and related literatures about the importance of both 'social' and 'technical' considerations for good systems design. In the case of CSCW, this was specifically targeted at supporting those people who worked together, often at a distance, and who were engaged in complex unpredictable collaborative activities. The turn to social science approaches as a way to understand social concerns and embrace the messiness of situations was particularly appealing for understanding such situations. To this day, how to embrace both social and the technical concerns for good systems design continues to be a topic that engages the community.

Not only does it engage the research community, but it is also an issue in industry, something I've experienced first-hand working in Sapient as a user experience researcher. We try to apply many of the 'social' approaches to understanding a range of client audiences and their needs and then have to convey this understanding to a multi-disciplinary team, working with them to design a 'good' solution. The issues here are brought into sharper relief compared with a research context because of the tight time and resource constraints involved in delivering to contract within commercial contexts.

This book is a contribution to this ongoing dialogue about how to design systems for the purposes of supporting people at work or play, and how to understand people's needs for the purposes of design. While much of the work underpinning the book was conducted some years ago, it is still entirely relevant. The main reason is that the very nature of the problem we are dealing with here — how to design systems that fit with people — is an example of a wicked problem where we never find *the* answer but learn more about both the nature of the problem itself and possible solutions through trial and error. I present the *Locales Framework* here as one possible solution. The *Locales Framework* is a shared abstraction that can sit in-between social and technical concerns and mediate communication between the two. I tell the story of the *Locales Framework* as a journey progressing through our own group's experiences with designing a collaboration system and trying to understand the needs of a group of people for whom we wished to deploy it, and then trying to use the framework in practice for understanding and designing. I tell the story as a journey to make explicit the experiences and concepts that fed into the development and use of the framework so that, in keeping with the wicked problem characterisation, others can learn from it and come up with yet better possible solutions, continuing the journey at the broader community level.

While it was tempting to re-write the journey from scratch from the position of current experience, I have focussed instead on revising it and shortening it to make it more readable, though I have brought in references to more recent literature where appropriate. While it is still a considerable number of chapters, they are written in a way that should make it easy to skip over some should the reader desire; for example, the case studies showing use of the framework are presented in separate chapters that are relatively self-contained. Further, the long discussion of each of the five aspects of the framework uses a number of devices that enables the discussion to be read to different levels of detail. It is worth pointing out now that, for the sake of arguments, I have used a number of rhetorical devices, such as talking about 'understanding' and 'designing' as if they were distinct activities. Wanting to embrace messiness and complexity, I do not believe that such distinctions and dichotomies actually exist either in practice or in the characterisation of the people involved. I invite the reader to consider these seeming dichotomies as if they are end points of a continuum where no such obvious boundaries exist but where it is perhaps possible to characterise the extremes for the sake of the discussion.

The main change from any previous discussions of the *Locales Framework* is in the articulation of the *mutuality* aspect. In the original formulation, I talked of presence and awareness, trying to pull apart the dual aspects required for awareness to be achieved, i.e., that some information has to be available to be perceived and that some perception of this information has to happen. The more recent work of my good friend Toni Robertson (2002) and Heath et al., (2002) provided a way to more clearly articulate these concerns. I now make it much clearer that awareness is an achieved outcome and talk instead of provision and perception as the informational and interactional processes entailed in awareness.

So, in short, the contribution of this book is not just the articulation of the *Locales Framework* as a shared abstraction for understanding and designing, but also the journey through which this framework has been developed and applied. It is presented as a contribution to the ongoing dialogue about designing systems that are better at fitting into the everyday lives of people they seek to support and transform.

Acknowledgements

A book is never produced by one person alone even if single authorship gives that impression. This book is no exception. There are so many friends, family and colleagues to thank for seeing me through the production of this book and the original work reported on here.

First and foremost, I am indebted to the generosity of my employer, Sapient Ltd, and to Colin Windsor in particular, for agreeing to give me the time and support to engage in this writing process. Many other Sapient colleagues, too many to mention, contributed in different ways as well, whether covering for work or helping me negotiate my way through the system.

Robbert van Berckelaer from Kluwer and Richard Harper, the editor, have provided much needed encouragement and support and pushed me to get finished, albeit later than they really wanted! Thank you for your patience.

Some colleagues have been encouraging me for years to turn the thesis into a book. They'll be pleased to know their nagging wasn't in vain. Thank you Kjeld Schmidt, Saul Greenberg, Volker Wulf, Tom Rodden, Kari Kutti, Bob Colomb, and Simon Kaplan for your encouragement. More generally, I'm very proud to be part of such an inspiring and collegial peer community, as the CSCW community is (and, too, HCI).

There are many other people to thank for their on-the-ground support. Yvonne Rogers has been an invaluable friend and support and also provided insightful feedback on drafts of some chapters, feedback I've tried to incorporate into this final version. Simon and Liza-Jane McBride provided much-needed sanity breaks; thanks for fun times, good food and wine, and your general support throughout.

For the conduct of the original work, I am indebted to Simon Kaplan, my supervisor for the major part of the PhD process, for enabling me to pursue odd ideas in a computer science department and to Tim Mansfield, my 'unofficial' associate supervisor and friend, for hours of discussions and making me articulate the ideas in my head that became the *Locales Framework*. I also had the pleasure of working with some great people at the University of Queensland, the Distributed Systems Technology Centre and the University of Illinois at Urbana Champaign, who provided stimulating supportive work groups over the years: including Jim Welsh, Ted Phelps, Rik Taylor, Bill Tolone, Doug Bogia, Andrew Loch, Bill Segall, Dave Arnold, Toni Robertson, and Storm Griffin. Thanks, too, to the members of the CSG, IEU and telehealth groups for allowing me the privilege of studying them as they went about their work and for being so generous with their time and knowledge.

For always being there for me regardless, I am indebted to both the Martin and Fitzpatrick families, Vonnie and Helen in particular. Dad and Gerry, sorry you're not here to see it. So Dan, do I get a new T-shirt now?

Most of all, my very special thanks to Mark, my best friend and love, who has endured more than should be asked of any husband and given more than I could ever hope to repay. His never-ending patience, love and encouragement and countless instances of practical support (and eagle-eyed proof-reading) have made the impossible possible ... again!

PART I

INTRODUCTION

Chapter 1

THE WICKED PROBLEM OF DESIGN

Software design is becoming increasingly complex and difficult. Advances in network technologies mean that not only are computers being connected together but so are people via computers. In considering how we might build applications to support people interacting with computers and with each other over networks, the problems to be solved are no longer just technical, e.g., how to distribute computational load over a number of processors; they are also social, e.g., how do we build systems that meet the real needs of the people who are asked to use them and that fit into their contexts of use.

Even if all the technical issues are solved, success is not guaranteed. Remember the old adage about "building the system right" not being the same thing as "building the right system"? There was a time when we could computationally verify that we had built the right thing against some clearly-defined systems requirements translated into formal specifications. This is no longer the case as computers become increasingly connected together into distributed multi-user environments and applications become embedded into people's daily lives and into unpredictable and uncontrollable social contexts of use. Our traditional software engineering techniques for understanding requirements and driving these through into design, such as data modelling or object-oriented modelling, are no longer sufficient in accounting for the complexities and uncertainties inherent in such socially-embedded systems.

This book is about finding an appropriate framework for both understanding requirements of complex social situations and for designing systems to support these situations in all their complexity. To this end, I will be presenting the *Locales Framework* as one possible approach to help us build better systems. A central notion underpinning the framework is that the design of socially-embedded systems is an example of a wicked problem. First then, let me introduce this notion of wicked problems.

1.1. Systems Design as a Wicked Problem

In their paper "Dilemmas in a General Theory of Planning", Rittel and Webber (1973) characterise two classes of problems they call *wicked problems* and *tame problems*. Tame problems are those that can be solved by a sequential process going from complete unambiguous problem definition to correct solution via established methods; tame here is used in the sense of being bounded rather than easy. Many traditional science and engineering problems fall into the category of tame problems.

Wicked problems are very different. They mostly arise in the social realm, where "the aim is not find the truth, but to improve some characteristics of the world where people live" [*op.cit.*, p. 167]. The following are some of the key properties of wicked problems:

- There is no definitive formulation of a wicked problem. The problem is only understood progressively as solutions are developed.
- Because problem definition and solution co-evolve, and because there are no criteria for determining when the problem is adequately defined, wicked problems have no internal stopping rules.
- It is not possible to exhaustively enumerate the set of possible solutions.
- Solutions are never true or false but instead are qualitatively judged as better or worse. A 'satisficing'[1] or 'good enough' solution is the realistic goal.
- There can be no immediate, ultimate, or definitive test of a solution because the consequences can possibly extend across time in any number of ways; also rigorous experimentation of possible solutions is not possible.
- The process of solving a wicked problem is inherently non-linear. Progress is defined qualitatively in terms of how much more is understood about the problem rather than distance from the solution.
- There are a number of stakeholders who are interested in how a wicked problem is solved. Each could make different qualitative judgements about the nature of the problem and the value of the solution.
- Every instance of a wicked problem is essentially unique.
- Every wicked problem can be considered to be a symptom of another problem. The problem should be settled on as high a level as possible.

The design of systems that support human activity, communication and interaction is a wicked problem. More than being an engineering problem, the design of such socio-technical systems is essentially a social realm problem where the systems are meant to fit into complex social contexts and help people in their daily lives, where there are multiple stakeholders from both the development context and the use context, where the definition of the problem and the solution co-evolve over time, and where the solutions can only be judged as better or worse rather than right or wrong.

Hence, I argue that to address this wicked problem of systems design, we need more than traditional software engineering techniques, even though we ultimately want to build hard-coded software systems that, at an engineering level, reduce to a tame problem.

1.1.1 CSCW Design as a Wicked Problem

However complex socio-technical systems are in general, Computer Supported Cooperative Work (CSCW) systems bring particular design challenges. Schmidt and Bannon (1992) define the research area of CSCW as being concerned with *understanding* the nature and requirements of cooperative work and *designing* systems to support that work. I will use the term 'work' here in its broadest sense to include all forms of activity and interaction, the 'work' of everyday living and relating.

The resulting CSCW systems (sometimes called groupware or collaboration tools, especially in commercial contexts) support people engaging in some collaborative activity together, often over a distance. Examples of CSCW systems include workflow systems, shared editing systems, shared drawing tools, shared calendaring tools, shared workspace tools, and so on.

The design problem for CSCW fits easily with a wicked problem characterisation. Because CSCW systems are used by multiple people and because of the interdependent nature of the human activity they support, they are firmly situated in the social and interactional realm. The design motivation is to improve how people work together especially at a distance. The design context is multidisciplinary, involving multiple stakeholders from various social science and technical disciplines. The user context involves numbers of people with individual and group needs. The problem of how to understand what cooperative work means and how to design systems to support that work is an inherently complex one that defies simple definitions and solutions, especially if the lack of pervasive use of CSCW systems despite many years of research[2] is anything to go by.

The history of research into CSCW provides evidence of an *ongoing dialogue* between understanding and designing, between problem definition and potential solutions. This dialogue is taking place at two levels. There is the dialogue at the *community level* about the design problem. From its early days, CSCW literature shows evidence of people collectively engaging in an iterative process of trying to understand the nature of cooperative work, designing systems to support work, evaluating the consequences, and learning how to understand and design in a better way. The evolution of workflow technologies over the years, to be overviewed in Chapter 2, is one example of this.

There is also the *unique instance of the wicked problem* of supporting collaborative work in each specific situation. Within the context of what is currently known at the community level, each specific workplace study, each system design, each evaluation, feeds into an understanding of that specific situation. Each also contributes to the more general community understanding about cooperative work and about new possibilities for system solutions. In this way the dialogue is not only between understanding and designing, but also between the community level and the instance level in engaging with the problem.

While we understand more about supporting cooperative work than we did previously because of this dialogue (which is defined as progress in the solution of a wicked problem), there is still a long way to go. One issue is the problem in communication between understanding and designing. To make this problem more explicit, I want to re-define CSCW as how best to understand work *for the purposes of designing systems*, and how best to design systems *for the purposes of supporting work*. This subtle re-framing changes the orientation of understanding and designing as relatively self-contained activities standing side-by-side to where they are firmly set towards the other and are mutually defined by the other.

1.1.2 The Abstraction Challenge

The CSCW community is a multi-disciplinary one; those concerned with understanding and those concerned with designing tend to come from distinctly different backgrounds, neither of which fully prepares their proponents to work at the intersection of the two areas or to orientate their work towards another discipline. It is not surprising that tensions have arisen among the people from all disciplines.

Computer scientists have found that traditional approaches to requirements analysis and design are not able to account for the contingent complexity of lived cooperative work. They struggle with how to make sense of socially-informed accounts of work and with how to translate 'social' insights, such as the situated nature of work, into the substance of design, see, for example, Bogia et al, (1993b). On the other hand, *social scientists* have found that their traditional perspectives, be they ethnomethodology, distributed cognition, activity theory and so on, are being asked to do a job for systems design that they were never intended to do. They struggle to understand what it is that computer scientists need for design and how to communicate their insights to influence design decisions (see, for example, Plowman et al, 1995).

A source of many of these tensions has been the *role of abstractions* or models in the different world-views. For many social scientists, abstractions are used to describe what has been studied. For computer scientists, abstractions are used more to prescribe and circumscribe the system to be built.

In line with Rittel and Webber's proposal that the problem should be settled on as high a level as possible, it is my contention that a reason for the communication problem is that the stakeholders involved in these different activities – social scientists, computer scientists (and users) – are more used to working in relatively self-contained ways and that they lack a set of *shared abstractions* that can support a mutual orientation between understanding and design and a re-definition of their own activities accordingly.

In a similar vein, Kuuti (1992) suggests that there exists no CSCW-design discipline because there is no appropriate *conceptualisation* of cooperative work that can take account of the emergent and situated features of work and give good design metaphors, i.e., take account of the needs of both 'understand-ers' and designers.

Looking for abstractions that can better facilitate the mutual orientation and dialogue between understanding and designing, and that can also be useful for both activities is a challenge given the differing world views on the role of abstractions; I return to discuss to discuss this challenge in more detail in Chapter 2 after exploring current approaches to understanding and designing respectively.

This book is about continuing the dialogue between understanding and designing, at the community level and at the instance level, not to find *the* answer because there can be no definitive answer, but to help come up with *better abstractions* so that we can gain *better* understanding and do *better* designing.

As such, this is not a traditional computer science text nor a traditional social science text. My agenda is fundamentally pragmatic. I bring together insights from social studies of work as well as an understanding of the needs of systems development to propose the *Locales Framework* as as a principled design framework that allows for construction of shared abstractions among stakeholders (social scientists, computer scientists, users), bridging the gap between social and technical concerns with a common language.

While this framework has been developed in specific dialogue with the CSCW design problem, its principles can be applied more generally to any socio-technical systems design.

1.2. A Research Narrative

For the sake of readability, I structure the book as if it occurred in some logical temporal fashion. However, in practice, multiple threads occurred together and informed and fed into each other. For example, the introduction to the work of Anselm Strauss (1993), the ethnographic study of the group of systems engineers, and the initial prototyping work of a CSCW system called wOrlds took place in parallel. The narrative of the journey told here is intended to better communicate the key issues and lessons learnt from these multiple threads.

It should also be noted that even though I seem to be setting up understanding and designing as distinct activities, I do so as a rhetorical device only to argue the case in this book. There might be activities toward end points of the understanding-designing continuum that are more distinctively one or the other but the conjunction of the two is fuzzily blurred. There might be people engaged in understanding who come from a social sciences background and people engaged in designing systems who come from computer science backgrounds, but often it is more to do with a person's philosophical position on those activities rather than with explicit training; I come from a computer science background, for example, but am deeply interested in how we understand requirements of wicked problem situations for design and how qualitative research approaches can be adopted and adapted for those purposes. In practice, understanding and designing are integrally a part of the other.

The *Locales Framework* story told here is structured in four parts as follows.

Part I: This introductory part continues in Chapter 2 with an overview of the approaches being taken to understanding and designing thus far in the CSCW community. A growing body of ethnographic studies of work gives us a view into the rich complex nature of work but offers little insight into how to actually go about designing and building systems to support such work. On the other hand, there is a plethora of systems designed to support cooperative work, often with little insight into the moment-by-moment nature of the work they wish to support. Many systems focus on a particular isolated task or function such as video conferencing or document co-authoring or structured email. Others are based on idealised abstractions of work processes, such as workflow systems. Yet others have been experimenting with systems based on a metaphor of space.

After overviewing different approaches to both understanding and designing, this chapter concludes with a discussion of the nature of the relationship between understanding and designing, looking at co-evolutionary influences, and arguing that shared abstractions are needed to better facilitate communication between the two in order to better support work.

Part II: Against this broad background of the community-level dialogue between understanding and designing, Part II tells the story of our own experiences with understanding and designing. It describes a project where a space-based CSCW system called wOrlds was developed (Chapter 3). The aim of wOrlds was to support a whole range of cooperative work activities that make up the workaday life of people — from formal to informal, from synchronous to asynchronous, from loosely coupled to tightly coupled, from individual to group work; these were aspects of work that we had learnt to be important from workplace studies reported on by others at the community level.

A further goal was to deploy a version of wOrlds for a group of systems engineers and to this end a qualitative study of the group at work was undertaken so that we could better understand their requirements (we had also learnt from work at the CSCW community level that such studies were better able to uncover important insights about how people work together than our usual software engineering requirements gathering techniques). The work of the systems engineers is described in Chapter 4 and a more detailed analysis follows in Chapter 5 of how they employed characteristics of both their physical and virtual domains in accomplishing their work.

Chapter 6 discusses some of the basic mismatches that we identified from the study between the wOrlds system and how the systems engineers currently worked. Since these mismatches would have constrained rather than enabled their work, plans to deploy the wOrlds system were put on hold. The mismatches lead to the critique of the basic assumptions and interpretations of spatial metaphors as embodied in wOrlds and other similar systems. Reflecting on our own experiences and those more generally, I propose instead that *place* as defined by interactional needs is a more appropriate metaphor for systems design than the simulation of physical space. Together these experiences lead to the development of the *Locales Framework.*

Part III: Part III introduces the *Locales Framework* — and its five aspects of locale foundations, civic structures, individual views, interaction trajectory and mutuality — as a shared abstraction that is better able to deal with the intertwined problem-solution space of wicked problems. Based on a metaphor of place as the lived interaction with space and resources, the *Locales Framework* can provide a coherent mediating framework to facilitate the understanding of the complex workaday world and the design of systems to support this world.

It can do this because the primary unit of analysis and design in the *Locales Framework* is *'locale'*. A locale doesn't exist *a priori* as does a space or a room. A locale is the place constituted in the ongoing *relationship* between people in a particular social world and the 'site and means' they use to meet their interactional needs, i.e., the space together with the resources and things available there, as shown in Figure 1.1. It is because a locale arises in the relationship between a social world and its use of space as place, that it is potentially suitable as a shared abstraction for both understanding and designing, albeit used with slightly different emphases for each: understanding activities can focus on the accomplishment of work within the space, while designing activities can focus on providing computer-based spaces and resources to better support the accomplishment of work.

Chapter 7 introduces these general framework issues, identifying 'locale' as the primary unit of analysis, and defining notions of 'perspectives' and 'centres' as key organising principles.

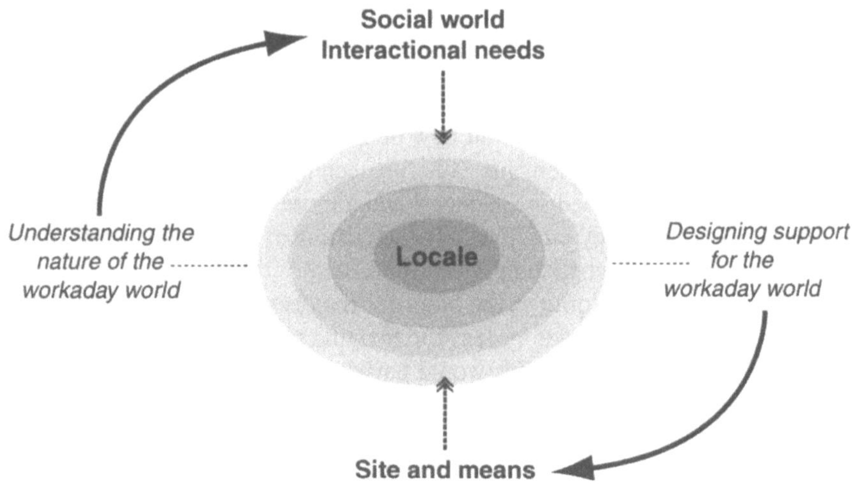

Figure 1.1. A locale, constituted in the relationship between social world and 'site and means', and providing a shared abstraction between understanding and designing.

Written to be read at different levels of detail, Chapter 8 is the core chapter in this book. It explores each of the five aspects of the *Locales Framework* in some detail and uses vignettes from the systems engineers study throughout to illustrate the aspects as appropriate. In summary the five aspects are concerned with the following issues:

- *Locale foundations* identifies the social world of interest and the spaces and resources (interchangeably called site and means) through which the people in the social world achieve their interaction.
- *Civic structure* identifies the relationship of this social world and its locales to the broader context, picking up on social, political, organisational, material, cultural, legislative, contractual, technological and other broader-sphere issues.
- *Individual view* identifies the different perspectives that individuals might hold of the one locale, together with an individual's aggregated view of the multiple locales in which they participate, as appropriate for the domain of interest.
- *Interaction trajectory* is concerned with actions and courses of actions, identifying the dynamic and temporal aspects of the living social world and its interactions within and across locales — past, present and future.
- *Mutuality* is concerned with awareness as an achieved outcome, identifying the mutual communicative processes through which awareness is achieved

— the provision and perception of information for awareness. It considers how spaces and things are made available and accessible to people and how people and their activities are made available and accessible to others through the spaces and things they use as locale.

In the nature of wicked problems, the discussions of these aspects do *not* constitute an exhaustive examination of each. Nor are they presented as complete and self-sufficient. Rather, they are meant to give a flavour of the sorts of issues that could be considered.

The *Locales Framework* aspects themselves are evolved through use by different people and in different understanding and design situations. Chapter 9 highlights the two-phase approach to using the framework for the purposes of understanding and designing, and gives a preamble to the actual use of the framework in Part IV. I also explore other work closely related to the *Locales Framework*.

Together, these five aspects capture the complexity of the workaday world and help position potentially isolated concepts such as 'group' or 'artefact' or 'context' into a coherent organising framework. Ultimately though, it is the questions that frame the particular design context, and the uniqueness of the situation at hand, that determines what issues are relevant, and to what extent the *Locales Framework* is useful for framing initial thinking or for organising complex research data or for framing design directions. What the framework provides is the broader locale context: by analogy, the focus given by the question at hand is like looking through a fish-eye lens onto the locale. Whereas a zoom lens excludes all but the focus from view, a fish-eye lens keeps the focus always in relationship to its broader locale context.

The main benefits provided by the *Locales Framework* can be summarised as the following:

- A common language for understanding and designing; a common approach for describing what is as well as envisioning what could be
- Potential to consider issues from group to individual, local setting to global context, micro scale to macro scale, and structure to process
- Applicability to a wide variety of spaces, physical, virtual or mixed
- A focus on the use of space and its affordances for support of interaction, space and its affordances being the very technologies that CSCW is concerned with building
- A framework rich enough to be sensitising to key elements of a collaborative environment but sufficiently generic, open and incomplete so as not to prescribe nor circumscribe all that is of interest

Part IV: Part IV begins the dialogue between understanding and designing arising from experiences of using the *Locales Framework* in practice for two cases studies and for the design of a collaboration system. Chapter 10 tells the story of a group of distributed researchers who were supposed to be developing closer collaborations following a directive from management. The *Locales Framework* was used for explaining why these collaborations did not come about, while at the same time another set of collaborations within a different group did. In particular, it drew attention to the civic structure issues that had a significant impact on the research synergies in both groups.

Chapter 11 illustrates how the *Locales Framework* was used in a telehealth project involving three Intensive Care Units, for understanding the interactions between the units and for framing the design of the telehealth solution to be deployed in terms of interactional needs. It was also used to explain some of the impacts, expected and unexpected, that happened following deployment. A key lesson here was that the *Locales Framework* was very useful for articulating systems requirements but was less useful for moving to the details of the design of the final system.

The implications of the *Locales Framework* for systems infrastructure and the use of the *Locales Framework* language at the technical end of the design spectrum are explored in Chapter 12 through the description of a prototype CSCW system called Orbit. Orbit was built around the notion of group-zones as one interpretation of a computer-based locale. The ultimate goal was for Orbit to provide a toolkit environment from which virtual locale support could be constructed for specific needs. I contrast Orbit with another application called Tickertape that spontaneously came to be used to support communication and collaboration within a group. I use concepts from the *Locales Framework* to explain why Tickertape worked while Orbit was less successful.

Finally, in Chapter 13, I reflect on the above experiences of using the *Locales Framework* for understanding and designing, drawing out a program of possible future work to continue the co-evolution of problem definition and solution. I conclude by reflecting more generally on the framework: on how it shares commonalities with more recent developments, suggesting that mediating frameworks and a focus on relationship are indeed appropriate directions to be looking in for solutions to wicked design problem; but also on reservations and concerns about the role of such frameworks, both for what they provide and what they hide, and on the role of people in arriving at better design solutions.

Notes

1 Herbert Simon (1960) coined the term 'satisficing' to denote 'good enough' decision making, i.e., because humans have bounded rationality rather than being truly rational creatures, they will make 'good enough' decisions based on limited information and rules at hand. Satisfice appears to be constructed from the terms 'satisfy' and 'suffice'.

2 The first CSCW Conference was held in Austin, Texas, 1986.

Chapter 2

THE CSCW DESIGN CHALLENGE

> "CSCW should be conceived as an endeavour to *understand* the nature and requirements of cooperative work with the objective of *designing* computer-based technologies for cooperative work arrangements." (Schmidt and Bannon, 1992) [Emphasis my own]

From its early days, the CSCW research community has been multi-disciplinary, involving not just computer scientists, but social scientists such as sociologists, anthropologists, psychologists and cognitive scientists. Our collective understanding of the nature of work and people's requirements for systems support, and of how to design systems to meet these needs and fit into their broader contexts of use, is drawn from contributions across all these discipline areas.

In this chapter, I present an overview of some of the approaches used within the CSCW community for understanding the nature of cooperative work on the one hand, and designing systems to support this work on the other hand. This provides the background against which my own journey took place, pointing to some of the methods, theories, concepts and systems experiences that were particularly relevant to the development of the *Locales Framework*. As such, this is a personal rather than exhaustive survey of CSCW research.

From this, I explore the nature of the relationship between understanding and designing and conclude by highlighting the need for better shared abstractions to help facilitate communication between the two.

2.1. Understanding Cooperative Work

Various methodologies and theoretical frameworks have been used in the conduct of workplace studies to understand work. From these studies, a range of concepts have emerged to become broadly accepted for characterising aspects of work and interaction. This section overviews some of these methods, theories and concepts for understanding work.

2.1.1 Methodologies for Understanding

While both quantitative and qualitative research methods[1] have been employed by CSCW researchers to gain an understanding of work, qualitative methods have perhaps been more widely adopted and produced the more interesting insights that have progressed the field. Because of their descriptive inductive approach, qualitative methods are imminently suitable for grappling with wicked problems because they do not seek to control or reduce the complexity of the domain to produce simplified rationalist accounts of complex phenomena.[2] I will overview methods here for data collection, data analysis, systems evaluation and meta-analysis.

Data collection for understanding requirements: Ethnographic[3] approaches are widely used for data collection. Ethnography is a qualitative, interpretative technique that involves the researcher engaging in some degree of immersion and direct observation of work in its natural setting over a period of time. Related qualitative techniques include in-context interviews, focussed observations, video diaries and interactive walk-throughs of spaces, processes or artefacts. Blomberg et al (2003, to appear) provide an excellent introduction to the use of ethnography for design. Proponents of ethnography argue its strength is the "study of work as it occurs, without imposition of specific research questions on the participants, as distinct from the experimental methods which are designed to investigate particular hypotheses". (Plowman et al., 1995, p. 311)

One breakdown of the different ways in which ethnography has been used in relation to design was derived by Plowman et al *op.cit* from a systematic overview of 75 reported workplace studies. They suggest that reports of such studies tend to fall into one of four categories: to provide detailed guidelines to inform the design of a specific system; to make general design recommendations; to report on basic research without direct comment on design implications; and to explore and evaluate the implementation of CSCW systems in the workplace. One issue evident in many of the studies they reviewed was the tension between providing explanatory accounts as well as usable design recommendations, and the different purposes that could be served.

Data analysis: While there are numerous approaches to data analysis, many informed by a preferred theoretical orientation, I focus on grounded theory in particular because it is the approach I will later use in the study to be discussed in Chapter 4. Developed by Glaser and Strauss (1967), grounded theory[4] is based on the premise that while theory is "indispensable for deeper knowledge of social phenomena", it must be "developed in intimate relationship with the data" (Strauss, 1987, p. 6) rather than deductively from grand 'armchair' theories. Working inductively then from study data, they seek to recognise, label, categorise and relate recurring phenomena in order to develop a conceptually dense theory that is grounded in data. By definition, such theory is always emergent as it can always be further developed by grounding in new data. An example of use of grounded theory in CSCW research can be found in Grinter's (1996) analysis of a configuration management system study.

Systems evaluation: Evaluation of systems in use, via qualitative or other methods such as surveys or system logs, is also particularly useful for gaining insight into the nature of cooperative work and how systems can support, constrain, and evolve that work. Examples of such evaluations can be found in Olson et al (1993) and Wastell and White (1993). Both the successes and failures noted in these evaluations are important for understanding the nature of support required.

Meta-analysis: Meta-analyses of the growing corpus of ethnographic studies and reports have also been useful for drawing out common themes and generalisations (Grudin, 1994; Hughes et al., 1994; Plowman et al., 1995; Robinson, 1993a). For example, Grinter (1997) drew out themes including status, making private work public, and providing information through spatial arrangements in her meta-analysis of various workplace studies.

For all of these methods, there are numerous theoretical perspectives from which the data can be collected and analysed. I now review some of these approaches in the following section.

2.1.2 Different Theoretical Approaches

The more common theoretical approaches used for understanding the nature of cooperative work include ethnomethodology, symbolic interactionism, activity theory, and distributed cognition. While ethnographic data collection methods can be used in all of these approaches, they each bring a different focus to the phenomena at hand and result in different insights into the nature of work. The key thing to notice, however, is that none have been developed specifically with systems design in mind.

Ethnomethodology

Ethnomethodological ethnography[5] (Garfinkel, 1967) is perhaps the most prominent of the social science approaches to understanding work in the CSCW domain. This dates back to Suchman's (1987) use of conversation analysis and ethnomethodology in her seminal study of photocopier use. It is from this study that the key notion of 'situated action' arose (this will be discussed as one on the key concepts). The prominence of ethnomethodology has continued, especially in the work of the social scientists from the UK CSCW tradition (Anderson et al., 1993; Bentley et al., 1992; Bowers et al., 1995; Heath and Luff, 1992; Hughes et al., 1993a).

Ethnomethodology is the study of the moment-by-moment nature of work as the practical ongoing accomplishment of everyday life. The output of such studies tend to be rich descriptive texts. Any attempt at abstraction or theorisation, or even suggestion for how the work might be improved, tend to be rigorously avoided by the ethnomethodological purist because they "reject that social order is an external 'given' which people 'enact' " (Shapiro, 1994, p. 418), rather, it is something to be studied. The compromise for many ethnomethodological studies reported in the CSCW literature is the near-ubiquitous "Implications for System Design" section near the conclusion of the report where suggestions for, and/or implications of, design decisions are (often reticently) highlighted (Plowman et al., 1995; Shapiro, 1994).

It is this analysis of the currently constituted sociality of work that is meant to underpin systems design (Hughes et al., 1994), and herein lies the paradox and problem of ethnomethodological approaches. Button and Dourish (1996) talk of this as the "paradox of technomethodology", the paradox being that the design of novel technical solutions is to be based on analytic studies of the existing detail of practical action. The wording of many study discussions still talk about 'design', but it is 'design' in the sense of general guiding principles or warning against what will not work rather than what will work. As stated by Plowman et al (1995), it is "*informing* systems design in the sense of 'imparting knowledge to' rather than '*giving form to*' " [the second emphasis is mine].

Even when ethnomethodology is used as part of requirements analysis, significant practical problems have been encountered. Firstly, there is the mismatch between the time and resources required for a traditional ethnographic study, and the time and budget constraints of systems development (Hughes et al., 1994). Secondly, there is the very important issue of how to effectively communicate the study results in a form that the designers can understand and use (Bentley et al., 1992; Hughes et al., 2000). These concerns are relevant to the other theoretical approaches as well. I will discuss approaches to address both these issues later in this chapter.

Symbolic Interactionism

Symbolic interactionism is another qualitative theoretical approach to collecting and working with ethnographic data. A symbolic interactionist approach assumes that "the organisation of social life arises from within the society itself and out of the processes of interaction between members of society" (Cuff and Payne, 1984, p. 137). The focus of symbolic interactionist research is to understand the symbolic meanings that people attach to situations and how these evolve over time through interpretive communicative activity between people. Researchers work explicitly at drawing out abstract conceptualisations from the data (often using a grounded theory approach). The concepts of boundary object (Star, 1989) and articulation work (Strauss, 1988; Strauss et al., 1985) are two such examples; they will be discussed later in the concepts section.

Anslem Strauss' (1993) *Theory of Action* emerged similarly through the drawing out of abstract conceptualisations grounded in data. Strauss spent over 40 years undertaking workplace studies and developing associated grounded theories. At the insistence of colleagues, he pulled together the recurring themes and concepts from across these studies and presented them as a *theory of action*. I will give a brief description of its key concepts: social worlds, actions, and interaction trajectory.

Social worlds: A social world is a group of individuals (or groups), bonded by a common, sometimes implicit, commitment to collective action. Social worlds are not necessarily bounded by traditional social or organisational boundaries but instead by the limits of effective communication. Membership of social worlds can be considered along a number of dimensions: size, longevity, the organisation of members into roles, the formalisation of membership and many more. Membership in a social world can range from highly informal and/or transient to highly formal and/or persistent. Social worlds may be composed of sub-worlds which themselves may be composed of sub-worlds and so on.

Social worlds constitute "the fundamental building block(s) of collective action" (Clarke, 1991, p. 131). Hence this concept captures both the structure and dynamics of the group. It also captures the resources for action since social worlds need 'sites and means' to facilitate their shared interactions and to provide shared contexts (Strauss, 1978).

Actions and Interactions: Another key concept is that of *continually permuting actions*. Members of a social world perform actions to accomplish the shared purpose of the world. These actions continually change to meet the contingencies of the situation at hand. Further, actions are always embedded in *interactions* and in systems[6] of meaning, past present and imagined future. Actions and interactions are carried out in relation to particular conditional influences, membership of a social world being one of the most significant conditions. These conditions and actions mutually shape and evolve each other over time.

Actions and interactions are carried out by one or more *interactants*. An interactant can be an individual, an aggregation of individuals or a collective. Interactants each bring a particular identity, biography and perspective to an interaction and, by their actions, are able to shape and manage the interactional course and systems of meaning.

Interaction Trajectory: The concept of interaction trajectory captures the emergence of a particular course of action over time — past, present, and future — together with the processes required to make it happen. Sub-concepts associated with trajectory include phase (sequence of interactions), projection (vision), scheme (plan), arc (accumulated actions to date), and management. Trajectory also includes both routine and problematic interactions.

In short, Strauss' theory of action provides an understanding of the working of social worlds to meet their shared goals, and a conceptual language to build further understandings. I will make extensive use of these concepts in the development of the *Locales Framework*. As with other theoretical approaches however, it does not, nor was it intended to, identify areas where collaborative technologies might be useful, nor how to go about designing appropriate support environments.

Activity Theory

Activity Theory is another theoretical approach used by CSCW researchers for understanding work situations. Activity Theory is based in the cultural-historical tradition started by Russian psychologists in the 1920s (Vygotsky, 1978) and has continued to be developed and expanded upon ever since, e.g., see (Engeström, 1991; Kuutti, 1991; Leont'ev, 1974). While there is consequently no canonical definition, the various evolutionary paths of Activity Theory all share some common theoretical commitments.

Similar to Strauss' theory of action, Activity Theory considers both the individual and the broader social cultural, historical and material contexts in which the activities take place.

The primary unit of analysis is "the socially distributed activity system" (Engeström, 1991) as the meaningful context for individual actions. It is analogous to a social world and its site and means in Strauss' theory of action. An *activity system* is composed of objects, subjects, actions and operations. An *object* is the environment to be transformed, i.e., the motive explaining why the activity exists. The *subject* is the individual or collective participating in the activity. The *community* defines those who share the same activity object. Activities consist of the subject's conscious and purposeful *actions* that have a particular *goal* relative to the object. Actions are composed of *operations*, which may become routinised and unconscious through practice. Activities are always evolving as conditions change (c.f. Strauss' notion of continually permuting actions). Hence, understanding their *historical development* is important.

Mediation is another basic principle of Activity Theory; the various relations between the subject, object and community within an activity are always mediated in some way by culturally constructed artefacts. For example, the relationships between subject and object are mediated by tools, between object and community by division of labour, and between community and subject by rules.

Activity Theory has been particularly strong in the Scandinavian tradition of systems design and is gaining wider acceptance in both Human Computer Interaction (HCI) (Bannon and Bödker, 1991; Bödker, 1991; Kuutti and Bannon, 1993; Nardi, 1995a) and CSCW communities (Bardram, 1997; Kuutti, 1992; Redmiles, 2002).[7] For CSCW in particular, Kuutti (1992) argues that Activity Theory is able to account for both the emergent nature of work and give suitable design metaphors. It offers a unit of analysis that is able to account for individual and social levels of activity in the one framework. It also deals with actions at a level of abstraction removed from the moment-by-moment performance of the activity itself (as is the emphasis in ethnomethodology) and so is potentially more amenable to informing systems design.

On the other hand, Activity Theory can be difficult to learn, as also noted in (Halverson, 2002; Kuutti, 1991; Nardi, 1995a; Truex III, 1991). There are a number of factors contributing to this. It is heavily based in Marxist philosophy. Its concepts are complex and richly elaborated, although some common terms are used in uncommon ways, e.g., object to denote motive not artefact. There are subtly different versions of Activity Theory that are continually being evolved; while signs of a healthy active community of use but none the less difficult for a newcomer to come to grips with.

Because concepts are so richly and densely elaborated, Activity Theory is generally presented as internally sufficient to account for emergent activity. For CSCW concerns however, the concept of 'community' has only been a relatively recent addition (Engeström, 1991). As such it is less well elaborated in a framework primarily evolved to account for the individual in context. Also, conceptualisation of the ways in which community is part of an activity is still being developed. Little explicit account seems to be taken of the interactional processes by which communities emerge and dissolve, arrive at shared understandings of object, negotiate the division of labour or the appropriateness of rules, or manage its evolution, although these issues could well be considered under 'historical development'. Much work is happening in this area however and new concepts such as coalition (Zager, 2002) and knotworking (Engeström et al., 1999) are starting to emerge.

Despite these concerns, Activity Theory is promising from a systems design perspective because it provides a relatively coherent framework that can be used for envisioning how things could be, and it does focus attention on the mediating artefacts for which computer-based support can be designed (symbolic interactionism can provide a similar focus on the role of 'sites and means' for work). On the other hand, symbolic interactionism and ethnomethodology are better able to account for the practical accomplishment of work in everyday interactional situations.

Distributed Cognition

Another approach that has also grown out of a psychological tradition, specifically cognitive science, is Distributed Cognition (DC) (Flor and Hutchins, 1991; Hutchins, 1995). While relatively new compared with the other theories presented here, it too is gaining greater acceptance within the CSCW community (Halverson, 1994; Nardi, 1995b; Rogers and Ellis, 1994). DC is concerned with the cognitive properties of a whole system rather than the individual, where the system is defined as "the distributed collection of interacting people and artefacts" (Nardi, 1995b). The actual composition of 'system' as a unit of analysis varies with the situation at hand.

A major focus of DC is the structure of representations, and the propagation and transformation of representational states between the artefacts and people within the system to meet a system goal; a critique of DC is that it makes little distinction between people and artefacts within this representational framing of cognition at a system level.

A differentiating feature of the DC approach is that it allows both social and cognitive concerns to be addressed, similar to activity theory; ethnomethodological and symbolic interaction approaches tend to omit the cognitive dimensions of work since they rely on what can be observed rather than what might be going on 'inside' a person's head (Rogers and Ellis, 1994). DC also draws specific attention to the human and artefact-mediated communication work involved in shared work activity and accounts of distributed cognition studies tend to provide detailed analyses of particular artefacts (Nardi, 1995b). However, DC has not been elaborated to the same conceptual richness as have Strauss' theory of action or activity theory; it seems to be better at providing questions about the cognitive properties and relations between people and artefacts, but not the language or constructs to describe them, letting this emerge from analysis of the study data (Halverson, 2002).

Rogers and Ellis (1994) state that the "utility of distributed cognition as an applied tool for informing the design of computing systems for collaborative work lies primarily in analysing how new systems might fit into or disrupt current working practices". Like the other approaches previously mentioned, its main value is for general requirements analysis, especially in relation to specific artefacts, or for gaining specific insights into work, e.g., the importance of the cursor in an automated Air Traffic Control system (Halverson, 1994), or for general analysis and redesign of work (Halverson, 1994; Rogers and Ellis, 1994).

Summary of Theoretical Approaches

Halverson (2002) argues that there are four attributes that we are looking for when we take a pragmatic view of theory in CSCW. The first attribute is *descriptive* power; by offering conceptual frameworks that helps us make sense of the world, all of the approaches just mentioned do this in their own ways. The second is *rhetorical* power; by providing named concepts, activity theory and Strauss' theory of action have stronger rhetorical power than DC, while ethnomethodology avoids naming concepts altogether. The third attribute is *inferential* power; all of the approaches are able to support some level of inference, for example, about the consequences of making some change. The fourth attribute is *applicability*; this is where the problem lies for CSCW design — these theories were never evolved with the pragmatic needs of system design in mind. As such, none are fully able to meet the needs of the designer, nor should they be expected to do so. If there is a critique, it is from the point of view of a systems designer "looking for a good theory of cooperative work [that can help] in finding new design metaphors" (Kuutti, 1992, p. 234).

The CSCW community is gathering together a rich corpus of workplace studies in a variety of domains, explored from different theoretical perspectives. Systems designers are still left with the substantial question of how to interpret these studies for their own ends, and how to go about designing systems that can support the full complexity of cooperative work as uncovered in these studies. For example, reporting on their experience with video technology, Fish et al (1993) found that "while social science literature was a useful basis for functional requirements, it did not provide the basis for detailed design" nor did it provide them with general principles that transcended the study medium. As stated by Hughes et al (1994), "... although there is a case for ethnography in CSCW systems design, at the present time it is a promissory note rather than a claim based on substantial achievement". Conversely, this is not to say that the sociality of work can be reduced to a set of 'tame' metrics or algorithms. What we are looking for is that something 'in between' social and the technical concerns to facilitate better communication and to start to provide general design principles. The challenge then for designers is that, while the problem domain for CSCW is wicked, they must ultimately design and build systems that are sufficiently bounded, specified and 'tamed' to be built as software — this is the CSCW wicked problem paradox. Finding the right abstractions that can account for a wicked problem domain but also guide design of tame systems is a key issue in meeting this challenge.

2.1.3 Core Concepts

While we do not yet have 'in-between' abstractions, various concepts have emerged from the workplace studies to gain some currency within the CSCW community as part of a shared language and common points of reference. While these concepts arise from different theoretical perspectives, they provide useful insights into the complex social and interactional organisation of work, aspects that were previously taken for granted or rendered invisible in more traditional modelling approaches used in software engineering.

I introduce some of the concepts that have been most influential in CSCW in general and my own work in particular. More detailed treatments of the concepts can be found in the referenced texts. These concepts include:

- Differentiating dimensions
- Situated action and work-practice
- Double level nature of work, including articulation work

- Seamless transitions
- Role of artefacts, including coordination mechanisms, common artefacts and boundary objects
- Awareness
- Workaday world

Differentiating dimensions: Attempts have been made to categorise a range of different dimensions about work. The most classic attempt is Johansen's *time-space* matrix (Johansen, 1991) which differentiates interactions based on whether they are synchronous or asynchronous, distributed or co-located. Others extend this matrix with dimensions such as *predictability* (predictable or unpredictable) (Grudin, 1993), or *groupsize* (Ellis et al., 1991). Another dimension that has been used independent of the matrix is the *degree of coupling* in work (loosely coupled or tightly coupled) (Haake and Wilson, 1992).[8] Yet another approach has been to distinguish between three functional aspects of cooperation: *communication, collaboration* and *coordination* (Ellis et al., 1991; Grudin, 1993; Grudin and Poltrock, 1993).

While each of these characterisations capture different elements of the nature of work, they tend to reflect a 'tame' view, suggesting distinct objective categories. Nonetheless they still provide useful tools for thinking about different aspects of work at any given point in time.

Situated action and work practice: One of the earliest and most influential concepts was *situated action* (Suchman, 1987). Suchman argued that "every course of action depends in essential ways upon its material and social circumstances" (*op.cit.*, p. 50). In so doing, she challenged the rationalistic understanding of the role of plans and planning in action, arguing that "plans are best viewed as a weak resource for what is primarily *ad hoc* activity" (*op.cit.*, p. xi, emphasis in the original). Situated actions have also been described as *emergent.* Schmidt (1991) suggests that cooperative work arrangements are transient formations, that emerge contingently and adapt dynamically to handle specific situational requirements.

Growing out of the concern to take account of the situated contingent nature of work comes the notion of *work-practice*, used within CSCW to refer to the organisation of work and the practices by which people handle the contingencies of work situations (Button and Harper, 1996).

Double level nature of work: A number of different concepts have emerged that capture some sense of the 'double level' nature of action, the two levels mostly reflecting a sense of the *core work activity* and the *work about the work.*

One commonly used distinction is between *formal and informal* work activities (Egger and Wagner, 1993; Kraut and Egido, 1988; Kreifelts et al.,

1991; Lonchamp, 1992; Perin, 1991; Rodden and Schmidt, 1994). The formal work activities concern the visible performance of the work. A workflow model, for example, captures the formal activities associated with a task. The informal activities are more to do with the conversations about the work, the casual ad hoc interactions and activities often rendered invisible in formal models of work (Star, 1991).

Strauss (1993), too, distinguishes between *action or work processes* such as division of labour, supervision, and the actual performance of tasks and the *interactional processes* or strategies such as negotiation around the work to be performed. Similarly, Schmidt and Bannon (1992) talk about *primary and secondary work.* Primary work is the carrying out of core tasks. Secondary work arises to deal with the interdependencies between multiple actors who need to interact through a common field of work. Hutchins (1995) also talks of two kinds of cognitive labour, "the cognition that is the *task* and the cognition that governs the *coordination* of the elements of the task" (p. 176, emphasis added).

Articulation work (Gerson and Star, 1986; Strauss, 1993; Strauss et al., 1985) is a concept closely associated with the 'work about the work', ensuring that individual activities help achieve some collective goal:

> "... individual yet interdependent activities must be coordinated, scheduled, aligned, meshed, integrated, etc. — in short: articulated. That is, the orderly accomplishment of cooperative work requires what has been termed *articulation work.*" (Schmidt and Simonc, 1996, p. 158)

While subtly different, each of these double level concepts express similar concerns. At their core is the distinction between doing the work, i.e., that which is most visible and normally forms the basis for models (workflows, procedure definitions etc.) of that work, and the work that goes on around the work, i.e., that which is less visible, and often excluded from models of the work. On first glance, presenting action in these dualistic terms seems to offer a similar 'tame' approach to the dimensions previously mentioned. Jirotka et al (1992), among others, argue that in practice, such basic dichotomies are hard to sustain. Despite this, they are still useful conceptual tools to draw attention to the less visible activities, and as a reaction to 'tame' rationalistic approaches to the conceptualisation of work that tend to focus on the more formal visible aspects. Further, discussions of such distinctions tend to highlight their interdependencies and complexities rather than their distinctiveness.

Seamless Transitions: As implied in the discussion of articulation work, cooperative work involves people who are engaged in inter-related individual work. This inter-relationship can take many forms and go through many transitions during the working day. Numerous reports have highlighted the way in which people make relatively *seamless transitions* between formal and informal work, individual and cooperative work, and synchronous and asynchronous work (Heath and Luff, 1996a; Heath et al., 1995; Moran and Anderson, 1990; Reder and Schwab, 1990; Rodden and Schmidt, 1994). All are inextricably interwoven and people often participate in multiple, interrelated activities at the same time.

Hughes et al (1991) argue against the very use of the term cooperative work as distinct from individual and other forms of work because *all work is socially organised.* While Schmidt and Bannon (1992) agree on this social organisation of work, they argue that a more specific definition of cooperative work can help designers understand different forms of work activity.

Role of artefacts: The role of artefacts in mediating and coordinating cooperative work has also been given rise to different concepts.

From studying articulation work in a number of settings, Schmidt and Simone (1996) coined the term *Coordination Mechanism*, or, in earlier work, *Mechanism of Interaction*, to characterise the specialised artefacts, such as a bug report form, that help reduce the complexity and overhead of articulation work by their structure and use in work processes.

Robinson (1993) coined the term common artefact to capture the "dimensions of communication that take place through, and are supported by a system" (*op.cit.*, p. 190). The dimensions that common artefacts support are predictability, at-a-glance peripheral awareness, implicit communication, an indexical focus for discussion, and an overview of work. Common artefacts also support the *double level* nature of work (Robinson, 1991; Robinson, 1993b). The *formal* level supports explicit communication by providing "a common reference point for participants ... a sort of 'external world' that can be pointed at, and whose behaviour is rule governed and predictable" (Robinson, 1993a, cited p. 42). The *cultural* level involves subjectivities, interpretation and viewpoints that support implicit communication. Examples of common artefacts that support interactions in these ways include hotel key racks, the flight progress strips in an air traffic control room, and the train timetable in the London Underground control room.

In a similar vein, Star (1989) has developed the concept of a *boundary object* to describe objects which support the maintenance of shared understandings of work across groups. The same boundary object, such as a document, can be used differently by different groups but still maintains a stable identity across groups.

Awareness: The concept of *awareness* has perhaps had the most influence on both social and technical research in CSCW, yet its definition becomes increasingly problematic. This is because it has become extensively and diversely qualified and used with reference both to humans and to technology (Robertson, 2002) yet at the same time remains relatively unexplored (Heath et al., 2002). What is generally acknowledged though is that awareness as an achieved outcome is a critical element of any cooperative work situation (Dourish and Bellotti, 1992).

The importance of awareness first started to emerge from studies of co-located work; the term *peripheral awareness* was coined to denote the ways in which people implicitly monitored each other and the local work environment while engaging in apparently distinct activities (Heath and Luff, 1992; Robinson, 1993b). For example, both Suchman (1996) and Heath and Luff (1996) describe the way in which workers immediately re-orient their activities to support a critical situation simply on the basis of overhearing a phone call or noticing a change in another's voice tone. Bentley et al (1992) similarly note the importance of a standardised display of the airspace to support air traffic controllers gaining at-a-glance awareness of the airspace others are controlling (as also mentioned under common artefacts). Many studies have also looked at the use of video-enabled media-spaces technology to support informal shared awareness across distributed offices (Dourish and Bly, 1992; Gaver et al., 1992; Gaver et al., 1995).

Full discussion of all the various approaches to the definition and qualification of awareness is beyond the scope of this book[9] though I return to consider technical approaches to the support of awareness later in this chapter; it will also become one of the key considerations in the *Locales Framework*.

Work and the Workaday World: Almost as a summarising concept, Moran and Anderson's (1990) notion of the *workaday world* is particularly useful for capturing, without needing to dissect, "the complex, unpredictable, multiform, relationships that hold among the various aspects of working life" (*op.cit.*, p. 384). They define the workaday world as "... the domain of people's mundane, everyday activities, relationships, knowledge, and resources (including technologies) ... the enclave that surrounds the accomplishment of work" described "from the view of a particular actor". They propose the workaday world as a new paradigm for CSCW design that puts technology in its proper perspective. The work presented in this book are design explorations motivated by this workaday world paradigm.

Summary of Core Concepts

In this section, I have given a brief introduction to some of the core concepts that have become part of the ontology of the CSCW community. They are also part of the foundations for the development of the *Locales Framework*. All of the concepts highlight the wicked, complex nature of work, drawing our attention to aspects that have previously been overlooked or not well understood, and providing explications beyond our common sense understandings of these terms. Ultimately though, cooperative work defies neat categorisation, as captured by the 'workaday world' concept. Indeed, even talking of 'work' is misleading because our interwoven activities are drawn from a wide spectrum of all that we are involved in, be it 'individual' or 'cooperative' work, leisure or paid work; all are socially organised and they exist not as distinct categories but as points along a continuum.

For the purposes of design, however useful the concepts are though, their usefulness is constrained by being part of a diverse collection of concepts, sometimes overlapping, mostly disjoint. They do not collectively form a coherent story about the nature of work for the purposes of design.

2.2. Designing Systems

Systems design largely draws from a background of computer science/software engineering practice. Traditionally, computer scientists have mainly been concerned with tame problems. Tame problems are those for which traditional linear problem-solving approaches apply: the problem can be completely characterised, a solution formulated and the result evaluated as right or wrong. This is not to say that such problems are easy, or that they can be solved simply or within polynomial time.[10] NP-complete (Non-Polynomial) problems such as the travelling salesperson problem, the Hamiltonian cycle problem and the time-tabling problem are all examples of classic computer science problems where there are no known polynomial time algorithms to solve them. Even though this is the case, however, it is still possible to completely specify the problem.

In the travelling salesperson problem, for example, the salesperson has to visit each of N cities exactly once, ending up where he started, and has to take the shortest route to do so. Even though no general algorithmic solution can be found to cover all cases, it is still possible to find a solution for any arbitrary case by trying all possibilities. This solution can be verified as the shortest route visiting all cities once, or not, i.e., as either right or wrong against the problem definition. Hence, while there might still be some traditional computer science problems that are regarded as computationally infeasible, they are not 'wicked' problems according to the definition set out by Rittel and Webber (1973).

For computer science problems that are computationally feasible within polynomial time, the *algorithm* is regarded as the central procedure by which the problem is solved. Its definition typifies a tame linear approach:

> "The algorithm consists of a sequence of steps which if faithfully performed will result in the task, or process, being carried out" (Goldschlager and Lister, 1988, p. 2)

A key component in finding the algorithmic solution is finding the right abstraction for every level of engineering design, from operating systems to user interfaces:

> "How then do good engineering theories arise? A necessary kernel is the development of an appropriate abstraction that discards irrelevant details while isolating and emphasising those properties . . . that are most significant for design." (Brooks, 1991, p. 53)

Abstractions are also considered key for 'requirements engineering' (RE). While RE emerged as a distinct field of practice within software engineering in recognition of the problems of understanding complex systems with multiple stakeholders that are embedded in the world, many of the definitions given for RE still reflect a tame orientation to how to address the problem:

> "RE represents a series of engineering decisions that lead from recognition of a problem to be solved to a detailed specification of that problem ... [where] modelling — the construction of abstract descriptions that are amenable to interpretation — is a fundamental activity." (Nuseibeh and Easterbrook, 2000)

This is the traditional 'tame' engineering background that systems designers (from a computer science/software engineering background) bring with them to the problem of design of CSCW systems.

For the design of CSCW systems, sometimes called groupware systems or, latterly, collaboration environments, finding the right abstraction(s) has been an elusive task. Even though many systems designers have been aware of the complexity of the CSCW design problem from the very beginning (Bermann and Thoresen, 1988; Bjerknes and Bratteteig, 1988; Bödker et al., 1988), especially through many of the workplace studies and concepts just discussed, new design abstractions have been slow to emerge. It is not surprising then that technical approaches to design, especially in the early years of CSCW, drew on the more traditional engineering approach and focussed on (what were thought to be) relatively well-defined functional tasks, resulting in point systems, or (what were thought to be) relatively well defined process flows, resulting in workflow systems where the interpretation of a workflow sat comfortably with the 'tame' definition of the algorithm given above. As the limitations of these approaches became obvious, designers started to explore the use of metaphors from the real-world; spatial metaphors then became popular as the basis for systems design and raised different sets of technical challenges. I will review each of these approaches in turn. This will not be a comprehensive nor representative survey of CSCW or groupware technologies. More recent work, for example, has seen increasing attention given to mobile and pervasive computing applications but these will not be discussed here. The following discussions illustrate some different technical approaches to the design problem for CSCW systems, chosen because they formed part of the background for the development of the *Locales Framework* at that time.

2.2.1 Functional Approaches

The categorisation of CSCW systems into discrete areas according to Johansen's (1991) time-space matrix corresponds with a comfortable tame approach to design. Not surprisingly, much early systems development focussed on functional piecemeal or point systems (Olson et al., 1993) that could be identified as belonging in a particular matrix cell, supporting a particular activity; consider, for example, structured messaging systems supporting different time/different place interactions (Dollimore et al., 1990; Malone et al., 1989; Shepherd et al., 1990); document co-authoring systems supporting same time/different place editing of documents (Harper, 1992; Leland et al., 1988; Neuwirth et al., 1990); and decision support systems supporting same time/same place meeting activities (Conklin and Begeman, 1988; Lee, 1990).

It soon became clear from experiences with many of these systems in use that while a system might be seen to fit neatly into a the time-space taxonomy, work did not (Ellis et al., 1991; Grudin, 1993). Further, people started to consider that groupware systems might have to consider work practices as wholes rather than as activities that fit inside boundaries and that "a comprehensive groupware system may best fit the needs of all the quadrants" (Ellis et al., 1991, p. 11). This was in line with the growing awareness of the complexity of work and the seamlessness of activities highlighted in previous discussions.

Both the successes and failures of these systems were important for beginning to understand the nature of support that people required (Grudin, 1988; Grudin, 1994; Olson et al., 1993; Robinson, 1993a). A major understanding was that piecemeal systems did not fit with the wicked reality of the workaday world:

> "This contradictory situation [of the large impact of CSCW concepts but the limited diffusion, and application failures, of CSCW tools] reflects the fact that, generally speaking, existing Groupware packages are focused on supporting one particular human interaction situation (asynchronous or synchronous electronic communication, meetings, ...) rather than on offering an effective support to the every day life of human beings during their work." (de Michelis, 1991)

2.2.2 Action-Based Approaches

Fuelled by the Business Process Reengineering trend in the early 1990s (Davenport and Short, 1990), action-based systems typified another early approach to the support of work. This involved capturing the sequential or repeatable aspects of work into a process model or workflow and then instantiating and enacting these in a process support or workflow management system, e.g., see (Bowers and Churcher, 1988; Kaplan et al., 1992; Medina-Mora et al., 1992; Sarin et al., 1992).[11]

Winograd and Flore's (1986) Language-Action theory (see also Winograd (1988)) was particularly influential as a theoretical underpinning for much work in this genre including the ActionWorkflow system (Medina-Mora et al., 1992), ConversationBuilder (Kaplan et al., 1992) and many others.[12] Petri nets (Gruhn and Jegelka, 1992; Hoffman et al., 1992; Victor and Sommer, 1991), role-activity diagrams (RADS) (Wastell et al., 1994), and various other 'tame' modelling formalisms were also used as the theoretical basis for process support and workflow applications. A shared underlying assumption of all these approaches was that work could be defined *a priori*, focussing on the more formal and visible activities, and that the resulting model could be used to some extent to predict and prescribe work — just as the algorithm was used to predict and prescribe computer programs.

Many of the reports of user experiences with workflow systems suggested that this was not the case (Bogia et al., 1993; Bowers and Churcher, 1988; Hughes et al., 1993b; Robinson, 1993b; Rodden, 1991; Sommerville, 1992; Suchman, 1994). People often found the resulting systems too rigid and inflexible (Wastell et al., 1994). The systems also offered little or no support for informal communication and had poor interoperability with external tools (Kreifelts et al., 1991). When users were forced to use the system, the systems were only seen to work because of the elaborate workarounds people engaged in to get their work done in spite of the system (Anderson et al., 1993; Bowers et al., 1995).

The main problem with these systems was that idealised workflow plans could not predict or prescribe work in situ, even if they appeared to abstract the patterns of past actions; as argued by Suchman (1987), plans are a resource not a prescription for action.[13] Further, even if support for routine, predictable, product-based processes might be desirable, the question that arises is, how much of work is in reality routine and predictable. Many reports suggest that the answer is very little (Bowers et al., 1995; Ellis et al., 1991; Suchman, 1983).[14] Reflecting on the failed application of a process support system that was modelled on clear and detailed work instructions, Wastell et al (1994) stated:

> "... routine work, which appears on the surface to be mundane and procedural, involves a considerable amount of extemporisation and problem-solving which is rendered invisible in procedural specifications and process models. Formal representations such as dataflow diagrams are normative idealisations; they inevitably hide what is most interesting and significant about routine work, namely its contingent problem-solving character and the interpretive work that is required to put procedures into action." (Wastell et al., 1994, p. 36)

Despite these ongoing criticisms, workflow technologies are the most widely adopted groupware tools in industry after email and calendaring systems (Radjou, 1999). In large part this is because workflow systems are promoted as technologies for organisational ordering and accountability (Bowers et al., 1995) and managers not users are the ones who make decisions about such purchases.

There has also been significant ongoing effort in workflow systems design to address the issues of flexibility, tailorability, support for informal communication, and a broader integration with other tools and activities (Abbott and Sarin, 1994; Klein et al., 2000). Examples of approaches being explored include: driving workflows by the products they produce rather than pre-specified controls (van der Aalst and Berens, 2001); providing support for a range of processes from highly-specified to unspecified and enabling users to change the level of specificity at run-time (Bernstein, 2000); and allowing for inconsistent and incomplete models and engaging users in situated interactive enactment of the model (Jørgensen, 2001).

In a different vein, Dourish (2001a) proposes a new conceptualisation of workflow as a visualisation technology that can bridge the dual roles of accountability for management, as well as support for users in the accomplishment of work.

While these directions are encouraging, there still remains a question about whether the codification of unpredictable, continually evolving actions is the most appropriate basis for computer-based support of work. In proposing the 'workaday world' as the guiding paradigm for systems design, Moran and Anderson (1990) similarly contend that task performance and segregating the formal from the informal should not be the focus for design.

What does it mean, though, to reject action-based models for the workaday world paradigm? How do we account for the fact that the very nature of computer systems software and hardware requires that at least some features or assumptions be fixed, yet the 'wicked' workaday world is unpredictable and evolving? This is one of the questions motivating this book.

2.2.3 Space-Based Approaches

In recent years, spatial metaphors have become increasingly popular in the design of CSCW systems; these came to be called collaboration environments. This move to space appears to make sense from a number of perspectives. As a reaction to action-based models, collaboration environments attempt to both contextualise actions, and enable and constrain a set of possible actions without focussing on actions *per se* (Fitzpatrick and Welsh, 1995). From an interactional point of view, they exploit our familiarity and intuitions about interacting in physical spaces (Benford and Fahlén, 1993; Kuhn and Blumenthal, 1996). From a technology point of view, they take advantage of evolving technologies such as improved graphical user interfaces (GUI), ubiquitous networking, Virtual Reality Modelling Language (VRML) and increasingly high-powered workstations.

Interpretations of space-based systems for CSCW are many and varied, as will be overviewed in the following discussion. Representations of virtual spaces can vary from conceptual aggregations of information, objects and tools into 2-D workspaces to higher-fidelity 3-D graphical depictions of real world spaces. Also, distinctions between previously disjoint technologies such as MUDs (Multi-User Dimensions, also called Dungeons and Domains), media spaces, and virtual reality environments are becoming increasingly blurred.

2-D renderings of virtual spaces such as rooms or offices have been used by developers for collaboration environments such as GroupDesk (Fuchs et al., 1995), TeamRooms (Greenberg et al., 1995), Mushroom (Kindberg, 1996), Diva (Sohlenkamp and Chwelos, 1994), TeamSpace (Geyer et al., 2001) and

CoLearn (Derycke and Kaye, 1993). These systems provide access to shared objects and tools by organising them into rooms or workspaces and providing some visual representation of the shared space at the user interface. Our own system, wOrlds (Fitzpatrick et al., 1995), fits into this category and will be discussed in Chapter 3.

3-D renderings of virtual spaces are also being explored. For example, DIVE (Benford et al., 1993) and MASSIVE (Greenhalgh and Benford, 1995) are collaborative virtual environments (CVEs) that use a 3-D virtual rendering of spaces such as a meeting room to support real-time interactions. The Populated Information Terrains (PITS) system (Benford et al., 1995) presents a 3-D rendering of an abstract data landscape in which people can interact with each other as well as with data.

Recreational *Multi-User-Dimensions (MUDs)* and *Objected-Oriented MUDs (MOOs)* (Curtis, 1992) have always adopted a spatial metaphor in using text-based rooms but there is now a trend to move away from purely text-based environments to graphical, often 3D, *virtual worlds* such as WorldsChat and Alpha World (Damer et al., 1996). There is also a trend away from recreation and fantasy to supporting real-world people, converging MUDs with CSCW concerns (Bruckman and Resnick, 1995; Evard, 1993). One such system used by a group of astronomers is called Jupiter (Curtis and Nichols, 1994). Jupiter's developers argue that they have been able to overcome the weaknesses of text-only MUD systems by providing audio, video and interactive windows. By accident of research trajectory, these systems are now amazingly similar to many of the 2-D CSCW environments just discussed that also use rooms augmented with video and audio capabilities.

Media spaces offer a rather different interpretation of the spatial metaphor (Adler and Henderson, 1994; Baecker, 1993; Dourish and Bly, 1992; Gaver, 1992; Gaver et al., 1995; Heath et al., 1995; Mantei et al., 1991). An augmented or embedded space is created between two or more distinct physical spaces through the integration of persistent audio and video connections. A media space can be sited between common public areas, such as Xerox Parc's video wall (Abel, 1990) and the VideoWindow system (Fish et al., 1990), and/or between people's offices (Dourish et al., 1996; Gaver et al., 1992) to support informal communication and collaboration among distributed co-workers. Most media spaces facilitate person-to-person or person-to-site communication through single fixed views.

Studies of media spaces in use suggest that media spaces are useful for promoting opportunities for serendipitous interaction (Bly et al., 1991), a sense of social cohesion and community (Abel, 1990; Bly et al., 1991; Dourish and Bly, 1992), and less obtrusive co-presence (Heath and Luff, 1993). Some of the studies also point to various problems. Interestingly, while not a representational rendering of space, media spaces are still often evaluated against real world spatial models and co-located interactions.

Gaver et al (1993), for example, found that people preferred task-related views rather than face-to-face views, but there were problems establishing joint frames of reference for such views. Heath et al (1995) raise a similar concern that media spaces provide people "with a poor and inadequate approximation of co-presence in which it is difficult to accomplish even the most simple collaborative tasks" (*op.cit.*, p. 88) and explored different configurations of media spaces providing multiple configurable views of workspace and objects as well as people to address this concern. In trying to evolve media spaces to support more focussed collaboration in these ways, media space work can be seen as converging with other work on 2-D virtual rooms with video connections, and MUDs incorporating video channels and support for real world work.

Issues for Space-Based Approaches

In the spirit of iterative problem-solution definition, the move to space-based systems has opened up new issues for computer-based support of work. This is largely because designers need to make explicit decisions about every aspect of the space, how people will see it and how they will interact with it (Gutwin and Greenberg, 1998). These are things we take for granted with physical spaces, a theme I will return to in Chapter 5.

One issue is about *embodiment*, that is, how people are identified and represented in the space. For example, textual MUDs rely on text-based descriptions of the player's identity and what they look like. In 2-D spaces, people are often represented by graphical icons or by live video images. In virtual reality spaces, players can take on graphical embodiments as avatars. While game-oriented 3-D spaces provide realistic user embodiments, people can in fact use even minimal embodiments of box polygons (giving a basic sense of 'face', 'front' and 'back') in similar ways to how they would interact using their physical bodies (Bowers et al., 1996); this suggests, for example, that 3-D embodiment features should only be added when they are found to be useful for social interactive purposes.

Navigation is another issue, especially for more complexly-constructed spaces. Navigation concerns how virtual spaces are represented and how people are able to find their way around in the world. Gutwin and Greenberg (Gutwin and Greenberg, 1998), for example, propose multiple workspace viewports to support navigation in their 2-D shared workspace environment. Physical world notions — such as Lynch's (1960) five legibility markers, and Hillier and Hanson's (1984) algorithm for spatial and social patterning — have influenced work on way-finding in 3-D virtual spaces (Bowers, 1995).

Perhaps the greatest effort has been directed towards the support of *awareness* in space-based collaboration systems, as well as coming up with appropriate models to base such support on. Early influential work in this regard was Benford et al's (1993) spatial model of interaction with its concepts of aura (presence subspace), focus (attentional subspace), nimbus (presence projection subspace), awareness (as a calculation of focus and nimbus) and adaptors (which can manipulate focus, nimbus and awareness); see also (Benford et al., 1995; Benford et al., 1994). Remembering the earlier comment about diverse uses of the term awareness, note that awareness here is defined as a computational function for the purposes of (3-D) systems design where position and direction can be measured. Rodden later generalised this model for non-spatial applications where location and proximity of action provide the frames of reference (Rodden, 1996). Sandor et al's (1997) Aether model and awareness engine builds on the same spatial model.

Event-based notification services are being used increasingly as the technical infrastructure for awareness services in collaboration environments. There are a variety of notification services in use with very different behaviours; see, for example, Lotus PlaceHolder (Patterson et al., 1996), Elvin (Fitzpatrick et al., 1999), AREA (Fuchs, 1999) and NESSIE (Prinz, 1999)). Fundamentally, they all enable a client that effects a change in some piece of data to communicate information about that change (the notification) to a (passive) client that wants to know (Ramduny et al., 1998).

Work is also being undertaken on specialised interfaces for conveying awareness information in 2-D groupware environments. Gutwin and Greenberg, for example, have developed a conceptual framework of different types of workspace awareness (Gutwin and Greenberg, 1996; Gutwin and Greenberg, 2002) and explored different types of techniques (Greenberg, 1996b), displays (Greenberg, 1996a), and widgets (Gutwin et al., 1996b) for making information available for awareness. There are numerous other examples, beyond the scope of discussion here, of the qualification and conceptualisation of 'awareness' and associated technical approaches to the support awareness (Benford et al., 1995; Dourish and Bellotti, 1992; Fitzpatrick et al., 1998c; Fuchs et al., 1995; Gutwin et al., 1996a; Hughes et al., 1997; McDaniel, 1996; Nomura et al., 1998).

Further issues of technical relevance for spatial models include *individual view* and *activity needs* versus shared group views and needs (Benford and Fahlén, 1995; Gutwin and Greenberg, 1998; Nomura et al., 1998), and the role of *boundaries* in supporting awareness, privacy, and security (Kindberg, 1996).

While spatially-based systems are starting to move away from 'tame' approaches, they are still problematic in different ways. I will defer further discussion of the ways in which they are problematic, leading to a critique of spatial metaphors in general, until Chapter 6, by which time our own 2-D space-based system called wOrlds will have been described in more detail and will form the basis of experience for the critique.

2.2.4 Summary of Designing Systems

In this section, I have given a high-level overview of three different approaches to the design of CSCW systems: functional, action-based and space-based. These systems have met with varying degrees of success but none has been entirely successful in meeting the situated workaday needs of the people they seek to support. Nevertheless, each has offered a different solution to the wicked design problem from which we have learnt more about the problem of design itself:

> "... the [technology] experiments provide indispensable insights, not only in the advantages and problems with applying those technologies for CSCW purposes, but also often – when the experience is carefully documented – in the (perhaps unforeseen) problems that can arise when such technologies are introduced in the social organization of work." (Schmidt, 2000)

What is interesting to note is that even though the problem of how to support cooperative work arrangements is a 'wicked' problem, systems designers have traditionally sought out tractable abstractions such as workflow or space to reduce the system design exercise to a tractable 'tame' problem.

The obvious need of systems designers to base their work on principled models or abstractions is evident in approaches to supporting awareness; both Benford et al's (1993) spatial model of interaction and Gutwin and Greenberg's (2002) framework for workspace awareness acknowledge the importance of awareness as a social and interactional concept (as reported in many workplace studies), but also point to the abstraction work they obviously feel they need to do in order to frame technical solutions. This same need for conceptual frameworks is also seen in much of the other work for supporting awareness. I will return to this issue of abstraction shortly but first want to explore some of the mutual influences between social and technical approaches in CSCW.

2.3. The Understanding - Designing Dialogue

The previous discussion introduced different approaches from the two ends of the design problem spectrum: understanding work for requirements and designing technical solutions. The nature of the relationship between understanding the 'social' nature of work and designing 'technical' support of that work is the subject of much discussion; see for example (Anderson, 1994; Button and Harper, 1996; Dourish, 2001b; Grinter, 1997; Hughes et al., 1994; Luff et al., 2000; Plowman et al., 1995; Shapiro, 1994). There is already evidence of the way in which this relationship is evolving as the experiences gained about understanding work and the experiences gained about designing systems start to influence and co-evolve the other. The nature of these mutual influences is the subject of the following discussions, along with the ongoing search for better abstractions to support both activities.

2.3.1 Influences on Designing

Concepts emerging from the understanding of work have had some impact on different aspects of design, although this impact is often more in the motivation for the system being developed rather than in the final product. For example, the developers of ConversationBuilder (Kaplan et al., 1992) were convinced by Suchman's (1987) argument about the situated nature of work and one of their stated aims was to provide flexible active support for situated action. In the end though, the degree of programming expertise needed to evolve the process model to achieve this flexibility was beyond many users. The difficulty here was in how to translate the motivation into actual system design and construction.

Other 'social' influences have been more at the systems infrastructure level. In response to the observed importance of flexibility in cooperative work, for example, both Dourish (1996) and Tolone (1995,1996) used reflective meta-level frameworks for building an open extensible CSCW toolkit and specification system respectively. Trevor et al (1993) developed a distributed systems platform to support the separation of policies and mechanisms so that the resulting application was not based on one particular model of work but could be tailored for many models of work. Much of the technical work around awareness, discussed in the previous section, is driven by the insights from workplace studies about the critical role of awareness in facilitating shared work.

2.3.2 Influences on Understanding

Technical design concerns have also had some impact on evolving approaches to understanding, especially in applying traditional social science approaches to novel design issues. We can interpret these evolutions as philosophical, methodological and conceptual.

Philosophical evolution: Proposals for technomethodology and for hybrid forms of social science are examples of shifts in philosophical positions to better meet the needs of design.

Button and Dourish (1996) propose *technomethodology* as a philosophical stand that attempts to bridge the concerns of both ethnomethodology and design. They acknowledge the methodological dangers of using ethnomethodological accounts as a basis for design, especially since ethnomethodology is concerned with explaining existing practice, not inventing the future. They propose that 'technomethodology' is a hybrid form that "can move [ethnomethodology] from design critique to design practice" (*op.cit.*, p. 19) emerging from a foundational connection between ethnomethodology and design where "design adopts the analytic mentality of ethnomethodology, and ethnomethodology dons the practical mantle of design" (*op.cit.*, p. 22).

Shapiro (1994) proposes *hybrid forms* in a different sense. He notes that not only are there problems between the social sciences and computer science but also in the relationships within the social sciences. These problems are highlighted by the many different and often divergent social science disciplines all trying to address CSCW design concerns, as we saw in earlier discussions. He proposes a model for interdisciplinary collaboration where hybrid forms of social science for CSCW are developed by drawing out a core set of propositions that "expose the inescapable character of the problems ... which are 'owned' by different disciplines" (*op.cit.*, p. 417).

The proposals for technomethodology and hybrid forms represent important *philosophical evolutions* in the application of the social sciences to the problem of design. What is lacking however, are demonstrations of how technomethodology would be used, or what the new hybrid forms of social science might look like.

Methodological evolution: Perhaps the greatest influence has been on methodological approaches to understanding work and communicating requirements.

As previously noted, there is a mismatch between the time and resources required for a traditional ethnographic study, and the *time and budget constraints* of systems development. Based on their own experiences, Hughes et al (1994) propose four different ways of using ethnography within design to address this issue: ethnography concurrent with systems development; brief ethnographic studies to give "a general but informed sense of the setting for designers"; ethnography to evaluate a set of design decisions; and a re-examination of previous studies to inform design thinking. In a similar vein, Millen (2000) proposes an approach called 'rapid ethnography' which outlines different field methods to help understand users and their environments in shortened timeframes.

Another problem area in trying to use social science approaches is how to *communicate* the rich descriptive output of ethnographic studies in a form that designers can understand and use (Bentley et al., 1992; Hughes et al., 2000). Plowman et al (1995) talk about this problem as the lack of a translation process whereby accounts of the social organisation of work can be translated into design information.

As a first step in this process, various researchers have experimented with different types of *tools* to help organise and communicate data. An early tool, no longer operational, was the 'Designers NotePad' (DNP) (Twidale et al., 1993). DNP provided a diagrammatic environment for the systematic and structured organisation of field study data around themes relevant for design such as people, processes and information stores. Pycock et al (1998) have used a virtual reality (VR) environment, both to represent study findings via modeling of work places and processes, and to envision new ways of working. Coming from an ethnomethodological perspective mainly concerned with describing 'as is', this also represents a significant philosophical evolution.

More recently, pattern languages (Alexander, 1979) have been gaining some popularity as an approach to representing requirements for design. One school proposes patterns as a retrospectively-derived resource to capture recurring design problems, grounded in existing studies of work and associated design solutions. These patterns then become a shared language for design (Erickson, 2000). Another school proposes an adapted patterns framework where the emphasis is on providing a descriptive framework for presenting findings; a structured template sensitises researchers/ethnographers to the needs of design and helps them structure their findings accordingly (Crabtree et al., 2002). This then becomes an input to design (rather than a shared problem-solution language).

In a commercial context (first at a company called e-Lab, then incorporated into Sapient), an approach called '*experience modelling*' (Blomberg et al., 2003, to appear) has been developed whereby patterns and principles arising from ethnographic data are developed into visual models at varying levels of scope and detail. These models are powerful tools for communicating ethnographic findings to the client and the development team, and as a basis for generating design concepts that are grounded in user data.

Bringing ethnographic findings even closer to the designer's world, Viller and Sommerville (1999) have developed UML (Unified Modelling Language) extensions in a design object diagram; the example they give is the representation of awareness in a UML diagram, based on fieldwork in a hotel office.

These evolved approaches — to address the time and resource problem and the communication problem — represent important methodological advances in making ethnography more appropriate for the pragmatic needs of design.

Conceptual Evolution: There has also been some evolution of conceptual frameworks to help with structuring and presenting ethnographic findings in a more accessible form for designers than descriptive texts. Sometimes this work has been tied in with development of tools for presenting and manipulating the data.

Associated with the DNP work above, Hughes et al (1997, 2000) describe a set of viewpoints for structuring ethnographic data and a set of framework dimensions for then presenting the data to systems designers. This was one of the first explicit attempts by social scientists (in collaboration with computer scientists) to draw out such a high-level conceptual structure relevant to design. Because this work is very similar to the *Locales Framework*, I will discuss it further in Chapter 9.

It is interesting to see this pattern repeated when social scientists and designers work closely together, as with the more recent MIME project[15] looking at media in the domestic environment (Diggins et al., 2001). The ethnographers and designers developed a structured representation for data called a Grounded

Innovation Map, organising data into concepts around design-relevant nodes of time, people, things, and space. Again, I will return to discuss this further in Chapter 13.

The *Locales Framework* has grown out of similar experiences; although I don't come from a social science background, I was undertaking studies informed from an ethnographic perspective and thinking about how to communicate the findings to the design team I worked with.

2.3.3 Finding Better Abstractions

Regardless of backgrounds, people engaged in understanding and people engaged in designing are starting to embrace the concerns and needs of the other and are evolving practices accordingly. There is still the more fundamental problem, however, of the communication at the junction of understanding and designing. One cause of this problem could be the lack of a common language and a set of shared abstractions to facilitate communication between the 'understand-ers' and the designers. While there has been a growing awareness of the complexity of the CSCW design problem, more realistic design abstractions have been slow in coming. Some of the methodological and conceptual work outlined in the previous section are important moves in this direction.

The search for a set of shared abstractions, however, is a non-trivial task. Button and Dourish (1996) suggest that social scientists and technologists have "very different ideas of the scope, form, nature and use" of abstractions. For technologists, abstractions are *generative* in that they give rise to, as well as characterise, system actions. The conceptualisation of work undertaken by systems designers around the awareness concept is an example of this. For social scientists, abstractions are *analytic* characterisations of observed action. The Grounded Innovation Map and descriptive patterns work provide such characterisations.

The concerns of CSCW push both generative and analytic abstractions beyond their current bounds. From a technical perspective, formal representations, abstractions and methodologies play an important role in communication among computer scientists (Button and Sharrock, 1995; Nardi, 1993) and in producing system behaviour (Button and Dourish, 1996). When these systems are CSCW systems, however, existing abstractions are not always able to meet CSCW needs, as we saw with some approaches to workflow support. Because distributed system technologies are being increasingly used to connect people and not just computers together, the very nature of design changes. Design is no longer addressing tame technical problems alone but also complex social problems. 'Good' technical abstractions can have 'bad' impacts on the way people work. Blair and Rodden (1991), for example, highlight some of the mismatches between constraints imposed by technical abstractions relating to distribution transparency in the Open Distributed Processing (ODP) model, and the visibility requirements people have in working together remotely; see also Rodden et al (1992).

In short, systems designers are being asked to address wicked problems that none of their traditional abstractions and methods were meant to deal with. On the other hand, while the problem domain may be wicked, the system to be designed ultimately has to be formulated as a tame problem if it is to be built as software and hardware. The challenge is to find new generative abstractions (and/or find new ways to apply existing abstractions) to meet both the technical and social demands made by CSCW systems and other systems that similarly sit within user contexts.

Conversely, from a social science perspective, analytic abstractions that explain or characterise observed work practices only tell part of the story needed by systems designers. Firstly, abstractions will be of most use to the designer where they relate to the work practices, artefacts or workplaces of primary concern in the design project. Abstractions about gender influences, for example, are likely to be of peripheral interest unless there were design implications. Secondly, abstractions are needed that will also help envision 'what could be' as well as explaining 'what is'. This is part of the concern that Button and Dourish (1996) raise for technomethodology.

A potential danger in creating such analytic abstractions is that they will make it easier to simplify or avoid the complexity of social life. Strauss (1993) expresses these concerns in the following way:

> "This is of course an old problem: Abstraction (theory) inevitably simplifies, yet to comprehend deeply, to order, some degree of abstraction is necessary. How to keep a balance between distortion and conceptualization?" (Strauss, 1993, p. 12)

Analytic abstractions still need to allow for analytic explanations. Coming from an ethnomethodological perspective, Button and Harper (1996) argue that if designers are to incorporate an understanding of work practice into systems design, it has to be grounded in analytic explanations of work that reveal how members handle contingencies. This is an admirable goal but where do these analytic explanations come from? That is, how do social scientists produce analytic explanations of work-practices that designers can understand and relate to appropriate system abstractions? Alternatively, if designers do not have access to such accounts, how do they go about trying to uncover their own analytic accounts? How are their designs to be grounded in an understanding of user needs?

For our purposes, the point is not to engage in a discussion about the generative-analytical duality. Rather, taking into account the demands of CSCW and other socio-technical endeavours on both generative and analytic abstractions, it is the search for a new abstraction that is grounded in, and can account for, the uniqueness of each workplace and the lived sociality of work in design. It also needs to account for the pragmatic needs of design in explaining that sociality.

This abstraction can sit between understanding and designing, be collectively owned, and serve as a shared communication framework by all stakeholders in the CSCW wicked design problem — an abstraction that mutually orientates and mediates social and technical concerns.

2.4. Summary

CSCW is a multi-disciplinary field because there is no one discipline that brings all the skills needed to address the wicked problem of how to understand the nature of collaborative work for the purposes of design and how to design systems for the purposes of work.

This chapter has provided an overview of the various approaches taken thus far within the CSCW community to understand work and to design systems, and to deal with the tensions between the two. In the nature of all wicked problems, we have learnt much about how to understand work for design and how to design systems for work. Notwithstanding, we are yet to see the pervasive use of CSCW technologies in the support of work. I have suggested that one of the reasons for this is the communication problem at the junction of understanding and designing for CSCW. Specifically, I have argued that new abstractions are needed to account for the sociality of work in design and the design of systems that fit into the workaday world of the people involved.

The subsequent discussions proceed as a dialogue between understanding and designing. This dialogue takes place at a personal level, through my engagement with our research group's experiences. It also takes place at a community level when I reflect on these personal experiences against those of the broader community to generalise or abstract learnings, and to evolve a new abstraction that can facilitate better communication between understanding and designing.

In line with the iterative nature of wicked problems, the dialogue builds from the background of work presented in this chapter. Various tenets from this work formed foundational positions, namely:

- That cooperative work is complex, dynamic, situated, and contingent, and is intricately and inextricably woven into the workaday world for the individuals involved

- That computer-based support needs to fit into this workaday world

- That systems designers need/use/like frameworks or abstractions as a basis for system design; that action-based models of work are an insufficient basis from which to provide support

- That the theoretical approaches currently being used were not developed to provide practical insights to design

Concepts from Strauss' (1993) theory of action, as previously discussed, were particularly influential. The reasons why I was attracted to this theory might help explain in a different way why I went on to develop the *Locales Framework*. As a non-social scientist, I appreciated the potential importance for design of the rich descriptions and ad hoc insights that I was reading about in the workplace studies reported in the CSCW literature. I was frustrated though by being unable to relate these together in any coherent or systematic way. Strauss' theory provided a coherent framework in which a lot of the ad hoc insights started to make more sense and I could begin to see how they could be used from a design perspective.Concepts,making sense of for design The discussion of the wOrlds system in Chapter 3 is an example of this. Perhaps also, the idea of a theory of action sat more easily with my 'tame' computer science background. At the same time, the emergent nature of the theory still allowed for the uniqueness of each workplace to emerge and the theory itself to develop (the importance of which I had also come to learn from other work in the CSCW area); this seemed to fit well with the wicked nature of the problem domain and the approaches required to understand it.

Reflecting the CSCW community in general, the dialogue to be continued here involves the intertwined paths of understanding and designing. In response to problems experienced with an action-based system, our project group designed a spatially-based CSCW system called wOrlds, attempting to interpret some of Strauss' concepts in the design (Chapter 3). A prototype version of wOrlds was to be deployed for a group of a systems engineers, so a study was undertaken to understand how they worked together in order to appropriately tailor the system for them (Chapter 4 and Chapter 5). As such, this research trajectory is similar to Hughes et al's (1994) notion of concurrent ethnography where design is influenced by an ethnographic study taking place at the same time. However, the deployment of wOrlds for the systems engineers never eventuated. I reflect on the reasons why, highlighting some fundamental problems in the underlying spatial metaphor of wOrlds (Chapter 6). Combining our specific experiences with a space-based system with experiences reported in the CSCW literature with similar systems, I draw out general lessons to be learnt for both designing and understanding. This leads to the presentation of the *Locales Framework* in Part III.

Notes

1 Quantitative methods involve measurements and often rely on experimental approaches. They can be characterised as rationalistic positivistic, and deductive, working from hypotheses to conclusions. Qualitative methods on the other hand involve descriptions and can be characterised as inductive and subjective, working towards understanding and explaining observed phenomenon. See Preece et al (2002) for an introduction to the range of methods.

2 On the other hand, there are issues for some about a lack of scientific rigour and validity around qualitative methods, a discussion for another time.

3 Some people, myself included, prefer to use the term 'ethnographically-informed approaches' to describe our more pragmatic use of ethnographic approaches for the purposes of design; this is in recognition of the depth of skills, knowledge and experience required to be a 'pure' ethnographer within a social science discipline (Forsythe, 1998).

4 The methodological approach of grounded theory was developed by Glaser and Strauss (1967) within a Symbolic Interactionist tradition. The grounded theory emphasis on "theory as an emerging, ever-developing entity, corresponds nicely with the Symbolic Interactionist view of social life itself as emergent and fluid." (Cuff and Payne, 1984, p. 205). Still, grounded theory is a technique that can be applied independent of that tradition as a way to draw out concepts from descriptive ethnographic data sets.

5 Ethnomethodology, a theoretical approach, is distinct from ethnography, a qualitative methodology, though the two terms are sometimes used synonymously in the CSCW domain.

6 'Systems' in this context refers to social systems not technical systems.

7 Activity theory has also been proposed for Information Systems (IS) research (Bodker and Pedersen, 1991; Kuutti, 1991) however discussion of such uses of Activity Theory is beyond the scope of this book.

8 More recently, Geyer et al (2001) have proposed a matrix based on work mode (individual, meeting and social) and tasks/activities (work-related, meeting-related and people-related).

9 For those interested in pursuing this further, I would direct the reader to the special issue on awareness of the Computer Supported Cooperative Work journal, volume 11, issue 3-4.

10 Part of complexity theory, polynomial algorithms are those algorithms whose behaviour in relation to input data of size n tends towards n, n^2 or n^c for some constant c (Goldschlager and Lister, 1988). Polynomial algorithms with practical input data sizes are generally computationally feasible, i.e., they take a practical length of time to compute.

11 'Process support' and 'workflow management' are terms that are often used synonymously. There is no universally accepted meaning to distinguish the two. From an historical perspective, 'process support' was the term used predominantly by the software process community and 'workflow management' by the business process community.

12 Other examples of workflow systems based on Language-Action theory include the following: (Bignoli and Simone, 191; De Michelis and Grasso, 1994; Gasparotti and Simone, 1990; Hanseth, 1991; Lonchamp, 1992; Schäl, 1996; Simone, 1993).

13 In Fitzpatrick and Welsh (1995), we draw a reverse analogy between workflow models and chaotic dynamics. In chaotic systems, early scientists had difficulty looking beyond the local chaotic apparent random behaviour to see the global order to be found there. Workflow modellers and process engineers, on the other hand, have difficulty seeing through the blurred abstraction of global order to see the local unpredictability and disorder at any point of action.

14 There are numerous other examples of reports that demonstrate the non-routine nature of work (Anderson et al., 1993; Bannon and Schmidt, 1991; Mi and Scacchi, 1991; Schmidt and Bannon, 1992; Suchman, 1987; Wastell and White, 1993).

15 The Multiple Intimate Media Environments (MIME) EU IST 2000 / 26360 project, funded by the Future and Emerging Technologies arm of the European IST program, involved Philips Design, Xerox Research Centre Europe and Nottingham University. Details can be found at www.mimeproject.org.

PART II

EVOLUTION TO THE LOCALES FRAMEWORK

Chapter 3

THE wOrlds SYSTEM

wOrlds was a computer-based environment developed by the wOrlds project group[1] to provide support for collaborative work through shared group spaces. Against the background of work and concepts outlined in Chapter 2, this chapter provides an overview of our experiences developing wOrlds, introducing the background motivation for the system and then giving a brief tour of wOrlds.

The wOrlds system grew out of experiences with another collaborative work system called ConversationBuilder (Bogia et al., 1993; Carroll, 1993; Kaplan et al., 1992). ConversationBuilder was a type of workflow or process support system that was "intended to provide flexible, active support for (collaborative) activities" (Kaplan et al., 1992, p. 378). The underlying action-model of the system was derived from Winograd and Flore's (1986) Language-Action perspective , which in turn was based on Searle's (1969) Speech Act Theory . The significant advance of the ConversationBuilder model over other Language-Action-based approaches to workflow systems at the time was that it allowed for unlimited forms of conversations, as opposed to the Language-Action perspective which required that all conversational utterances be one of a pre-defined number of forms.

The developer group had experiences using ConversationBuilder for the development and maintenance of ConversationBuilder itself and for paper writing activities. While it proved particularly useful for some forms of work such as software bug tracking, they found that it suffered problems similar to other action-based systems, e.g., (Kreifelts et al., 1991; Wastell et al., 1994), as discussed in Chapter 2. Firstly, it was not flexible enough to handle the contingencies of situated work efficiently. When contingencies did arise, users were required to change the underlying action model but there was no support for evolving the action model in a coherent way that maintained the integrity of the underlying database. Secondly, ConversationBuilder did not provide any support for the 'informal' communicative aspects of work. While this was less of a problem for the development group, as they all shared the same room, they recognised it as a potential problem for distributed groups.

Prior to joining this group, and in response to other reported experiences with similar workflow-type systems, I had also proposed a notion of process spaces that contained elements to support both formal and informal aspects of work and where people could dynamically compose their own workflows (Fitzpatrick and Welsh, 1995).

These collective experiences led to the initial motivations for the move from ConversationBuilder to the wOrlds system — to provide integrated support for both the formal and informal aspects of work, and where the support for the more formal aspects would be evolvable in a responsive, reflective, and user-friendly manner.

For the design approach to the wOrlds system, we drew upon Strauss' (1993) theory of action to motivate what was needed to support cooperative work. Specifically, we drew upon Strauss to argue that:

- Interactions take place in some context (including, for example, organisational, spatial, technological,and moral conditions) which shapes the possibilities for interaction.
- People who engage together in some cooperative work can be viewed as a social world whose activities require site and means.
- Site and means are part of the spatial and technological conditions for work.
- Since spatial and technological conditions constitute the more stable, persistent elements of collaborative work situations, they are far more amenable to instantiation in a computer-based support system than representations of actions that are continually evolving.

We saw a spatial metaphor as a way to embody the more stable contextual conditions for action without making any *a priori* assumptions about how that action should proceed. In contrast then to ConversationBuilder with its action-based model, wOrlds was built using a variation of a spatial metaphor.

The goal of the wOrlds system was to provide spaces for shared work. In principle, we wanted to view a wOrlds space as being more than just a container for actions and resources; it was also to embody the way in which members of social worlds would use, evolve and make sense of the space in their interactions, i.e., actions in and with the space creating ongoing context and meaning for further actions.

To capture more of this notion, we called our spaces *locales*, influenced by Giddens' (1984) use of the term to refer to the "use of space to provide settings of interaction, the settings of interaction in turn being essential to specifying its contextuality" (*op.cit.*, p. 118). In short, locales were to be regarded as collections of conditions which both enabled and constrained action possibilities, that together with 'action in and with setting', become context for further actions. In practice, however, wOrlds locales ended up being more like containers for actions and resources. For this reason, I will call a wOrlds locale a *room* in this discussion to distinguish it from later use of the term locale in relation to the *Locales Framework.*

In the remainder of this chapter, I will overview the design of the wOrlds system via a brief wOrlds tour. A more detailed description of the system can be found in (Fitzpatrick et al., 1995).

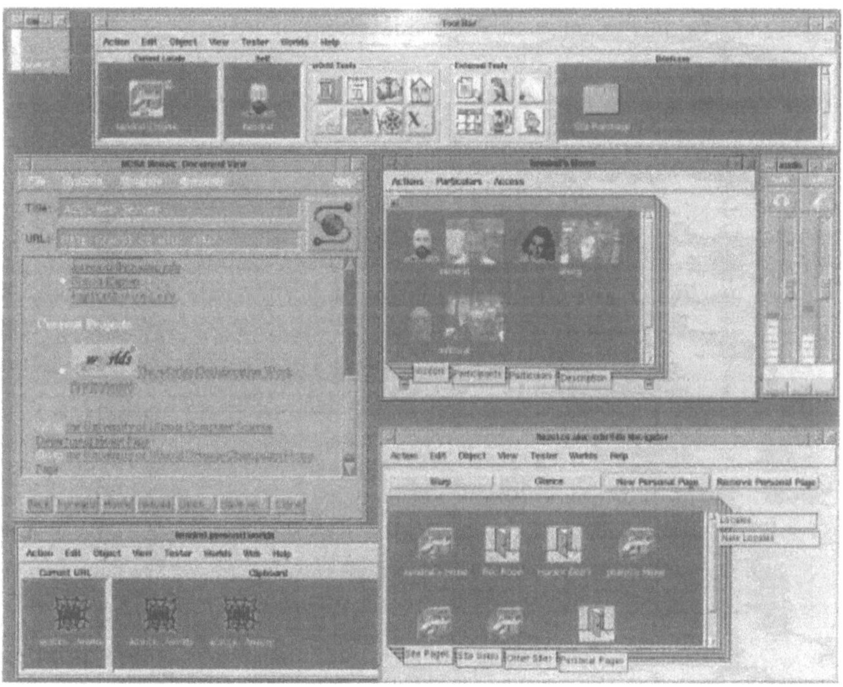

Figure 3.1. wOrlds A screen shot of an example rooms-based work environment in wOrlds.

3.1. A Brief wOrlds Tour

The wOrlds system was a collaborative environment that provided room-based aggregations of facilities and resources to be shared by a particular group of people working together. Each room contained appropriate furnishings, including integrated external tools. Full video and audio facilities were available to visitors concurrently in a room, together with integrated email and notes facilities for all the participants in the room. Hence, rooms could facilitate a broad spectrum of social world interactions.

Figure 3.1 shows a typical rooms-based work environment in wOrlds. The wOrlds tool bar, at the top of the screen in Figure 3.1, provided generic user-tailorable functionality such as identification of the user's current room, access to standard tools such as a web browser, and a navigation tool.

Navigation around rooms was supported by warp and glance mechanisms and a site navigator. Warping is the direct movement from one room to another while glancing models the more socially acceptable practice of peering into a room before being invited to enter. The navigator, shown in Figure 3.2, depicts all the rooms and users registered at that site, other rooms of group interest beyond the current site, and users' personal pages of sites.

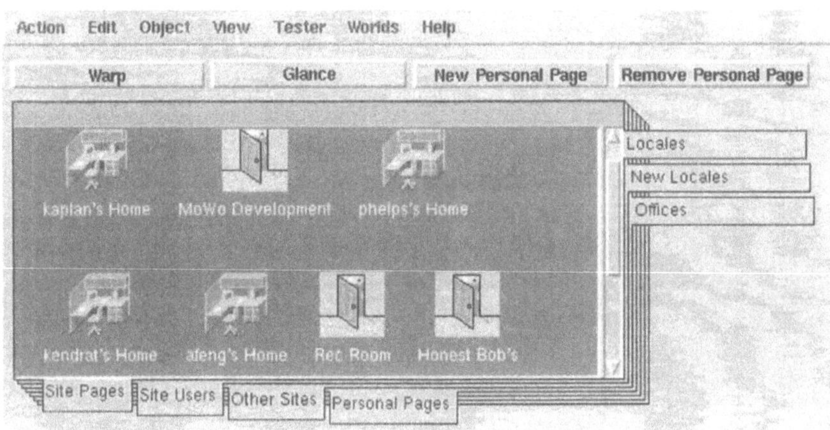

Figure 3.2. The rooms navigator, accessible from the tool bar.

A wOrlds room was defined to support a particular social world's activities. It can be characterised by four main components as shown in the room pane page of Figure 3.3 and outlined here:

- The *description of the primary work purpose* for which the room had been created.

- The *particulars* or furnishings of the room, i.e., the artifacts, tools, resources, and possible actions that furnished the room, as shown in Figure 3.3.

- The *people* who can participate in, and interact with, the room. Here we distinguished between *participants* and *visitors*. Participants had one or more roles assigned according to the social world's negotiated division of labour. Visitors were the people currently present in a room. A visitor may or may not be a participant.

- The *sub-rooms* of the room.

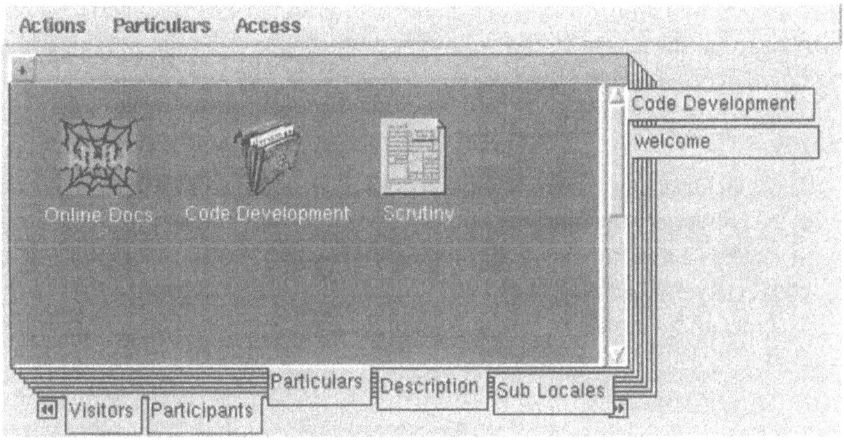

Figure 3.3. A typical room pane, currently showing the particulars in the room.

Interactions in wOrlds were supported by rich communication channels including video and audio, email, post-it notes and an answering machine facility. These supported both synchronous and asynchronous interactions, and were particularly useful for facilitating informal serendipitous interactions.

The more formal aspects of work were also supported by codified *actions* and *processes*. Pre-defined actions with user-defined semantics, such as a 'distribute minutes' action in a meeting room, could be invoked from the menu at the top of the room pane as needed. Facilities for specifying process schemas (or trajectory schemas) were provided to automate standard aspects of work, such as a 'bug report tracking process'. Process schemas could potentially span rooms and also provided a way of grouping rooms together. The reflective toolkit, Introspect (Tolone et al., 1995), supported the representation and evolution of these process schemes.

3.2. Summary

wOrlds was developed to provide the members of a social world with the basic infrastructure and mechanisms to create and evolve computer-based rooms as their settings for interaction. These rooms could be richly furnished with shared tools and resources, and a variety of communication channels, as well as with more formal reflective process models and pre-specified actions as needed.

Typical of the wicked problem of understanding and supporting collaborative work, the wOrlds system will not be the stopping point of this story. Just as wOrlds grew out of experiences and critical reflection on the ConversationBuilder system, another system called Orbit will grow out of experiences and critical reflection on the wOrlds system. This will happen in light of the findings from a study of a group of systems engineers for whom we had hoped to deploy wOrlds, to be discussed in the following two chapters and the articulation of the *Locales Framework.*

Notes

1 The wOrlds project group was based in the Department of Computer Science at the University of Illinois at Urbana-Champaign (UIUC). I joined the group in 1994 as a visiting exchange student. The group moved from UIUC to the University of Queensland in 1995. More detailed discussions of the wOrlds system can be found in (Fitzpatrick et al., 1995; Kaplan et al., 1997; Tolone et al., 1995).

Chapter 4

SYSTEMS ENGINEERS AT WORK

The systems engineers in this study were part of the Computer Support Group, hereafter called CSG. CSG was part of the computer science department of a large university. Its role, as outlined in the departmental guide, was to "operate all the [department's] general instructional and research computing ... resources." These resources were used by over 600 undergraduate students, 400 graduate students, 40 academic staff and 30 support personnel. Access to the computing resources was facilitated by over 400 workstations and 100 dumb terminals, hooked into one of 15 networks, and spread across two buildings. The software configuration making up the department's computing system was extensive, diverse and continually changing. Apart from the PCs used by the clerical and administration staff, it was predominantly a Unix environment running on three different platforms, and offering standard Unix facilities.

CSG was divided into two subgroups. One group of two people looked after the hardware components. Another group of six people were responsible for the software and overall functionality of the system. The six systems engineers of this software group — Alan, Frances, Tom, Kate, Helen, and Sue — were the main focus of this study.

The study took place contemporaneously with the wOrlds system development because, as stated previously, we (the wOrlds project team) had hoped to deploy a tailored prototype of the wOrlds system for this group on the basis of the understandings gained.[1] Data was collected over a three month period using qualitative ethnographic techniques. These techniques included naturalistic observation, formal and informal interviews of both CSG members and their clients, attendance at meetings, subscription to mailing lists and newsgroups, and access to hard-copy and on-line materials. In working with the data, I used grounded theory techniques (Glaser and Strauss, 1967), previously discussed in Chapter 2, to draw out emerging themes and concepts. The social world concepts from Strauss' (1993) theory of action proved useful for describing aspects of the observed phenomena.[2]

The discussion of the study is broken across two chapters. Fictitious names are used to preserve anonymity. Quotes from members of the group are presented as reconstructions of conversations from notes made during and immediately after the event and every effort has been made to be faithful to the speaker's style and perceived intent. In this chapter, I explore the nature of work for the systems engineers whose work is largely defined by a complex virtual work object, i.e., the computing environment, and is largely carried out within that environment. I describe their day-to-day work and also call out two particular instances where problems occurred. These breakdown instances will be re-visited frequently in subsequent chapters.

In the following chapter, I analyse the study to understand how they achieve their work; in particular to understand the strengths and weaknesses of the virtual and physical aspects of their environment for the support of group work, and how the engineers work with the strengths and around the weaknesses. Ultimately, this will lead to a review of the appropriateness of spatial metaphors for the design of collaboration systems. It is the insights from this study, together with experiences with wOrlds, that lead to the evolution of the *Locales Framework.*

4.1. Appearance of Work in Isolation

It was easy to gain an initial impression that the work of systems engineering was largely carried out by autonomous isolated individuals. This was because of the primary role of the computer as both work place and work object for these people as they sat in separate offices. Each member of CSG had their own office along one side of a corridor. Most preferred to keep their door closed to minimise interruptions, though some of them used their door in deliberate ways to control interruptions.[3] A large portion of their working day was spent alone in front of a computer screen, typing in silence at a keyboard.

A typical computer-based workspace that a member sat in front of is shown in Figure 4.1. Because this screen shot is composited from observations of different engineers, I shall attribute ownership of it to Sue for the sake of discussion.

Sue used a window manager that allowed her to have multiple virtual workspaces. The lower right hand corner shows thumbnail representations of each of these workspaces. Only one is active at a time. Some have specific labels, others are miscellaneous workspaces. The labelled ones indicate that one workspace is related to a file server, another to the electronic locking system and another to a student subject CS342. In the main workspace currently active on the screen, there are multiple windows, each labelled in the top border. The 'printer queue' window was where Sue worked on her printer software module.

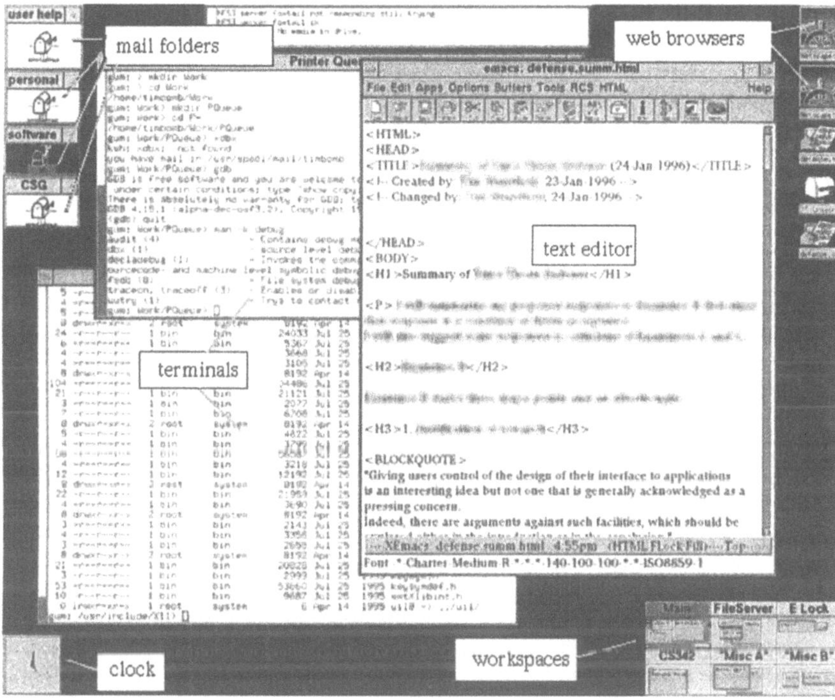

Figure 4.1. Screen shot of Sue's work environment as presented at the interface. (Content blurred to preserve anonymity.)

Another window has a document opened in a text editor. Another has a prompt waiting for a command to be executed, with evidence of the output of previous commands. There are multiple mail icons, where mail is filtered into different folders. There are other tools that have been iconified as well.

Each of the engineers had a similar collection of windows and tools on display, depending on the different partitions of the systems they wanted to access and view, and on their preferred way for constructing and managing those views.

This apparently isolated screen-based work was interrupted by occasional periods of intense collaboration, for example, to deal with an emergency such as a server crash, when two or three people would sit around a terminal trying to solve the problem together. There were periods of other social contact as well — people attended regular weekly meetings, visited each other, had lunch together, shared coffee, and so on. In the main however, they worked physically alone.

The technology they used reinforced the perception of isolation by creating a sense of virtual isolation. Indeed, one of the specific design goals of multiprocessor operating systems has been to give each user the look and feel of being the only one on the system (Rodden et al., 1992).

This appearance of work in isolation belies the highly interdependent and collaborative nature of the work they do. To illustrate, the following composited scenario is a snapshot of our typical CSG member, Sue, supposedly at work 'alone' in her office but in fact engaging in multiple interactions with different people:

> Sue is seated at her desk typing commands in one of the windows at the interface. The last command starts a job running a printer queue program which she knows will take some time. She moves the cursor to another window and reads the new email that has just arrived into her user-help mail box. It is a message directed to her via the help-line facilitator from a professor with a software problem. She moves to yet another window on the screen, logs in to another machine and opens up the software program. She cannot determine what the problem is on visual inspection. Someone else has written this program and she finds it hard to follow. She decides to run a debugging tool. Still no solution. Every now and then she looks back to the first window to see if the first job has finished. She phones the professor to seek clarification on exactly how he experiences the problem. She then emails Tom to see if he can help. He responds almost immediately, suggesting that she check whether the program relies on a particular group of C libraries because he knows a new version has been installed recently. He concludes the email by asking if she has finished the printer-queue program. It is the job that is still running. Tom needs this program module so that he can finish the upgrade to the printing application. She gives him a time estimation by return email then returns to the professor's problem, finds the library calls and makes the necessary changes. A small window pops up on her screen reminding her that she has a meeting in five minutes. Her running job is still not finished. Tom pops his head in the door and says he will walk with her to the meeting.

This scenario will figure frequently in discussions in the subsequent chapters analysing the nature of the engineers' work.

4.1.1 Collaboration and System Complexity

One of the main reasons for many of the interactions that Sue was engaging in can be attributed to their highly complex virtual environment. Having evolved over a period of more than 20 years, the computing environment in this department was complex, multi-faceted and in a continual state of change. It also played multiple simultaneous roles in their work; it was both work object and work tool(s), in that the engineers were constructing the environment and using it at the same time. The environment could also be viewed at multiple levels of abstraction, from the basic operating system infrastructure and network partitioning, to the functional infrastructure (such as window managers, printing, email and news services), to the specific suites of software applications. This complexity went some way to explaining why the departmental administrator, Voss, described software as a nightmare:

> *Voss*: "There is a fundamental difficulty with the software people. The hardware people get things done and are reliable. Even though there are only the two of them, they seem to manage well, despite all the equipment they have to look after. But software has been a nightmare since day one back in the late 70's."

The hardware engineers within CSG presented an interesting counterpoint to the system engineers because of the tangible nature of hardware work as well as the lower overheads of communication and coordination in a smaller group. The work place for the two hardware people was focused on a large open-plan workshop. They worked mostly with the physical network cables, hardware boxes and other equipment. Their environment was, in the main, tangible, visible and largely knowable. Indeed, they were able to draw up a map of the complete layout of the network cabling, with labelled connections and locations of machines and equipment. A network management tool enabled the complete state of the network to be visualised at a glance. Problems could be readily identified through auditory alarms and visual display changes.

The work of the systems engineers, by contrast, was not so tangible, visible or knowable. They did not have manuals or diagrams or plans to show the overall structure of the system and to indicate the relationships between the various components and levels. They could not pull a cable and see or feel the results. Yet the whole software environment was significantly more complex and in a constant state of flux. Because of this, the system was basically unknowable in its totality; each person had only a partial knowledge of the system.

In spite of this reality, one member of the group, Alan, defined a good systems administrator in the following way:

> *Alan*: "...who can look at the big picture all the time and not just at each individual problem in isolation. You always need to be thinking of how this problem fits into the bigger picture and what else would break if you do something."

This was easier said than done when the bigger picture was not able to be known. The high degree of uncertainty that the engineers worked with was typified by the comment of another member, Frances:

> *Frances*: "You never know what's going to break. You think you've accounted for all possibilities then you find out that there was something you didn't even know about that depended on [the change just made]. Sometimes the thing breaks fairly soon but sometimes it may be months later and it can take you ages to figure out what went wrong."

4.2. Breakdowns in Work

While the systems engineers mostly managed to provide a stable functional computing environment for the department in spite of these complexities, breakdowns and crises did occur. The breakdowns were mostly due to one or more of the following factors:

- A lack of communication about actions or system state changes which have consequences for others

- A lack of knowledge of the total system state

- A lack of awareness of the work of others and the presence of others in the system

Two particular incidents illustrated such breakdowns. One concerned the preparation of the student laboratories for the start of a new student year. The other involved an upgrade to the electronic locking system for the doors in the department. These incidents will be referred to frequently in discussions in the following chapters, in particular in the presentation of the *Locales Framework* where they will be used as illustrative vignettes. For now I introduce the incidents as they occurred.

4.2.1 Student Computer Laboratories

The student laboratories, hereafter called the labs, were used by computer science students for their course-work. There were three labs, each comprised of different hardware and software configurations. Historically, the labs had been administered separately from CSG to meet government funding requirements. After a recent change in recurrent funding arrangements, it was decided to bring the labs under the CSG umbrella. Kate, who was responsible for the labs, then became part of the CSG team.

To meet the new funding requirements, CSG had to re-arrange student accounts and write special accounting software programs. Coincidentally, a decision had been made to upgrade one of the older operating systems in the labs. Both the accounting and upgrade jobs were supposed to have taken place over the summer break before the start of the new semester. Helen, the senior administrator of CSG, was under the impression that Kate had been making appropriate progress on both tasks, because Kate had told her so.

Unfortunately, when the students returned from holidays, the labs were in a chaotic state and the students were unable to do their programming assignments. All three of the labs, not just the one involved in the upgrade, were found to be in disarray. The problems were attributed in part to Kate's inexperience, and in part to the number of people who had worked in the area over the years, doing things their own way and using too many short-term ad hoc solutions to problems. The cumulative effects did not become obvious until major changes were attempted.

It became a priority for the group to get the labs operational as quickly as possible. All members of CSG were co-opted away from their normal responsibilities to work in the labs. This entailed a whole new set of complexities and overhead in coordination of tasks and communicating the state of the labs to people unfamiliar with them.

For one particular task, Frances had spent a long weekend installing some software packages at Helen's request. These were "absolutely necessary for the machine to run properly" [Frances]. On the Tuesday after the long weekend, Helen asked Alan to re-partition the machines, as they had never been partitioned in an efficient way, and then re-do the operating system upgrade. There were three ways that Alan could have approached this work. Because Kate was the primary person responsible for the labs, he asked her which one he should use. Whether Kate was unaware of Frances' work, did not realise the implications of the different options, or just forgot, no one is sure, but she gave Alan incorrect advice and all of Frances' work from the weekend was undone. Incidents such as this were not uncommon.

Two weeks after the start of semester, the labs were finally ready for the students.

4.2.2 Electronic Locking System

Another episode involved the electronic locking system for all the doors in the department, hereafter called the *elock* application. Every staff member and student in the department had their nine-digit social security number and a two-digit 'lost card' number encoded on their identity card. The central university Administration Branch maintained a current database of all numbers for everyone on campus. The administration database was down-loaded at regular intervals into the CSG area and then applied to the elock application. When users swiped their card through the card sensor at a door, the elock application matched the number to the entry from the database to determine whether could they gain access or not.

The elock application was written a number of years previously by an external contractor, Tex, from a software company some thousands of miles away, in close collaboration with Helen. Part of Tex's contract required that he provide ongoing maintenance as needed. Helen had maintained primary on-site responsibility for the elock application with Frances carrying secondary responsibility, until recently when they swapped roles.

Helen still maintained a close eye on the area as she was aware that Frances was new and that they were entering a critical period of upgrade to the application. The upgrade was needed because the Administrations Branch had decided to change the format of the number on the identification cards.

Helen communicated the required changes to Tex on Frances' behalf as she knew him better. Tex proceeded to make the changes to the code remotely and used a test set of data provided from the Administration Branch to check that they worked. He re-installed the new code and then went away on holidays.

When the complete database was next downloaded to CSG, no-one was able to gain access to rooms in the building with their card. Frances and Helen were unable to contact Tex. Eventually, they found that Tex's interpretation of the new number was incorrect and they were able to make a temporary correction until Tex returned from holidays.

However there were still intermittent problems with the system that they couldn't understand. After days and nights of looking and trying everything they could think of, Helen happened to open up the database manual to a page that had a note about the use of file permissions. She recognised this as the source of the problem and informed the Administrations Branch that they would need to change the permissions format on the main database.

4.3. Summary

The previous discussions gave a brief overview of the work of the CSG system engineers. They highlighted that, despite the outward appearance of work in isolation, systems engineering work was in fact highly collaborative and interdependent. However, the virtual environment that primarily defined this work was complex, unknowable, and with little inherent support for the collaborative aspects of their work. This was evident in the breakdowns associated with the labs and the elock application. In the following chapter, I explore how the systems engineers managed to work with this environment and why breakdowns occurred.

Notes

1 An earlier report focusing on additional aspects of the systems engineers work can be found in Fitzpatrick (196). An abridged discussion of the analysis of the study can be found in Fitzpatrick et al., (1996).

2 I saw several advantages with drawing on concepts from Strauss' theory of action. Firstly, it placed the current study in a more general context of understanding because it built upon a theory of action that was already grounded in numerous other ethnographic studies undertaken by Strauss during his lifetime. Secondly, it made explicit some of the background and biases I brought to the field. Thirdly, it involved an explicit effort to develop a conceptually dense framework from studies of work.

3 Alan's door was always closed whether he was in or not. Frances kept her door very slightly ajar to inhibit visual access but still conveying that she was available. Tom usually left his door wide open; people tended to assume that if his door was closed, then he was not in, something that Tom used to his advantage when he really did not want to be disturbed. Helen used her door in less consistent ways so people always tended to knock to check.

Chapter 5

HOW SYSTEMS ENGINEERS ACCOMPLISH WORK

The computing environment in which the systems engineers worked was described in the previous chapter as "complex, multi-faceted, and in a continual state of change" and as being "basically unknowable in its totality". Despite this complexity and unknowability, CSG succeeded most of the time in providing a functional environment for the students and staff in the department, and the systems engineers mostly managed to make sense of the environment and achieve their work together on a daily basis.

How did they do this? How did each individual make sense of this complex virtual work environment to get their work done? In the representative screen shown on page 56, for example, why did Sue choose to represent these particular tools, machines and activities in her workspace? And why would each of the other systems engineers be likely to make different choices? And how did they integrate work across different physical and virtual workspaces?

This chapter explores possible answers to these questions about how the systems engineers were able to manage their work. In particular, the discussions focus on the following aspects:

- The ways in which they used their participation in multiple social worlds to make sense of a complex environment

- The ways in which particular characteristics of their physical and virtual environments enabled and constrained different aspects of work

- The strategies they developed for working with the strengths, and working around the weaknesses, of different virtual and physical aspects of their environment.

Throughout the discussion, the term 'virtual environment' is used to mean the computing environment that was both workplace and work object for the systems engineers.

5.1. Making Sense of an Unknowable Environment

Strauss' (1993) concept of social worlds, and the perspectives given by each individual's participation in different social worlds, proves useful here for explaining the ways in which the engineers were able to make the virtual domain sufficiently comprehensible for their current levels of involvement and how they managed different activities in the one screen interface. The suggestion is that they implicitly used two levels of structuring or sense-making, the first based on a shared *social world* perspective of the environment, and the second based on each person's unique perspective from their participation in *multiple social worlds*. I will discuss each in turn.

5.1.1 Social World Structuring of Locales

In talking of social worlds in a city environment, Strauss (1961) states:

> "... the various kinds of urban perspectives held by the residents of a city are constructed from spatial representations resulting from membership in particular social worlds." (Strauss, 1961, p. 67)

Relating this to my own experiences, for example, I do not have complete knowledge of the city of Brisbane where I grew up; I have various perspectives of the city resulting from where my family lived, where I went to school, where I socialised with my friends, and so on. As such, there will be some parts of Brisbane I know intimately, other parts I have limited knowledge of, while yet other parts I know nothing about at all based on the social worlds in which I participated.

There was an analogous process at work for the systems engineers in the virtual 'city' of the department's computing environment. How each of the engineers saw the environment, and what they knew of the environment, i.e., their perspective of it, was based on their membership and activities in particular groups or social worlds. Some of the social worlds were formally designated by management such as the two-person teams with responsibilities for particular software areas, such as elock. Other social worlds were emergent, self-selected, or ad hoc, as when all CSG members were co-opted to be part of the group addressing the lab crisis.

The concept of social worlds can also be used to interpret the scenario about Sue presented in Chapter 4. Sue was a member of the systems engineers sub-world of the CSG social world, which was itself a sub-world of the Department. Sue was also a member of various other sub-worlds within the software group.

The electronic locking system world included not just herself and her fellow CSG member, Helen, but also Tex from the external company. Others were worlds that evolved for a particular need; one example was the world formed by her cooperation with Tom to write a new printing package although it was not on her formal responsibilities list. Hence, in complicated environments such as the CSG domain, social worlds (and sub-worlds) provided a way of dividing tasks and interactions into related 'chunks'.

For each of these worlds, there would be a particular set of objects, files, resources, and so on, that were part of their perspective of the virtual environment. That is, the social world became the lens through which relevant parts of the computing environment became accessible and comprehensible. This collection of relevant aspects constituted a virtual *locale*[1] to provide the site and means of work for the members of that group. For example, the printer files and the tools needed to work on those files were part of the printer locale for Sue and Tom. The elock locale was constituted by the elock application, the data file from the Adminstration Branch, the database used by the application, and so on.

The locale as a group view of the system provided a basis for building shared representation and understanding both within and between social worlds. It helped to make the necessary parts of the system more comprehensible, identifying and relating relevant parts, and drawing these into sharper focus for its members than less relevant parts. It should be noted that these locale structurings were abstract views, not hard-coded divisions within the system. They only had meaning in relationship to the social worlds that created and used them, and to their related worlds.

5.1.2 Individual View Over Multiple Locales

Based on this social world structuring of the virtual environment into relevant locales, the individuals in social worlds engaged in a further level of structuring, or sense-making, of the environment by using the perspective of their own participation in multiple social worlds. That is, just as each CSG sub-group didn't need to know about the whole of the computing environment, so each person didn't always need to know everything about the locale in which that sub-group interacted. Some aspects of the locale were important than others. What was important at any point in time was based on the person's current level of interest or involvement in the life of the group.

Referring to Sue's working screen again, even though Sue was a member of the printer and elock social worlds, we did not see all aspects of each of the locales on her screen. Instead, she worked with a filtered view based on her current involvement at any point in time. For example, the printer locale that Sue and Tom used to develop new printing functionality was constituted by all the modules and applications being written for that purpose, as well as the various tasks and/or communication tools deployed by them. Sue's current involvement, however, was focussed on one particular module and she only had that module and related tools visible on her screen. This was her perspective on that social world locale at that time. Sue was also a member of many other social worlds and for each of their locales she made similar choices about what became part of her perspective.

Hence, the windows, tools and activities displayed at the interface indicated the various social worlds in which she was participating at that point in time. The degree of focus and attention she gave to her interaction in any given social world context was indicated by the prominence of those windows/activities at the interface, e.g., iconified or open, in the foreground or background, large or small, active or inactive. This was similar for all the systems engineers.[2]

What is of particular interest was the way in which the systems engineers unselfconsciously made use of features and mechanisms of their virtual environment, firstly, to manage the simultaneous representation of multiple locale views at their interface, and secondly, to manage their work in multiple locales. Many of these features and mechanisms did not have a strong correlation with their experience of similarly intentioned actions in the physical domain.

For example, the activities and artefacts from multiple social worlds could be visible simultaneously in one screen, whereas activities of different social worlds were often located in distinct spaces in the physical domain. Also, seamless and fluid transitions between different social world activities were supported in their virtual domain by the minimal, subtle effort required to move a cursor from one window to another or to type in a new command. They could quickly change their levels of involvement in different social world activities by choosing to iconify or close one object and opening or making active another. Hence, there was minimal physical effort in changing social world contexts or moving to a different locale. There was no obvious change in scenery nor tangible time lapse while the transition took place as would occur when they moved from one physical place to another.

The following section explores in more detail some of the particular characteristics of both their physical and virtual domains and how these characteristics enabled or constrained certain types of working.

5.2. Working with Workspace Characteristics

While the discussion thus far has focussed on the virtual environment of work for the systems engineers, their total locale of work was derived from an interesting juxtaposition of both virtual and physical spaces, as described in Chapter 4.

The virtual computing environment and the physical environment were similar in that they were both richly populated with tools to support the core engineering activities of CSG software and hardware work. There were other ways, however, in which these environments were very different and thus facilitated very different styles of working. The differences were derived from the mechanisms by which core activities could be undertaken, activities in multiple locales represented and managed, and collaborative work needs supported. Some of the more fundamental differences could be explained in terms of the characteristics of the topology and physics of the spaces, and the related possibilities for embodiment and sensory perception. The following discussion explores both physical and virtual characteristics of their environments in these regards.

5.2.1 Physical Workspace Characteristics

As with *physical workspaces* in general, the engineers' physical spaces, at all levels of scale from buildings, to rooms, to objects, were tangible, knowable, and relatively stable. *Location* in space could be defined by Cartesian coordinates relative to some axes and referred to by absolute addresses, e.g., room 102, Building X, 10 The Street. *Distance* between points could be measured in exact units. The *physical properties* of the space supported phenomena such as the transmission of sound waves, and the propagation of light as energy waves. People and objects in the physical workspace had tangible, physical, and relatively constant form. They were bodily and perceptually immersed in the space:

> "We do not perceive the world in front of us, like a picture. We are in it. ... The human body immerses itself, spatially and temporally, in its lived world. This immersion is both constituted and maintained by perception." (Robertson, 2002)

A consequence of bodily form and bodily immersion in space was that people and objects could only be in one location at a time. Another consequence was that physical movement, passive or active, between locations required the traversal of all points in between (Benedikt, 1994).

These characteristics of bodies in physical space were used implicitly in the organisation of workspaces and the creation of social world locales. Each of the engineers was assigned an office space that became known as their home location. These office spaces were clustered in one corridor of one floor of the departmental building — the CSG locale of The Department. The CSG locale and its assigned offices provided a visible persistent point of access to the CSG members as well as providing physical loci of work, while the arrangement of objects within the offices provided other visible and readily accessible markers to aspects of the engineers' work. The separation of their offices and different uses of doors also provided ways of controlling visual and auditory distractions and increasing privacy. Locales for other social worlds, such as the departmental administration group, were in distinct identifiable locations elsewhere in the building. To physically engage with this different locale required bodily movement from one space to the other.

The work of the systems engineers in the physical domain, especially the collaborative aspects, was afforded by relatively unconscious use of the inherent properties of their immersion in physical space, and the availability of 'free' perceptible information. If two people were co-located, and working on the same physical object, such as a printer, they could not help but see, hear and possibly feel the presence and actions of each other and the object they were working on. Other mechanisms for the coordination of work were able to be constructed as tangible, persistent and visible artifacts, as in the group whiteboards.

Most of the work of the hardware people in CSG was carried out in this physical domain — this could explain why their work was relatively unproblematic when compared with the systems engineers. The importance of such sensible peripheral cues for mutual awareness in work has been widely reported in many workplace studies; see for example Heath and Luff (1992) and Suchman (1996).

5.2.2 Virtual Workspace Characteristics

In contrast, the systems engineers' *virtual workspace* was intangible, complex, largely unknowable, and continually changing. *Location* could be defined in a number of ways including relative addresses, e.g., a virtual machine address, a user account area, or a path giving a file's position within a directory tree. Files could also be accessed via a number of different addresses, where all but one of the addresses was a symbolic link to the actual address and where the indirection was not always transparent. *Distance* between points was relative to locations in a directory tree or network partition and so on. *Physical laws* of behaviour did not extend into the virtual space. Objects within virtual space, e.g., files and applications, were intangible.[3]

If a virtual locale happened to correspond with network partitions or directory structures, then it was relatively stable and could be uniformly accessed. For most of the systems engineers' locales, such as the elock locale or the printer locale, this was not the case. These virtual locales were conceptual aggregations of related objects rather than persistent, addressable aggregations. An advantage of this was that the engineers could evolve their virtual locales relatively easily. They could also change their representative view on the locale at the screen interface relatively easily. A disadvantage was that it was more difficult to represent and share this locale with others not intimately involved in it.

While the systems engineers are embodied in physical form outside of the virtual space, their 'presence' in their virtual locales was mediated by technology and was intangible, asensual and disembodied. They were represented by their system user name. Their interaction in and with the computing environment was mediated by limited indirect sensual engagement via the screen interface. They could see the bitmap representations of files and objects on the computer screen. They could manipulate the virtual space via keystrokes or mouse clicks.

Their position in virtual space was dislocated from, and independent of, their bodily position in physical space. This facilitated great flexibility in working arrangements. Referring back to the scenario from the previous chapter, the physical location of the workstation that Sue used was irrelevant so long as the virtual area was accessible across the network. She could access multiple virtual locations from the one physical location. Disembodiment meant that she could also 'be' in more than one location at the same time. People at different physical locations could also 'be' in the same virtual location at the same time. This enabled Sue to engage in multiple streams of activity concurrently.

However, Sue's virtual location and the effects of her actions were not freely or sensibly available to others as they would be in a co-located physical space with a physical target. The only observable physical activity that Sue engaged in was the movement of her fingers as she typed. If Sue's conversations and activities in her virtual locale were translated into the physical world, there would have been a flurry of movement from one location to another for the different tasks she was undertaking, the sound of activity as she engaged in different tasks, and the chatter of voices as she talked to different people. In the physical world, this activity could be seen and heard by others; in her virtual world, frenetic work activities and conversations took place silently and were almost invisible. Cues for virtual location or virtual activity in this environment had to be explicitly sought out by the use of Unix commands such as `finger` or ps or by looking at a retrospectively-annotated log in a version control system.

On the other hand, without the constraints of embodiment, movement in virtual space cost little in terms of time or effort. Seated at the one workstation, Sue could just as easily 'go' to a file on a server on the other side of the world as she could to a file on a local server (assuming she was permitted access). Further, even though Sue accessed a particular file by giving a directory path, she had little sense of having 'travelled' through a world-wide network or through parent directories to reach that file.

Connections between objects and between locales within the virtual workspace were also intangible; an engineer's actions on one object were not transmitted to be 'felt' by an engineer working on a connected object. Further, no sensible trace, e.g., footprints, fingerprints, perfume, etc., of past actions or presence were automatically left. There was no way, for example, that Tom could just 'happen' to notice that Sue had been working on the printer application. Finding out such information required explicit effort such as asking her directly or visually inspecting the code or running the application to look for changed functionality.

The breakdowns in the labs and the elock locales, described in the previous chapter, could be attributed in part to the intangible nature of the virtual workspace and the lack of support for shared representation and mutual awareness. Helen was not aware, for example, of the precarious state of the labs, an analogy for which would be a car engine increasingly being held together by rubber bands and pieces of string. Because she could not 'see' the lab state, her perception of it was based on verbal reports from Kate, and from knowing that they had worked well enough for the students to date. Similarly, it could be argued that Alan undid all of Frances' work on the labs because he could not 'see' the work that Frances had just done, nor how that work was connected to the work that he was to do.

5.2.3 Implications of Workspace Characteristics

What are the implications of these workspace characteristics for how work was achieved? The key role for the systems engineers was to maintain and evolve the software computing environment for the department. By definition then, it was the virtual workspace much more so than the physical workspace that shaped and defined their core work activities, and it was the virtual workspace where these activities took place (albeit via embodied actions at the physical screen interface). The engineers exploited characteristics of their virtual workspace very effectively to accomplish their work at an individual level. These characteristics enabled them to do the following:

- Easily represent aspects of their different locales in the one workspace
- Move relatively seamlessly from one locale's activities to another
- Easily change the level of involvement in different locales
- Engage in multiple locales simultaneously

These ways of working were not so easily facilitated in the physical domain because of the constraints of embodiment and tangibility. On the other hand, there were other characteristics of the virtual environment that made the collaborative aspects of their work difficult. The system engineers' work in this virtual space was highly interdependent and collaborative, despite the appearance of work in isolation. In their physical workspace, inherent characteristics, including the nature of embodiment and the laws of physical behaviour, did much to facilitate the perceptual availability and accessibility of spaces and actions, and hence the achievement of awareness important in collaborative activities. Robertson (2002) highlights why this is so:

> "For participants in a cooperative process to be aware of anything, it must be publicly available to them. And this public availability of anything is dependent on its perceivability." (Robertson, 2002)

There were no such characteristics to support collaboration in their virtual environment as currently constructed, yet this was where many of their collaborative work needs arose. While their virtual environment was richly populated with tools to support individual engineer-to-system interactions, such as code compilers and debugging tools, there were few mechanisms, inherent or constructed, to support the shared representation of locales of work, the mutual perception of actions in a shared space, and the management of interdependencies in work. Again, Robertson (2002) highlights nicely the reason for this lack of inherent support, drawing on the work of phenomenologist, Merleau-Ponty:

> "Reversibility [of relations between the perceiver and perceived] is a fact of embodiment in physical space *because* of the material properties of our bodies and the physical world in which we are embedded. Reversibility does not hold in virtual space where the public availability of actions and artefacts does not rely on their being made of the same stuff but on their transformation and representation by the mediating technology. ... People and physical space are made of the same stuff, but people and virtual space are not." (Robertson, 2002, emphasis in the original)

Surprisingly though, breakdowns, such as those around the labs and clock, did not happen often despite the lack of virtual domain support for their collaboration needs and, in the main, the computing environment ran smoothly. A major reason for this was the explicit effort undertaken by the systems engineers to *work around* the constraints of virtual space interactions. This is discussed in the following section.

5.3. Work Around Strategies

The engineers succeeded most of the time in maintaining a functional computing environment by making use of a variety of strategies, often in concert, to compensate for and work around the constraints of their virtual environment and to facilitate their collaborations. Many of their strategies involved externalising the system work via surrogate representations as publicly available perceptual resources, and making satisficing use of mechanisms in the physical domain rather than where the need arose. The strategies considered here include the division of responsibilities and use of surrogate spokespersons, external visible representations, verbal representations, and representation in software tools. I discuss each in turn, commenting on the degree to which they succeeded or not.

Division of responsibilities and surrogate spokespersons: To deal with the complexity of the environment, CSG management decided to *divide up responsibilities* among the CSG members to create areas of specialisation, with one CSG person designated as the primary person, and a second person assigned as back-up. These can be defined as sub-worlds of CSG responsible for particular machine types, or particular software or system functionality. The sub-world for the elock application, as an example, was made up of Frances as the primary person and Helen as the backup, with Tex as a peripheral participant.

An important consequence of this decision was that the designated people came to act as *surrogate spokespersons*, providing visible reference points to that virtual locale. When the elock system failed, people went to Frances to talk about it rather than look at the application files themselves. Frances was the physical pointer and spokesperson for that locale.

In general, this strategy made sense in light of the unknowability of the total system — people only needed to know their own area and they could always talk to someone else who knew something about the other parts of the system. Problems still arose arise however. For example, Kate was not a very effective spokesperson for the labs and it took a critical incident before others became aware of this. Also, the designated areas were often not discrete or independent and a spokesperson for one area might not be aware of all the related areas. In the scenario, Sue was responsible for fixing the professor's problem but not for the changes in the C libraries that caused the problem to arise in the first place.

Hence, specialisation could fragment the representation of the system in simplistic arbitrary ways that were not always visible and could give management a false sense of system coverage. The division of responsibilities was still generally useful though for providing representative spokespersons for parts of the system and for giving high-level cues about others' likely work activities.

External representations: The software engineers also created persistent external representations of work going on in the virtual domain as another way of making work more visible and giving surrogate perceptible forms in the physical domain of imperceptible virtual activity in a virtual environment. An example of an external representation was the list of outstanding tasks that management asked each person to write. These tasks were posted to an on-line group directory and supposed to be updated as tasks were completed. The lists were to provide a balance to the formal division of specialised responsibilities by reflecting the reality of day-to-day work.

This strategy met with mixed success. While the on-line lists helped meet management needs for understanding what was going on in the group, they were rarely used by the members themselves. Very few of them kept their on-line lists current and even fewer accessed the lists to monitor others' work.

Instead, they chose other forms of external representation that were more immediately visible and accessible within their physical workspaces and easier to keep up to date. Most of the systems engineers kept the more current but informal version of the on-line list written on their whiteboard or pinned to the wall in their office. This list became part of the background information in their environment. They could easily attend to the list by a quick glance. Visitors to their office could also gain a quick overview of what that person was engaged in. Being visible, they were also more often reminded and inclined to keep this list up to date.

Even though these representations only provided a high-level overview and were displaced in time and space, they were still a useful visible form in the physical domain for work in the virtual environment that would otherwise be invisible.

Verbal representations: Talk and personal interaction provided some of the most important forms of surrogate representation of the system in the physical domain. The creation of transient verbal representations of work were important because there were no implicit forms of peripheral communication within the virtual environment whereby the engineers could be aware of what others were doing and so coordinate their work together.

The regular weekly meetings provided a formal forum for talk within the group. The meeting was a regular synchronisation point for each of the members to discuss their past week's work as well as plans for future work and served to re-orient people to the 'big picture'.

The engineers also took advantage of a wide range of informal opportunities for talk. In particular they made use of features of their physical workspace to pop heads around doors, shout through walls, cluster around coffee machines, have lunch together, and so on. They also made extensive use of electronic tools such as phones and pagers for distributed forms of talk.

Formal and informal opportunities for talk were often able to generate synergies with other strategies by bringing together spokespersons and external representations. While each strategy on their own might have been a poor technique, the engineers were able to meet many of the shared work needs by using strategies together.

Representation via software tools: As well as persistent external representations and transient verbal representations, the system itself, in its role as tool[4], was also used to create visible or explicit representations of the engineers' work in their virtual locales. Email was the most widely used tool. It was used for both personal and group communication, supporting more asynchronous forms of talk than the forms discussed in the previous section.

The systems engineers occasionally used other tools, such as configuration management and version control tools, to provide explicit forms of representation of access to a virtual file. These tools provided a trace of past actions that otherwise would not have been available inherently in the virtual locale. They could also show when someone else was working on the file at the same time. As such, they were useful tools for basic coordination of work by providing limited awareness across time and potentially making actions visible (Grinter, 1995). These tools were only useful to the extent that members chose to annotate their access record as requested by the tool — in this group, most tended to providc minimal annotations.

5.3.1 Comparison of Work Around Strategies

In summary, this group of systems engineers used a variety of strategies for meeting collaboration needs that arose from work in a shared virtual workspace environment. Most of the strategies involved creating surrogate representations of parts of the system as a focus for interaction in the physical world. They needed to use these strategies because the virtual environment, as currently constructed, provided little or no inherent support for the mutual awareness of work within it. Some strategies produced relatively persistent representations, e.g., the division of responsibilities. Other strategies produced more transient representations, e.g., verbal reports of system state. Some strategies were relatively interchangeable, e.g., email contact and talking to someone. The implicit choice to use any particular strategy depended on personal preference and the perceived strengths, weaknesses, and best uses for each strategy.

The breakdowns that did occur might in part be because the surrogate representations were displaced in time and space and attempted to give a sensible presence to something that was not inherently physical or sensible. Sometimes these satisficing strategies were not able to 'sufficiently sufficed'.

5.4. Summary

In this chapter, I have explored how the CSG systems engineers managed their workaday world when their primary work object and work environment was complex and virtual, yet their work was highly collaborative. The CSG people worked with an interesting juxtaposition of both physical and virtual features of their environment. By exploiting features of virtual space, such as lack of embodiment and ease of movement, they were able to engage in multiple social world activities relatively seamlessly. Because of the complex nature of their environment, and the relative lack of support for the collaborative aspects of their work, they also had to engage in significant other work to make the necessary parts of the system comprehensible and to create surrogate representations of their work and the current system state to support shared virtual work activities.

Many other CSCW studies involve work defined to a large extent by the physical world. Where computers figure in the workplace, they are often in the role of tool for work (Bowers et al., 1995), or communication medium (Bellotti and Sellen, 1993), or immersive space (Benford et al., 1995). For the systems engineers group in this study, the computing environment played multiple roles, not just as tool and communication medium but also workplace and work object. The contribution this study makes to the corpus of CSCW studies is around understanding the nature of work in a predominantly virtual domain and on a virtual work object, and how people can use features of particular virtual environments to manage their involvement in multiple social worlds. These are important since, with an increasing emphasis on the development of integrated environments such as wOrlds, more and more work can potentially take place in and on a virtual environment.[5]

In conclusion, the main issues from this study can be summarised in the following:

- Understanding how people accomplish their work day-by-day requires consideration of both the multiple social worlds or groups they participate in, and the mix of physical and virtual environments in which they work.

- The physical and virtual environments offer different advantages and disadvantages for the representation of shared work, the management of work in multiple locales, and the support of collaboration.

- Meeting work needs is the driver for getting work done, and people will make creative use of any available features, physical or virtual, to meet those needs.

The next chapter draws out the lessons from this study for understanding and designing, focussing in particular on the implications of these lessons for the use of spatial metaphors in systems design.

Notes

1 Strauss (1978) states that social worlds need sites and the means to carry out their collective tasks. I use the term locale (Giddens, 1984) or place to signify the site and means that a particular social world uses. For example, when CSG move into a meeting room for their weekly meeting, that meeting room becomes a locale for the duration of their interactions, albeit short-lived. However, locales may not necessarily have spatial dimensions or configurations as the meeting room does. This will be discussed in more detail in Chapter 8.

2 Interestingly, a similar phenomenon was observed when they were sitting at their desks: the papers opened at the centre front of the desktop being the centre of attention, the papers stacked towards the back of the desktop being readily available but not the current focus of attention, and objects sitting on bookshelves or in drawers still further from focus.

3 While all virtual workspaces can be presented ultimately as a configuration of zero and one switches on a physical memory chip, when I talk about the virtual workspace here, I refer to the way in which that virtual workspace was understood and interacted with by the engineers as software rather than hardware devices.

4 The virtual environment lent itself to the development of software tools for the support of group work. Indeed, this was the very work of software developers in the CSCW community. However, while CSG had gathered together a vast array of software tools to assist them in their individual work activities, e.g, code compilers, debuggers etc., they had only a limited, albeit very useful, range of tools to support needs arising from interdependence in their virtual work.

5 Other insights gained from the systems engineers study reinforce similar findings from other studies. One example is the observation of the multiple social worlds with which an individual is involved, and the different perspectives that the individuals hold of those worlds, e.g., see (Suchman, 1996). Other examples include: the seamless and fluid transitions people make between different forms of work, e.g., (Heath and Luff, 1992); the importance of peripheral awareness of others' activities, e.g., (Bentley et al., 1992; Goodwin and Goodwin, 1996; Heath and Luff, 1996a); the use of features of the space of work for getting work done, e.g., (Suchman, 1996); and the ability of people to creatively adapt and make satisficing and, at other times, novel use of technology to get work done, e.g., (Adler and Henderson, 1994; Bowers et al., 1995; Dourish et al., 1996; Heath and Luff, 1993; Hutchins, 1995).

Chapter 6

MOVING FROM SPACE TO PLACE

One of the motivations for undertaking the systems engineers' study was to understand their needs in order to populate and tailor a version of the wOrlds system as a collaborative environment to support their work. At a very early stage in the study, however, it became obvious that the spatial metaphor embodied in the wOrlds system did not match the way in which these people worked.

The main lesson drawn from engaging in the design of wOrlds and the study of the systems engineers concerned the appropriateness of the spatial metaphor of the wOrlds system for the support of work. This can be framed as a mismatch between basic concepts from wOrlds and from the reality of the systems engineers' work. One of the reasons for this mismatch is that the wOrlds system was based on a metaphor of space and attempted to simulate, albeit inadvertently, features of the physical world in a virtual environment. Since wOrlds was similar to many other space-based systems by accident of research trajectory, this critique was broadened to the use of spatial metaphors in general for the support of collaborative work.

This and other experiences with space-based systems ultimately motivates the need for a different approach for understanding and designing collaborative systems — an approach that starts from a notion of place and the meeting of social world needs, and that seeks to exploit (or create) virtual environment mechanisms in their own right rather than simulating features from the physical world.

Before discussing this move from space to place, I want to first highlight another lesson about the difficulty in interpreting and presenting ethnographic data for the purposes of design.

6.1. Ethnography to Design

This first lesson is a personal one but reflects experiences more broadly in the CSCW community — the difficulty in translating the output of an ethnographic study to a form relevant for systems design and for deciding on appropriate systems support (Plowman et al., 1995).

I came from a computer science background, and undertook this study with the express goal of gathering requirements and translating them to systems support. In understanding the limitations of more traditional requirements gathering techniques in complex collaborative environments (and for socio-technical systems more generally), I chose an ethnographically-informed approach because of the critical design insights that could be gained in understanding the workaday world in such a way. (Some of the concepts and insights emerging from studies have been discussed in Chapter 2.) Despite this background, it was still very difficult to find a language with which to describe such a complex work domain in a way that made sense to the other people in the wOrlds project group. The key issues I struggled with were the following:

- How to structure and communicate rich descriptive data so that it could be used to answer the questions of if and how technology could help and if so what were good design options, without losing sight of the workaday world
- How to position a design solution into the broader context of use and suite of strategies and resources that the systems engineers already used to meet their collaborative needs
- Conversely, how to abstract out the needs of the group from how they were currently meeting those needs so that the design solution wasn't constrained by what is but what could be, yet was still grounded in the context of use

This study experience highlighted the need for a framework in which to interpret study outputs and for describing the domain requirements for systems design.

6.2. wOrlds Away From the Systems Engineers' World

The major lesson concerned the appropriateness of the wOrlds system, and the spatial metaphor it embodied, compared to the reality of how the engineers currently worked.

As discussed in Chapter 3, the wOrlds system grew out of an experience with the ConversationBuilder system (Kaplan et al., 1992). The motivation for wOrlds was that since work was highly situated, a wOrlds' room as 'context for work' was thought to be a more appropriate basis for the support of work than *a priori* action schemes. We (the wOrlds project team) anticipated that the collaboration needs of a group like CSG could be supported in a wOrlds room by providing containers for shared objects and providing full audio and video capabilities. Indeed, it could be argued that it was precisely because the system engineers' virtual medium as currently evolved did not support such features that so many of CSG's problems arose.

Rather than solving many of their problems, the study indicated that wOrlds would have introduced an entirely different set of constraints.[1] There were two major ways in which wOrlds would be a less than optimal solution for the members of CSG. Firstly, because of this simulation approach, there was a mismatch of basic concepts between the wOrlds system and the way the systems engineers worked. Secondly, wOrlds used many features simulated from a physical domain to enable work in 'familiar' ways, whereas the systems engineers were already exploiting features of their virtual domain to work in novel ways that wOrlds couldn't support. I explore each of these in turn.

6.2.1 A Mismatch of Basic Concepts

The differences between the rooms-based approach of wOrlds and how the systems engineers currently worked was brought into focus by looking at the mismatch between basic concepts inherent in both. The interpretation of a wOrlds room can be captured by the notions of group, space, boundaries, and binaries whereas the way in which the systems engineers work which can be better captured by notions of individuals-in-groups, place, centres and continua.

Group versus individuals-in-groups: The *group* or social world was the primary unit for the definition of a wOrlds room. While the systems engineers did indeed form the group, CSG, each person also belonged to a number of different groups — hence the notion of *individuals-in-groups* — that could be formally defined or more ad hoc. Supporting the work of the group required a focus beyond the group to the individuals-in-groups and their workaday world.

The wOrlds system provided reasonable support at the group level, although only for more formally-defined groups. On the other hand, it would have constrained the individuals-in-groups compared to the way they currently managed their multiple group involvements by exploiting features of their virtual environment.

Room versus place: In wOrlds, it was assumed that the activities of a group or social world could be mapped to one virtual *room*, i.e., all the resources used by the group could be contained in one *space* and that this would constitute their shared context.

Even though the systems engineers worked in both the physical space of their offices and the virtual space of the computing environment, their work was rarely framed in terms of a discrete spatially-bounded 'containers' such as a wOrlds room. Rather, their work environments were more fluid and conceptually defined by emerging relationships among physical and virtual spaces, objects and resources as needs arose.

Think of the distributed evolving collection of spaces and resources that constituted and was constituted by the elock work. This was a combination of the individuals' separate offices (Tex's office being in a totally different city), telephones, email, the system folder containing the code of the elock application, the version management tool used with the code, the central university database used by the elock application, and so on, all given meaning within the cultural and historical life of the group. Think too of the different ways different people in the elock group worked with these. Strategies for meeting work needs made use of the best available resources from any of these components - primacy was not given to the virtual space.

Place rather than space is a better way of conceptualising this work environment; that is, place as the lived relationship with the spaces and resources that afforded the group's satisficing communication and interaction strategies.

Boundaries & binaries versus centres & continuum: Entailed in the basic concepts of group and rooms was the notion of *boundaries*. Boundaries ended up forming an implicit organising principle for how wOrlds rooms were defined. Objects and people were located inside the room as distinct and separate from those outside the room. At the code level, boundaries were implemented via the room containment object. At the user interface level, boundaries were defined by separate virtual screens for separate rooms.

A boundary notion carried certain *binary* constraints. Objects and people were either in a wOrlds room or out of the room. A person could only be in one room at a time. The room was a fixed entity that was available to all in exactly the same way; people saw all of the room or none of the room.

The 'fixed group view' provided in wOrlds' rooms does not support the individual's idiosyncratic views of rooms, as evidenced in Sue's interface (page 56). The 'all or nothing', 'in or out' engagement with rooms did not support multiple simultaneous foci of work nor different levels of engagement. A significant reason for this was the design decision to link participant or visitor 'presence' to one room at a time — a simulation of the physical world and being made of the same stuff (Robertson, 2002). Sue on the other hand was able to engage in many different activities almost simultaneously by having multiple windows open, different jobs running, and different mail folders active. She could do this precisely because she and her virtual environment were not made of the same stuff.

Boundaries in the traditional spatial sense then were not relevant for how the systems engineers experienced place. A more appropriate notion is that of *centres*. Social worlds have centres, to do with core purpose or core people and so on. Individuals also act as centres. The configuration of windows, applications and tools in Sue's interface could be interpreted as Sue being a centre, drawing into her focus what she needed from various group places. Those that were 'opened' in her workspace were more relevant to her current work foci than those that were iconised, and these in turn were more relevant than those applications and tools not represented at her interface.

Centres allow for varying levels of relationship and varying levels of boundaries. We can think of these levels as ripples around a central point, a *continuum* of relationships from the centre to the periphery. The notion of centres is a more appropriate metaphor than a bounded room with binary constraints for how the systems engineers managed involvement with multiple groups.

6.2.2 Simulate Physical Features or Exploit Virtual Features?

A key reason for the basic mismatches between wOrlds concepts and the concepts characterising the workaday world of the systems engineers was the use of the physical world as a baseline metaphor in wOrlds, albeit unintentionally.

The appeal of using physical space as a metaphor is understandable. Benford and Fahlén (1993), for example, suggest that the reason for the popularity of spatial approaches to collaborative systems is "their strong relation to physical reality and therefore their highly intuitive nature" (p. 10). They also talk about exploiting the interactional affordances of space, and the way in which people use the properties of space to manage social interaction (Benford and Mariani, 1993; Benford et al., 1995). Kuhn and Blumenthal (1996) similarly argue for exploiting experiences of physical space:

> "Spatialized user interfaces *exploit*: the *experience* ... of living and acting in space; the *affordances* offered by spatial environments and artifacts; the role that spatial layout plays in human *memory*; ... ; the range of *cues* space offers for navigation, decision, and tracing history." (*op. cit.*, p. 176, emphasis in the original.)

What these arguments fail to take account of is the shared material properties of the physical world and bodies that make such exploitations possible. People and virtual spaces do not share the same properties and, as such, a simulation of space does not provide for "the alternative relations between people and the perceivability of actions and artefacts in virtual spaces without this common stuff" (Robertson, 2002).

The virtual environment is only rendered sensible through an arbitrary representation, on the wOrlds interface for example. We cannot bodily and sensibly engage directly with the space but interact with it through indirect mediation. Consider a window on the computer screen signifying a wOrlds room, with digital images (or even video images) of two people there and a graphical icon of an object that can be manipulated indirectly by mouse clicks; this is not the same experience as those same two people being bodily co-present with a tangible object in a physical room with the richness of perceptual resources available to them.

Simulating physical features in a virtual environment, intentionally or unintentionally, and expecting similar consequences by analogical use seems not to make sense.[2] A simulation approach puts the emphasis on the features themselves rather than on *why and how* the features might be used in the physical world: what collaborative need they meet, what capabilities are required to make use of those features, and whether the features are optimal for meeting that particular need or whether other options might be available.

A simulation approach also fails to explore and *exploit features of the virtual environment* in their own right. wOrlds makes only a rudimentary attempt at such exploitation. Warping is one example, where visitors were able to move instantaneously from one wOrlds room to another. But the systems engineers in this study showed how other features of the virtual domain could be created and exploited to work in new ways that have only a weak correspondence with the physical domain. For example, the window management software and underlying UNIX operating system enabled them to move rapidly between different activities in quite a different way to how they managed different activities in the physical domain, e.g., by arrangement of objects on the desktop, walking from one room to the next, and so on.

A simulation approach removes the system from the *broader context* of its users and the strategies and mechanisms they use across domains to meet their interactional needs. Simulated space-based systems often provide alternative independent spaces rather than spaces integrated with the workaday world for the support of work.

6.2.3 Other Experiences with Space-Based Systems

The simulation approach and basic concepts embodied in wOrlds were similar to those embodied in many other space-based systems. While these systems all utilised and rendered spatial metaphors in very different ways — whether 2-D or 3-D depictions of space or MUDs/MOOs — they could all be characterised as offering a bounded room-as-container model, simulating real world spaces to varying degrees of veracity. This was because many of the interpretations of space for virtual environments were largely drawn from experiences with, or insights from, use of physical space, as discussed in the previous section. As people gained experience using other space-based systems for the support of collaborative work activities, various criticisms started to emerge, many reflecting our own experiences with wOrlds.

In relation to the potential of virtual offices with 3-D objects for information management, Shum (1990) cautioned that "it is far from clear whether this cloning of the real world, especially the visuospatial [sic] aspects, is a productive direction to take". Derycke (1995) questioned the appropriateness of the rooms-based metaphor to provide virtual spaces for learning and social encounters, as implemented in the Co-Learn system (Derycke and Kaye, 1993). He argued that a rooms metaphor was too static, that it represented an administrative rather than user viewpoint, and that it was unable to support activity-time relations. England (1995) critiqued the spatial models used in the COMIC project (Benford and Mariani, 1993) as only providing a model of presence through syntactic or surface awareness but not of general awareness of semantic and contextual relationships.

Some instantiations of space-based systems, while based on the physical world, moved beyond a true simulation of space. For example, as the COMIC collaborative virtual environment work evolved, they created virtual boundaries to be "permeable to sound, vision and transit in ways which do not necessarily correlate with each other ... 'reparametrising' what is familiar from real spaces" [John Bowers, personal communication, 1996]. Büscher et al (2001) deliberately exploited features that were not possible in physical spaces and explored parallel, folded, and tunnelled properties in their digital spaces for architects.

While such approaches started to take fuller advantage of the mechanisms that virtual spaces could afford (and exploited specific technologies such as virtual reality), many were still doing so from the basis of familiarity with physical space. The ways in which the metaphor was 'broken' can be instructive, especially where reparametrising what was familiar from real spaces led to breakdowns in the spatial metaphor. The Alpha World system (Desmond, 1995) was a case in point.

Alpha World[3] was a simulated world of green spaces, buildings etc., where people could take on avatar representations to move around and interact with the world. In this world, avatars weren't restricted to walking on thc paths provided; they could also fly above the world (though they did not have any wings or other devices to suggest how such movement was afforded). Because many people chose to fly rather than walk, doors to houses, while still depicted, became obsolete as entry points to buildings. Instead, people could now fly into buildings through openings in roofs!

While not seeking to simulate space in the same way, experiences with the use of media spaces have also found them wanting in comparison with co-located face-to-face interactions. For example, Heath and Luff (1993) point to the loss of gaze awareness and (all but macro) gestures for the management of the interaction, both of which are used extensively in face-to-face interactions.

Dourish et al (1996) take a different perspective when reflecting on 10 years of media space exploration and use. They argue that it is important to evaluate media space as a communicative medium in its own right rather than use real world face-to-face interaction as the baseline, a position also argued in Bly et al., (1991). The authors found that their work-practices and communication practices co-evolved over time as they became more familiar with the medium and that the technology came to be used in novel ways by other people in the environment who were not directly engaged with it.

6.3. From Space to Place in Systems Design

Architect William Mitchell (1995) argues that the new 'City of Bits' that is this virtual environment will require the re-definition of many of our basic notions from physical space:

> "The network is the urban site before us, an invitation to design and construct the City of Bits... But this new city will turn classical categories inside out and will reconstruct the discourse in which architects have engaged from classical times until now. This will be a city unrooted to any definite spot on the surface of the earth, shaped by connectivity and bandwidth constraints rather than by accessibility and land values, largely asynchronous in its operation, and inhabited by disembodied and fragmented subjects who exist as collections of aliases and agents. Its places will be constructed virtually from stones and timbers, and they will be connected by logical linkages rather than by doors, passageways, and streets." (Mitchell, 1995, p. 24)

Approaches that simulate aspects of physical space clearly have limitations. If space is not the most appropriate metaphor for collaborative systems, then what should we use for the new city of bits that our systems will become? The notion of *place* rather than space can provide an alternative starting point, where place is defined as the lived relationship with the spaces and resources that afford the group's communication and interaction strategies.

What does a move from space to place mean for systems design? Instead of trying to simulate features that work because people and the space are made of the same stuff, we should instead focus on what needs those physical features meet, and then consider if and how we can meet those needs with virtual-space mechanisms. For example, if a wall is useful for separating spaces, for minimising the information that is freely available across spaces etc., then what mechanisms can we use in a virtual environment to meet similar needs? This is an abstraction level away from spatial metaphors. It is still possible to choose a spatial representation for the graphical interface of the system, but the choice of representation would be driven by social world needs, current or projected, and the availability and appropriateness of different options to meet those needs.

A place-based approach, then, is driven by a clear understanding of interactional *needs*, exploits the *best features of any space*, physical or virtual, to meet those needs, and is *integrated* into the broader context of how people construct and engage with their workaday world.

6.3.1 The General Move from Space to Place

In line with more general critiques of space-based systems, the importance of place and the relationship between space and place, albeit interpreted in slightly different ways, are becoming common themes in CSCW and other literatures.

In her study of the work in an airline operations room, Suchman (1996) defines place as being "constituted by, rather than container for, culturally, historically, and locally meaningful forms of lived activity" (*op.cit.*, p. 35).

She goes on in some detail to explore the moment-by-moment production and transformation of personal and shared spaces in the room, and the boundaries between them, while the operators resolve a relatively routine problem. Using the term 'workspace' similar to the notion of place here, Suchman notes that "Even those occupying the same physical space, insofar as their orientations are different, may be inhabiting separate attentional and interactional workspaces" (*op.cit.*, p. 53). This is a similar observation to the ways in which the systems engineers worked with a social world perspective over the spaces they worked in.

The constitution of place through use of space is a notion shared by others as well. In talking about use of media spaces, Dourish et al (1996) argue that "It is important that we allow for the way that place-orientations *emerge out of* the flexible, exploratory and *creative* use of the space by its occupants" (*op.cit.*, p. 58, emphasis in the original). Harrison and Dourish (1996) extend this argument to critique spatial models in general, arguing that although designers use models of space to support interaction, it is notions of place which shape behaviour: "space is the opportunity; place is the understood reality" (*op.cit.*, p. 69). Behavioural patterns cannot be transferred to a virtual domain simply by simulating structural features from the physical space in which those patterns were observed.

Strauss (1978) similarly notes the need to look beyond the space itself to what is actually happening in and with the space and how this is given meaning. In relation to his observations of life in the city, he states:

> "The important thing about any given urban world is not that it is rooted in space. That is merely what often strikes the eye first... What is important about a social world is that its members are linked by some sort of shared symbolisation, some effective channels of communication." (*op.cit.*, p. 67)

The space catches our eye first but it is the lived experience of the space that constitutes place. This lived experience can be framed in terms of interactional needs within a social world perspective, where the needs, in the social world context, frame the production, use and transformation of the space and resources there for the experience of place.

This use of space for place-making is in the spirit of Hollan and Stornetta (1992) who argued for the framing of problems in terms of needs, media and mechanisms rather than being blinded by "being there", i.e., in the space. We should instead be focussing on the communication *needs* that people are trying to meet, the *media* available to mediate the communication, and the *mechanisms* enabled by that media. As also found by Dourish et al (1996): "when the medium changes, the mechanisms change too; but the communicative achievements remain" (*op.cit.*, p. 59).

6.4. Summary

The experience with the wOrlds system and the systems administrators' group highlight the difficulty in designing systems to support cooperative work needs. These needs take into account the whole of a person's workaday world, and their idiosyncratic involvement in multiple social worlds and possibly with different types of spaces. The design difficulty is further reinforced when we look at experiences with other spatially-based systems and studies of work.

A main argument of this book is that place defined by interactional needs rather than space is a more appropriate metaphor. But how do we design systems that have place, not space, as the driving metaphor, that take account of the whole environment in which the work gets done or is to get done? How do we use the output of ethnographic studies for the purposes of design based on a notion of place? How do we interpret studies so that the primary focus is on identifying interactional needs and not the physical features used to meet those needs? How do we analyse features and mechanisms of any space, not as an end in themselves, but for how they can both enable and constrain the meeting of needs?

These questions form the motivation for the *Locales Framework*: that the *Locales Framework* is able to provide a shared language that can be used to structure workplace studies, frame system requirements, and inform the systems design for the support of wicked problem situations such as the support of collaborative work. The *Locales Framework* is the focus of discussions in the following chapters comprising Part III.

Notes

1 While it is true that any technology, hard or soft, will always entail a different set of possibilities and constraints for action, it was postulated that the tradeoffs in this case would constrain the systems engineers to work in 'unnatural' ways for their virtual domain.

2 This touches upon the whole debate about the appropriate role and limits of metaphors for systems design, e.g., (Madsen, 1994). It is not my intention to further this debate here but rather to question the appropriateness of simulation in this instance.

3 This system was seen during a demonstration at CHI'96, based on the paper (Damer et al., 1996).

PART III

THE LOCALES FRAMEWORK

Chapter 7

INTRODUCTION TO THE LOCALES FRAMEWORK

Wicked problem situations involve creative unpredictable people interacting in and with complex and dynamic contexts involving social, organisational, physical, and technical dimensions. These interactions and inter-dependent contexts are not amenable to the simplifying design abstractions that have served systems engineering well in the past, approaches that are more suitable to where problems can be fully articulated and solutions verified as right or wrong. This is not the case with wicked problems. Yet while ethnography and similar qualitative techniques seem better able to account for the complexity of wicked problem situations, they entail a different set of problems to do with communication between understanding and designing. And while a metaphor of space seems to be better than an action-based approach for the design of collaborative systems that address wicked problem situations (because we are all familiar with space and actions do not need to be specified *a priori*), these too are proving problematic.

In this chapter, I introduce the *Locales Framework* — and its five aspects of locale foundations, civic structures, individual views, interaction trajectory and mutuality — as a shared abstraction that is better able to deal with the intertwined problem-solution space of wicked problems. The *Locales Framework* builds from a number of strands of work, drawing these together into a coherent mediating framework based on a metaphor of place to facilitate the understanding of the complex workaday world and the design of systems to support this world.

One strand is from the background of work undertaken in the CSCW community, as presented in Chapter 2. This includes the many important but ad hoc concepts, such as awareness, that have emerged from workplace studies and point to critical elements in the achievement of collaborative work. It also includes the ongoing explorations of the relationship between understanding and designing that we continue to learn from.

Another strand is from our own iteration through the problem-solution space of the systems engineers world and the wOrlds system, drawing on the lessons learnt about the difficulties moving from ethnography to design and about the limitations of spatial metaphors.

The other major strand is the work of Anselm Strauss (1993) and his theory of action. Not coming from a traditional social science background, Strauss' work provided a conceptual map for me against which many of the ad hoc insights emerging from the workplace studies started to make more sense. The key notions from Strauss' theory that underpin the framework in particular are social worlds, action, interactions, and sites and means. A *social world* is the fundamental building block of collective action (Clarke, 1991). A social world is a group of people who share some commitment to collective action. *Actions* always take place in relation to other actions and are continually evolving; as such they are always embedded in *interactions*. Social worlds need '*sites and means*' to facilitate their shared interactions (Strauss, 1978).[1]

A related strand, reinforced from the systems engineers' study, is the understanding that *interactional needs* are paramount. By this I mean that people appropriate and construct spaces and things as places, and that their use of space can only be interpreted in terms of the interactional needs that the use fulfills. A focus on needs also points to the fact that people will be resourceful and creative in making use of whatever is available to meet those needs – they will use a shoe as a hammer if that is all they can find to hit a nail into a wall.

In the nature of wicked problems and the co-evolution of problem understanding and solution development, the framework itself becomes another strand in the evolution of better approaches as we gain more experience with understanding and designing for complex environments.

The following discussion positions the concept of locale as the primary unit of analysis, overviews the organising principles of perspective and centre, then introduces the framework aspects that will be discussed in more detail in the following chapter.

7.1. Locale as Unit of Analysis

The primary unit of analysis and design in the *Locales Framework* is '*locale*'. Locale doesn't exist *a priori* as does a space or a room. A locale is the place constituted in the ongoing *relationship* between people in a particular social world and the 'site and means' they use to meet their interactional needs, i.e., the space together with the resources available there, resources including whatever constitute the 'things' involved in the accomplishment of work, be they objects, artefacts, tools, features, mechanisms and so on. As such, the framework is based on a metaphor of place as the lived interaction with space and resources.

It is because locale arises in the relationship between a social world and its use of space as place, that it is potentially suitable as a shared abstraction for both understanding and designing, albeit used with slightly different emphases for each.

For understanding, the researcher looks at locale with a focus more on people and their actions/interactions, i.e., on their appropriation and evolution of 'site and means' as place for the *practical accomplishment of their work and meeting their interactional needs* (Fitzpatrick et al., 1996; Harrison and Dourish, 1996). This allows for the complex, dynamic and situated 'interactional' aspects of work to be accounted for but not in isolation from where and how those interactions happen.

For designing, the designer looks at locale with a focus more on the *'site and means' used to meet those needs*, and on how those needs could be better supported through the design of different sites and/or means. This allows for the pragmatic needs of design, focusing on the more stable 'environmental' aspects enabling interaction but not in isolation from their use.

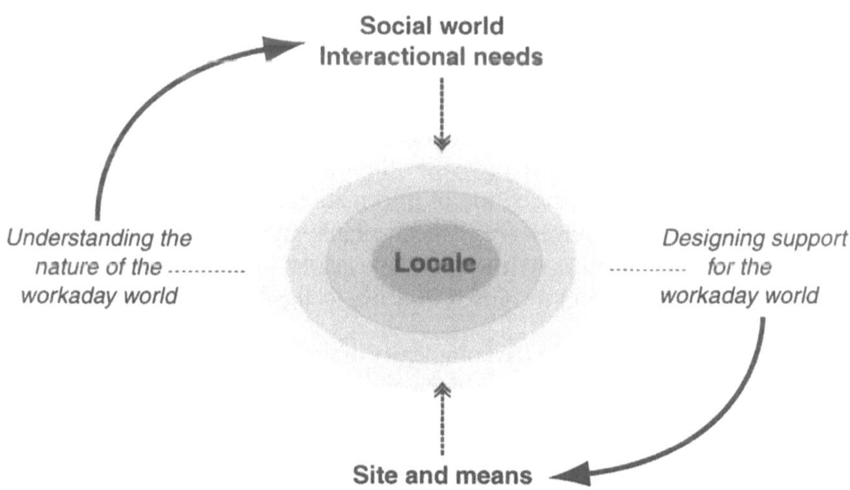

Figure 7.1. A locale, constituted in the relationship between social world and 'site and means', and providing a shared abstraction between understanding and designing.

Even though both activities have a different focus, it is always connected to the total context of the situation at hand because locale, by definition, always includes both the social world and the spaces and resources they interact with and through. This interplay between locale and activities of understanding and designing is depicted in Figure 7.1.

7.2. Overview of Framework Aspects

Given this unit of analysis, the *Locales Framework* is defined in terms of its five aspects: locale foundations, civic structures, individual views, interaction trajectory and mutuality:

- *Locale foundations* identifies the social world of interest and the spaces and resources (interchangeably called site and means) through which the people in the social world achieve their interaction.
- *Civic structure* identifies the relationship of this social world and its locales to the broader context, picking up on social, political, organisational, material, cultural, legislative, contractual, technological and other broader-sphere issues.
- *Individual view* identifies the different perspectives that individuals might hold of the one locale, together with an individual's aggregated view of the multiple locales in which they participate, as appropriate for the domain of interest.
- *Interaction trajectory* is concerned with actions and courses of actions, identifying the dynamic and temporal aspects of the living social world and its interactions within and across locales — past, present and future.
- *Mutuality* is concerned with awareness as an achieved outcome, identifying the mutual communicative processes through which awareness is achieved — the provision and perception of information for awareness. It considers how spaces and resources are made available and accessible to people and how people and their activities are made available and accessible to others through the spaces and resources they use as locale.

These five aspects capture the complexity of the workaday world and position potentially isolated concepts such as 'a group' or 'an artefact' into a coherent organising framework. Together they can provide a principled approach for the following purposes:

- As a heuristic guide for the analysis of work in complex situations that has an ultimate design purpose; building on understandings of previously-seen concepts and patterns of interaction, but still allowing for the emergent situated nature of the specific situation
- For the design of systems to support such work where the design is motivated from an interactional rather than technological perspective.

Moreover, the *Locales Framework* provides a shared set of abstractions and a common language to facilitate communication between the two activities. To this end, the *Locales Framework* purposefully frames the study of the target domain in terms more relevant to what systems designers can ultimately do, which is to construct either new locales of work, or additional tools to support or augment existing locales of work, either physical or virtual. It frames design in terms relevant to interactional needs.

While these aspects are presented as if they are separate orthogonal entities, they are in fact interdependent and overlapping. They are also not meant as an exhaustive nor prescriptive set of issues with which to solve the design challenge. Some aspects will be more relevant or important for a particular domain than others, and concepts and issues beyond the framework will emerge specific to the situation at hand.

The point of the aspects, as previously stated, is to suggest different perspectives on the same phenomenon, bringing aspects to the fore that can otherwise be forgotten. Where concepts and issues specific to the domain of interest do emerge, they can be used to provide feedback to the ongoing evolution of the framework itself.

7.3. Centres and Perspectives

Two important organising principles for the concept of locale in particular and the *Locales Framework* in general are centres and perspectives. These principles come about because locale is based on a metaphor of place and arises from lived interaction with space and resources.

A metaphor of place embodies a principle of *centres*, giving rise to notions of peripheries and relationships (Fitzpatrick, 2000a).[2] In contrast, a metaphor of space embodies a principle of boundaries. When reflecting on the appropriateness of the wOrlds system for the systems engineers, one of the mismatches identified was between a wOrlds room defined by boundaries and the systems engineers group defined by more fluid relationships around their central tasks. Strauss (1993) also questions the appropriateness of boundaries. In noting the variation and relative fluidity of social world boundaries, he suggests that "perhaps it would be better to discard the concept here of boundaries and substitute something like peripheries" (*op.cit.*, p. 214). If we do adopt the concept of peripheries, then peripheries only make sense in relation to something at the centre.

A locale is constituted in the relationship between the social world and its use of space and resources; the shared purpose of the social world provides a centre around which the people, spaces and resources come into relationship. Individuals (or a space or an object) in a locale can become another type of centre, drawing the most related things nearer. For the purposes of the *Locales Framework*, I define a centre as an attractor that relates together, and give sense to, the relevant people, site and means around it.

A principle of centres allows for varying levels of relationship and varying levels of boundaries, as depicted in the representation of 'locale' in Figure 7.1.

We can think of these levels as ripples around a central point, a *continuum* of relationships from the centre to the periphery; where distances from the centre can potentially be defined along multiple different dimensions as appropriate; and where something can be considered as more or less central and more or less marginal. Centre relationships also suggest the possibility of variation and movement along the continuum towards or away from the centre.

Using a centres-based principle, the effect of boundaries, and hence the affordances provided by boundaries, can still be achieved by the degrees and limits of relationships or distance from the centre. This boundary effect, however, is not strictly binary, static and inflexible in the way that physical boundaries are interpreted. Further, the effect of multiple different boundaries can be achieved because different proximity relationships can define different arbitrary boundaries at points that are better differentiated than others.

Because locale arises in a *lived* relationship, everything is defined from some *perspective* or point of view, rather than from a position of absolute objectivity. Perspective, as another organising principle for the *Locales Framework*, plays out in multiple ways.

Each of the *Locales Framework* aspects provide a different perspective or way of understanding the locale of interest, as if turning an object around and studying it from different angles. Consider the student labs in the systems engineers study. We could look at how the labs are physically laid out in the building (foundations). We could look at the departmental regulations about student use (civic structures). We could look at Kate's involvement in the labs as the person primarily responsible for them, or Helen's perspective as the group manager, or the students' perspectives as users of the lab (individual views). We could look at how the software configuration of the labs has evolved over the years (trajectory). We could look at how Helen became aware of the crisis, and how others in the group were made aware (or not) of the current state of the labs so that they could help (mutuality). Each aspect invites us to look at the same thing from different perspectives, asking different questions, and helping to build up a more complete picture.

There is the perspective of each of the entities involved in the locale — the social world, the individuals, the spaces and the things — and how the locale can be viewed and experienced differently from each of their perspectives because of their particular relationships with the locale.

The researchers and designers engaged in understanding and designing look at locale from the perspective of the particular questions that frame their relative interests. They also bring the perspective from their own life trajectories, in terms of experiences, skills, theoretical backgrounds, and so on.

There is the perspective of the question or issue that brings the researcher and designer to the engagement in the first place. With systems engineers, for example, we could have focussed on the one specific episode involved in fixing the elock application or we could have focussed on the how the whole department worked, where CSG is only one of many sub groups.

A major implication of these principles of centres and perspectives is that the *Locales Framework* can be applied at any level of *scale*, from the most focused to the most generalised, from short time frames to long time frames. In the fuller discussion of the *Locales Framework* aspects, the application and influence of these principles will become more obvious.

7.4. Summary

The *Locales Framework* is presented as on ongoing work in progress, a starting point for stakeholders to address the issue of designing support for the work of social worlds in a way that takes account of the broader context of use, and that is applicable to a wide range of domains, physical and virtual. It is meant as a generic framework to be used intelligently and creatively by the researcher/designer as a sensitising device to open up the important elements of a wicked problem context and to be evolved through use.

This chapter introduced some of the general *Locales Framework* issues by discussing the background of the framework, introducing locale as the primary unit of analysis and the five framework aspects, and overviewing the organising framework principles of perspectives and centres. The next chapter explores each of the framework aspects in more detail.

Notes

1 While this theory played a critical role in the evolution of the framework, it is not needed in the application of the framework; ultimately the framework perspectives can be motivated, used and populated independent of Strauss' theory. Understanding that there are other conceptualisations of group and cooperative work for which the *Locales Framework* holds, I use the two terms 'social worlds' and 'groups' interchangeably.

2 A fuller discussion of centres as an organising principle can be found in Fitzpatrick (2000a).

Chapter 8

LOCALES FRAMEWORK ASPECTS

Having laid out the broad background of the *Locales Framework*, this chapter explores each of the framework aspects in some detail. Together these aspects provide a coherent framework for taking account of the group, the individuals in the group, the broader context, how activities happen over time and how a sense of shared place is enabled. Ultimately though, it is the questions that frame the particular study or design context, and the uniqueness of the situation at hand, that will determine what issues are relevant, and to what extent the *Locales Framework* will be useful for framing initial thinking or for organising complex research data or for framing design directions.

The discussions here give a flavour of the sorts of issues that could be explored, but not as an exhaustive or self-sufficient account. One reason is that, in the nature of wicked problems, the aspects can never be completely specified. Another reasons is that more comprehensive discussion of any one of the aspects could take up a book in its own right. Understanding of the aspects themselves will be evolved through use by different people and in different research and design situations.

Each aspect is explored using a variety of techniques so that the discussion can be read at different levels. The *main body* of the discussion provides a basic introduction to the aspect, motivates why it is important, and then introduce some of the issues entailed in the aspect.

Where appropriate, *vignettes* drawn from the systems engineers study are used to illustrate parts of the aspect.

The vignettes from the systems engineers study will be presented in italicised text like this so that they can be easily identified, and skipped over, if desired.

A *boxed text figure* is also used to summarise some of the basic *properties* of the aspect, and the *dimensions* along which these properties can be thought about. This technique of using properties and dimensions to characterise the

Locales Framework aspects is drawn from Strauss (1993). It gives a sense of the kinds of questions that could be asked about the aspect properties. The dimension labels should be interpreted as points on a continuum rather than discrete binary end points or absolute dimensions. For example, if a dimension was 'small ... large' for a property of membership, the researcher or designer might re-phrase this as a question about the size of the membership and the implications of size for design of some supporting solution. An example of the property-dimension figure is given in Figure 8.1.

Property possibly followed by a short definition
Typical Dimensions: a list of typical dimensions, presented in the style of 'this ... that'
where 'this' and 'that' are significant points along some continuum;
These dimensions can be re-phrased as questions where they prove relevant.
Typical Issues: other issues to ask about the property, many of which will be trajectory-related process issues.

Figure 8.1. An example of the technique for summarising properties, dimensions and issues for an aspect.

Whether the properties and dimensions make sense, and how they make sense, will necessarily be context-specific. Some situations might be characterised by relatively stable position along some property dimension, e.g., relatively stable membership size. Others might be characterised by continually changing positions within some (possibly identifiable) range along a dimension, e.g., a membership size that fluctuates between two and ten. For others, the properties might not be relevant at all.

The following discussions address each of the aspects in turn: *locale foundations*, *civic structures*, *individual view*, *interaction trajectory* and *mutuality*.

8.1. Locale Foundations

Locale foundations identifies the social world of interest and the spaces and resources (interchangeably called site and means) through which the people in the social world achieve their interaction.

Why is the *locale foundations* aspect important? *Locale foundations* addresses the axiomatic notion that activities are embedded in social contexts or social worlds. Understanding these social worlds is critical for understanding and designing support for activities since social worlds are "the fundamental building block(s) of collective action" (Clarke, 1991, p. 131). For CSCW in particular, much of this social context can be understood through the group of people engaged in some shared collaborative work. Foundations also addresses the equally axiomatic notion that the workaday world is always constituted in and through some physical and/or virtual contexts, providing the space(s)and resources, or sites and means, that enable actions and interactions, and provide shared context and resources for social worlds (Strauss, 1978).

Some of the generally well-accepted concepts that have emerged within CSCW, and discussed in Chapter 2, also help underpin and motivate this aspect, including: coordination mechanisms, common artefacts, and the concerns of Distributed Cognition and Activity Theory in the mediating role of artefacts.

The interactional needs of a social world and the site and means used to meet those needs are the basic components of the relationship by which *locale* is constituted; hence the naming of this aspect *locale foundations*. The other four aspects build from these foundations, positioning the locale within broader contexts and shedding different kinds of perspectives on the life of the social world in its relationship to its locale.

This section explores in more detail issues relevant to *locale foundations*:

- Characterising the group(s) or social world(s) of interest
- Characterising the spaces and things or site and means that become the locale they use to achieve their goals

A characterisation of a group's needs and the design of appropriate site and/or means to support the workaday world and collective activities of the group is the crux of the CSCW design problem, indeed of the design of socio-technical systems more generally. Foundations is still relevant, for example, where groups might be defined more by common patterns of behaviours or needs or attitudes than by the interdependent and more tightly coupled actions of collaborative groups. This is often talked about in industry as 'target audience segmentations', made up of individuals loosely coupled by shared approaches to individual goals rather than by ongoingly negotiated approaches to shared collective goals. We still need to understand the characteristics of audience segments as a group and the spaces and things they use.

8.1.1 Characterising the Social World

Understanding the primary social world(s) of interest is about asking why the group exists or what makes this a group, who are the people involved, and how is the group constituted and defined. Sometimes, the primary social world(s) is easily identifiable by the framing questions for the study or design exercise, as it was for the systems engineers study. Other times, the framing question entails trying to identify the primary social world(s) involved, as would have been the case if the framing question for the study just mentioned had have been "How is the department's computing environment run?"

The social worlds concept can encompass such diverse groups as the two hardware engineers from the study, the systems engineers group, the builders renovating the house next door, all the employees of Sapient, the people attending the Manchester United football game tonight, the fans of The Beatles music, the set of people who shop online for books in a similar way, the community of World Wide Web users. These social worlds are richly complex, dynamic, and fluid entities. Any attempt to characterise them will necessarily be located from a specific perspective in time and space and from the perspective of the framing questions brought to the exercise. Some of the characteristics that can be used to understand a social world include: collective goal; membership; duration and life-cycle. Examples of the issues for goal, membership and duration for social worlds are summarised in Figure 8.2 and discussed subsequently.

Goal or shared purpose of the social world:

Typical Dimensions: single ... multiple; simple ... complex; concrete ... abstract; specific ... vague; agreed upon ... the subject of dispute and/or negotiation; fixed ... changing; easy to evaluate ... difficult to evaluate; defined in terms of outcomes ... defined in terms of processes;

Typical Issues: how is the goal negotiated and re-negotiated within the group.

Membership of the social world:

Typical Dimensions: clearly defined rules ... no clearly defined rules; small ... large; closed ... open; stable ... unstable; knowable ... unknowable;

Typical Issues: what are the different levels of membership or association for the group; what are the different limits of communication, degrees of commitment, and levels of participation for members; how do people join/leave the group; how do levels of membership relate to privacy, security and access issues; who decides; how does the membership change over time.

Duration of the social world:

Typical Dimensions: short lived ... long lived; new ... old; well planned ... emergent; changing over time ... relatively stable over time; characterised by cycles or patterns ... no cycles or patterns;

Typical Issues: how does the group come into being; how does it dissolve; what are its cycles or patterns.

Figure 8.2. Social world properties of goal, membership and duration.

A social world can be characterised by the nature and focus of its *collective goal* or collective interest — what is the defining feature that makes this a social world. This goal or interest might not necessarily be well developed or completely knowable. It might be general or specific. It might not be totally agreed upon. The goal itself will likely be the focus of ongoing negotiation and evolution in the group as the life of the group unfolds.

The collective purpose of the social world acts as a centre to gather and relate together the various members of the group and the spaces and resources they need.

The systems engineers group share the general collective purpose of maintaining and evolving an operational computing environment for the department. The elock sub group has the more specific goal of updating the elock application, which becomes even more focussed to fixing the elock problem when a problem arises. The day-to-day meaning of the goal is the subject of ongoing interpretation and negotiation among members of the group and their clients.

Social worlds can be characterised by the nature of *membership*. Social world membership can be highly variable and dynamic, both in terms of how well defined membership is, and who constitutes the members at any point in time. Membership of social worlds can be considered along a number of dimensions such as size, formality, openness, stability, knowability, and many more.

The systems engineers group is relatively stable and clearly defined in terms of employment contracts with the university department. Six people form the core of the group. Other people are co-opted as needed, for example the people who had previous student lab experience.

Strauss' conceptualisation of social worlds suggest that membership can also be characterised from a centres-peripheries perspective with respect to a number of other dimensions, depicted in Figure 8.3:

- Degree of commitment
- Limit of communication
- Level of participation

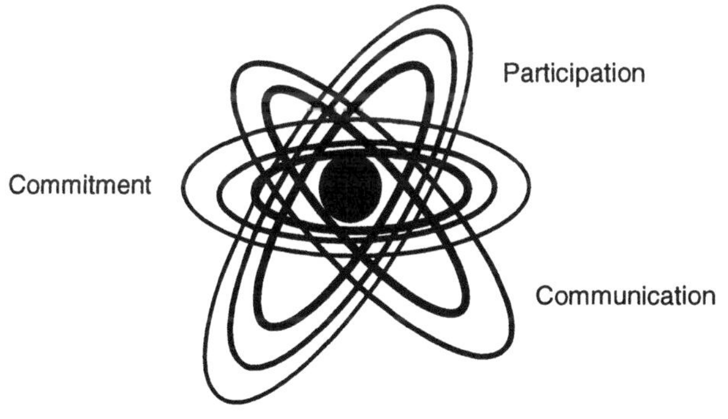

Figure 8.3. A social world centre with multiple peripheries defined by commitment, communication and participation.

These are multiple dimensions along which the effect of multiple boundaries can be seen in a social world. Differentiated peripheries might exist around the degree of commitment to the social world purpose. This can vary from intense commitment to wavering commitment. Differentiated peripheries can exist according to the limits of communication. These might vary from co-located face-to-face communication to geographically and possibly temporally dispersed communication via different technological media. Differentiated peripheries can also be described according to different levels of participation - these can vary from actively involved in core activities to passively involved in marginal activities.

The varying levels of commitment, communication and participation, i.e., the movement between the centre and the peripheries along these dimensions, can be highly dynamic in space and time: across time with the temporal ebbs and flows, phases and cycles of social world activities; and across space as people and artefacts move around the sites used by the social world to support their work practices.

Consider Tex's participation in the elock group. Tex can be seen as a more peripheral member of the group compared to Frances and Helen. His commitment to the group is via the engagement of his company to support the elock application. His communication with the group is limited to email and phone, except for the times when he works on-site. His participation is mostly passive, except for the period of intensive work when he upgraded the software.

Social worlds can be characterised by *duration*, whether they are transient or permanent, how long they have been a group and so on. Related to this are life-cycle issues, how the group came into existence, and the rhythms and patterns of group over time.

CSG is a long-lived group. The group was instituted soon after the department came into being, though its size and membership has changed over the years. There is an expectation that there will always be a systems engineers group as long as the department exists.

Other characteristics that can be used to understand a social world include structure, roles and culture; associated dimensions and issues to be discussed are summarised in Figure 8.4.

Social worlds can be characterised by their internal *structure*. The group could, for example, be strongly hierarchical or relatively flat in structure. It can be composed of sub-worlds, which in turn are composed of sub-worlds, and so on.

CSG is composed of many sub-worlds. Some of these sub-worlds correspond to the formal assignment of primary and secondary responsibilities for a particular area, e.g., Frances and Helen who looked after elock. Some also include external participants, e.g., Tex by contractual arrangement in the elock group. Other sub-worlds are more emergent and often less formally recognised, such as the group of people seconded to help with the student lab disaster.

Roles within the group can be ways of designating particular responsibilities to particular people. Other roles can be more informal, and often self-selected.

The primary and secondary responsibility lists for the CSG members constitute part of their formal role within the group. Alan took on the self-selected role of

Structure of the social world:
Typical Dimensions: hierarchical ... network ... flat; composed of sub-worlds ... includes overlapping worlds; corresponds to formal groupings ... independent of formal groupings; rigid ... flexible; strong ... weak;
Typical Issues: how does the structure emerge and evolve.

Roles fulfilled within the social world:
Typical Dimensions: fixed ... fluid; imposed ... socially agreed upon; assigned ... self-selected; generic ... specific;
Typical Issues: how do roles arise and evolve; how do roles relate to the effect of boundaries via access and security issues.

Group culture, conventions, rules, policies, etc. that are part of the 'soft' means and resources of the social world:
Typical Dimensions: weak ... strong; implicit ... explicit;
Typical Issues: how do people become enculturated into the group; how do these 'soft' means support various social world processes.

Figure 8.4. Social world properties of structure, roles and group culture.

sending notices to the group of any interesting new technologies he came across that he thought they might be interested in.

Internal *culture*, conventions, rules, policies and the like can also frame, as well as reify, the nature of the social world. Other issues such as status, power, gender might also be relevant for the social world at hand.

The issues of the *focus* or object of the group's activities in relation to the goal, and on the *tasks* involved in achieving the goal are also important for understanding social worlds. While an overview of these issues is provided in Figure 8.5, they will be explored more fully in identifying the locales of interest and in the trajectory aspect.

Focus of work in relation to the goal(s):
Typical Dimensions: single ... multiple; physical ... virtual ... conceptual; simple ... complex; existing ... to be modified ... to be created;
Typical Issues: how is the object known, represented, shared.

Tasks in achieving shared goal, both primary and secondary:
Typical Dimensions: directly related to goal/object of work (core) ... indirectly related to goal/object of work (peripheral); easy ... difficult; plannable ... emergent; independent ... interconnected; simple ... complex; unitary ... decomposable into sub tasks;
Typical Issues: also the relationship of tasks together, the relationship of tasks to object(s) of work, the degree of coupling between tasks.

Figure 8.5. Focus and task properties of social world.

8.1.2 Characterising the Locales of Interest

Along with understanding the social world of interest, we also need to identify and characterise the 'where' and 'with what' people use to accomplish their activities. We can talk about these as the 'site and means' or 'spaces and resources' from which locale or locales are constituted. This is a key part of the *Locales Framework* because it is ultimately talking about the kinds of support that systems designers can provide through computer-based spaces and things.

Relationship of Locales to Sites

What is the relationship then between this notion of locale and site or space? As stated previously, a locale is more to do with the notion of place as experienced and defined by members of a social world. It is constituted in the relationship between a social world's needs and the sites and means (spaces and resources) used to meet those needs.

The principles of centres and perspectives come into play here. A social world perspective enables members to filter and structure the broader environment and make relevant parts of it comprehensible and useful. The social world and its needs act as a centre for creating the relationships among the relevant sites and means; those spaces and resources that are most relevant are drawn close and into sharper focus, other less relevant parts are more towards the background, while yet other parts that are not relevant at all remain totally out of view.

The spaces that form locale can be physical spaces or virtual spaces (in the sense of being electronic or computer-based). Locales can also be constituted from a mix of overlaid or intermeshing sites and means.

The elock locale arises from intermeshed and overlapping spaces. The centre of the elock locale is the software comprising the elock application which is located in a particular network directory – a virtual space. Frances and Helen often work on the application from the computers on their desks in their offices – a physical space – but can also access the elock application from any computer connected to the network. Tex accesses the application from his office thousands of miles away – another physical and virtual space. As well as software tools, they also use a physical file of notes about the application and hard-copy software manuals. They often use email and telephone calls to communicate with each – a different sort of virtual overlay. The data the application uses comes from the central administration branch – overlap with another set of spaces.

There is not necessarily a one-to-one mapping between social worlds and spaces. One space can be a different locale for multiple social worlds.

The same machine room is a different sort of locale for both the CSG hardware group and the CSG software group. They see it and engage with it in different ways with respect to their different collective purposes and their different kinds of activities.

There can be different kinds of mappings between locale and spaces. Some form persistent mappings, others are more transiently mapped.

Part of the CSG locale is strongly and persistently mapped to the individuals' offices in the departmental building. On the other hand, the departmental meeting room is a shared space that is appropriated by CSG as their meeting locale for the duration of the meeting only. Their virtual locales are mapped to their virtual site in a less tangible and visible way.

Locales exist in relationship to other locales (the nature of these relationships will be discussed more fully in in relation to *civic structures*). Locales can be comprised of sub-locales.

Our wOrlds research group was physically located in a large office in a building on campus — the wOrlds locale. This locale is divided into a number of sub-locales by the positioning of dividers and desks corresponding to individual work spaces. The table in the centre of the room is a different sort of sub-locale, being used by all people in the room for ad hoc meetings.

Figure 8.6 begins to capture some of the characterising dimensions of sites or spaces as fields or domains of activity. Apart from the dimensions noted, other characteristics of site could be captured in drawings of the layout and configuration of the site, diagrams of movements around the site, and so on.

Site or space as the domain or field of activity:
Typical Dimensions: physical ... virtual ... mixed; geometric ... non-geometric; distributed ... centralised; public ... private; inhabited ... visited; persistent ... transient; strongly mapped to a particular social world ... weakly mapped to a particular social world ... intermittently mapped to a particular social world; stable ... changing slowly ... changing rapidly;
Typical Issues: the layout of the physical space or the configuration and representation of virtual space; the features of the space; people's positions and movements within the space; and the position and relationship of objects within the space.

Figure 8.6. Dimensions of sites or spaces making up locale.

In summary, a locale can be constituted from many different sites and means, in dynamically varying configurations, in so far as they are used by the people in the social world to achieve their central purpose. The fact that moment-by-moment interactions of a social world may be mapped to certain spaces at certain times is only of importance in relation to the interactions themselves. Also, a social world can have multiple locales in which it works; whether these are considered as sub-locales of a larger conceptual locale for the group, or whether they are regarded together as the aggregation of locales used by the group, depends on what makes most sense for the purposes at hand. As stated by Strauss (1961) (and previously quoted on page 85) in relation to his observations of life in a city:

"The important thing about any given urban world is not that it is rooted in space. That is merely what often strikes the eye first ... What is important about a social world is that

> its members are linked by some sort of shared symbolisation, some effective channels of communication." (Strauss, 1961, p. 67)

The locale concept captures the supporting 'site and means' by which this shared symbolisation and effective communication occurs.

Means

Sites are furnished with the *means* or resources that people in the social world use to accomplish their activities; Figure 8.7 begins to capture some of the characterising dimensions of the means.

> **Means** or resources as the created or inherent 'furnishings' or 'things' of the site – the features, objects, tools, artefacts etc.:
> *Typical Dimensions*: tangible ... intangible; physical ... virtual; persistent ... transient; stable ... evolving; private ... public; familiar ... new; core ... peripheral;
> *Typical Issues*: how is the object identified and known about within the group; how accessible and available is the object; what are the relationships between objects; what is the object's relationship to the site.

Figure 8.7. Dimensions of means that make up a locale.

Means encompass a whole range of features and objects, some connected directly with the performance of the work, others connected more indirectly by facilitating interaction about the work (c.f. Chapter 2). Means also include the media and mechanisms discussed by Hollan and Stornetta (1992) (and noted on page 85); these will be discussed in more detail in the *mutuality* section.

These 'means' can be created or inherent features of the domain. The following lists some examples of the types of created things that could be part of the available means for a group:

- Objects or artefacts as the focus of the social world activities
- Tools used to create or modify other objects
- Objects used to facilitate communication around the work, e.g., common artefacts (Robinson, 1993b; Robinson, 1993c), or mechanisms of interaction (Schmidt and Simone, 1996) (c.f. Chapter 2)
- Reference materials such as policies, guidelines, prototypes, etc., that help inform the work — these are not usually modified during the course of the work

Means also include the created and inherent infrastructure of the space itself. Created infrastructure includes features such as doors, windows, walls, etc., in a physical space, and (interpreted more loosely) network partitions and file types in virtual space. Inherent features also include the presence of air, and the laws of sound and light transmission in physical spaces, and the absence of sensory support in a virtual space.

CSG offices are situated down one side of a corridor, with the machine room, meeting room, and printing room opposite. There is one person per office. The offices are furnished with desks, chairs, filing cabinets, bookshelves, phone, computer, etc., that each person has arranged in a unique configuration. Doors and locks are an important access and security mechanism. Each of the members uses their door in different ways to provide privacy. (In a fuller discussion of these issues, we could go on here to draw examples of office layouts, the relation of desks to doors, etc. We could also go on to describe the layout of the machine room, etc.)

Means can also play a role in facilitating access and supporting privacy and security in the group locale, often complementing the group's social processes and protocols in these regards. This is summarised in Figure 8.8.

Access and security, as facilitated by features of the site, e.g., to support boundary-like affordances:
Typical Dimensions: closed - regulated - open; rigid - flexible; implicit - explicit; implemented at an object level - implemented at a locale level;
Typical Issues: who decides on appropriate access and security levels; how are these negotiated, communicated, monitored, enforced, etc.; how are features or resources of the site used to facilitate access and security.

Figure 8.8. Access properties associated with site and means of locale.

Use of the office door in the previous vignette is one example of a site feature being used by members to control access to their own office spaces. Passwords, differentiated permissions on files, dial-in access, and moderated mailing list memberships are other mechanisms used in their virtual domain.

Together, these site and means ultimately serve to both enable and constrain possibilities for social world interactions. This creates an interesting tension between locales and interactions in terms of their relative rates of change. Many features of space and things change relatively slowly, if at all, e.g., a physical building structure, the speed of computer network, etc. Brand (1994) identifies six layers of a physical building that are all changeable at different rates with use. All of these can also be interpreted as different layers of the available site and means:

- *Site:* used in a more specific sense than Strauss' use of 'site', to mean the geographical setting, the urban location of a building
- *Structure:* the foundation and load-bearing elements
- *Skin:* the exterior surface

- *Services:* the working infrastructure of a building, e.g., the communications wiring, electrical wiring, plumbing, etc.
- *Space plan:* the interior layout of walls, doors etc.
- *Stuff:* the furniture, e.g., chairs, desks, phones, pictures, etc.

Site is the most stable layer, while the other layers are changed progressively more frequently until the stuff layer which can be changed on daily (or even more frequent) basis if necessary.[1] Actions, on the other hand, are continually permuting to suit the contingencies at hand. Within the constraints of the locale, people are continually exploring its enabling possibilities and using space and resources as locale in creative ways to meet their interactional needs. At a slower rate, the locale itself is also evolved to meet new needs, and on it goes. Paraphrasing Winston Churchill, Brand (1994) notes:

> "First we shape our buildings, then they shape us, then we shape them again — ad infinitum. Function reforms form perpetually." (Brand, 1994, p. 3).

Locale Foundations Summary

This section has outlined the foundational issues of who is the social world, and what are the sites and means used by the social world in constituting their locale. Ultimately, the outcome of the design process will be new or enhanced sites and means that can become locales for some group. Before deciding on what these new locales might be, the other *Locales Framework* aspects will provide different perspectives to better understand how social worlds interact in and with their locales, in both a local and global context.

8.2. Civic Structure

Civic structure identifies the relationship of the social world and its locales to the broader context, picking up on social, political, organisational, material, cultural, legislative, contractual, technological and other broader-sphere issues: a view of the 'world' from the perspective of the locale of interest.

Why is the *civic structure* aspect important? Just as actions don't take place in a vacuum, so social worlds and their locales don't exist in a vacuum, as we saw in the systems engineers study. *Civic structure* is about trying to uncover and understand this broader interactional context that both impacts on, and is impacted by, social world actions in the locale of interest. In so doing, 'public sphere' issues, including social, political, organisational, material, cultural, legislative, contractual, and technological issues, can be made more visible in the design process.

In many ways, *civic structure* takes the other *Locales Framework* aspects but asks the questions at the global scale from the perspective of the social world of interest. Instead of talking about members of a social world, we talk about social worlds as members of the larger 'world'. Instead of talking about a locale, we talk about the world of locales. Interactions, navigation, and life-cycle processes address *interaction trajectory* concerns on a larger scale. *Mutuality* aspects consider how the various social worlds and locales maintain a sense of their shared relationships and interdependencies in the global sphere. *Individual view* is about the view each of the component locales might have of the global space.

Civic structure is a relatively recursive notion, depending on the granularity and perspective of the locale of interest.

> *If the whole of the CSG locale is the focus, the elock group would be regarded as a sub-locale and* civic structures *for CSG could include the departmental users of the software. If, instead, the elock group is the focus of attention, then it might make more sense to think about the other CSG sub-locales as part of the civic structure for elock.*

In the spirit of the *Locales Framework* as an aid for understanding and designing, there are no right or wrong answers; it is not critical whether a locale be labelled as 'in' or 'out' of the civic structure layer but rather by applying similar concepts at varying levels of interactions between groups and their locales, we might be able to identify dependencies and overlapping concerns that weren't previously obvious.

The rest of this section covers the following issues in turn: the structuring of locales in the broader sphere and the relationships between locales, including the mutuality and interaction between locales and the external influences on a locale; the navigation around locales; and the life-cycle processes of locales. (Note that talk about locales here, by definition, also includes the social world for which the locale has meaning.)

8.2.1 Inter-locale Relationships

Social worlds and their locales exist in a broader sphere of dynamically changing and fluid relationships with other social worlds and locales. The relationships of particular concern in the *Locales Framework* context are those centred around the locale, or locales, of primary interest. The first question to ask, then, is what are the other social worlds relevant to the social world of interest.

> *The social world of primary interest in the CSG study is the systems engineers group. Some of the social worlds that have direct impact on the work of the systems engineers include the student body, the teaching staff of the department, the departmental administration staff, the central Administration Branch, and so on. Less involved but still relevant social worlds include the software and hardware supply; also the government funding body that determines how resource usage should be accounted for, which in turn influenced the earlier decision to administer the labs separately from CSG.*

At any point in time, some relationships will be stronger, or more important or relevant than other relationships, depending on the interactional needs of the group.

During the elock crisis, the central Administration Branch locale came into closer relationship with CSG, specifically with the elock sub-locale, because of the changes they made to the student number format. Previously, their relationship was much more peripheral.

One way to represent the centres-nature of these relationships is via a conditional matrix diagram (Corbin, 1991). A conditional matrix is a technique for capturing some of the conditions that influence or impact on the phenomenon at the centre of the matrix. In Figure 8.9, a conditional matrix illustrates some of the social worlds relevant to the elock group during normal maintenance times. The distance from the centre reflects the relative importance of the relationships along some dimension, in this case the daily maintenance of the system. The inner rings are those features that have the closest influence on the centre while the outer rings have the least.[2] (By way of example, a different form of representation is used in Chapter 10 to show the relationship of the different social worlds making up the civic structure for a distributed research group.)

These relationships help identify the potential source of external influences and inter-dependencies. These can be of many different forms — organisational, professional, financial, contractual, legislative, ethical, cultural, political, technological, production-related and so on. Further, the relationships can have either a unidirectional or a bidirectional effect.

Consider the relationship between CSG, the student labs, the Engineering College and federal legislation. The labs were initially administered separately to the rest of CSG to conform to the (unidirectional) federal accounting requirement. When the Engineering College increased the recurrent funding for the department, the departmental managers and university auditors were able to bring the labs under the CSG umbrella while still conforming to government requirements.
Another example we could give here is the relationship between CSG and their hardware and software suppliers (bidirectional), and between CSG and the lecturers whose teaching requirements largely influence what is bought and whose work is in turn influenced by the computing environment able to be provided (bidirectional).

There can be varying levels of interdependence between social worlds and their locales, ranging from a general interest to a tight coupling.

The elock group are directly dependent on the central Administration Branch to maintain the central database of students and staff. Moreover, the elock application directly downloads the database at regular intervals and so depends on a consistency of format and access. When the Adminstration Branch decided to change the format of the student number, the elock application had to be changed accordingly.

Having identified the relevant social worlds, we then need to identify their respective locales, and, more specifically, how inter-locale interactions are supported.

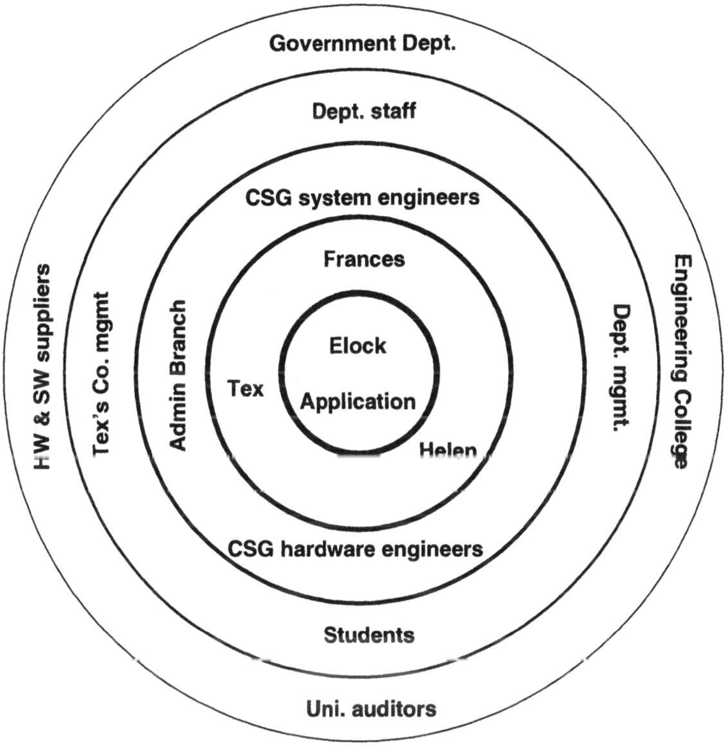

Figure 8.9. A conditional matrix representing civic structures around the elock application. The first concentric ring encapsulates the elock social world. Consecutive circles indicate increasingly distant aspects of the civic structure.

The Administration Branch locale is a mix of physical offices and computer-based spaces. For interactions between the elock and Administration Branch locales, people use various communication media, such as paper-based inter-departmental memos, email, and person-to-person phone calls. The elock application can also be coded to directly interact with the Administration Branch database.

As with the *mutuality* aspect, the different ways in which a locale can be made present, available and accessible in the public sphere need to be considered. This brings in issues of identity and representation. Most social worlds, through their locales, create different interfaces for different *civic structures* relationships. This enables them to differentiate between that which is internal and private, and that which can be made available to the external world. These various interfaces can create the effect of boundaries around the world and locale. A locale can have multiple different forms of boundary information available to satisfy different relationships.

The interface between elock and the students and staff of the department is the functional door access system. When the system has problems, the people within elock interact more directly to explain what is going on, a different interface between elock and students and staff. The interface between elock and the Administration Branch is via their database schema definition. Again, when there are problems or changes in these public-facing interface, the people involved in the social world serve as additional points of access.

One mechanism for the representation of this information may be *boundary objects* (Star, 1989). A boundary object can encapsulate the publicly shared information that constitutes the locale's presence to those external to, or less involved in the detail of, its work. A boundary object can be used differently by different social worlds. A further issue then is what are the processes for deciding what information is to be made available to whom and in what form and how do worlds engage with boundary objects.

The government policy document on university accounting procedures is an example of a boundary object by which the government encapsulates information to be made available to the universities in the country.

Figure 8.10 summarises some of the dimensions and issues that can be used to characterise inter-locale relationships.

Relationship between locales:
Typical Dimensions: formal ... informal; known ... unknown; simple ... complex; direct... indirect; close ... distant; uncoupled trajectories ... loosely coupled trajectories ... tightly coupled trajectories; information-based ... influence-based; unidirectional ... bidirectional; conflictual ... supportive;
Typical Issues: What is the nature of the relationships, e.g., organisational, professional, financial, contractual, legislative, ethical, cultural, political, cultural, technological, production-related, etc.? How are the locales identified and known in the public sphere? How do the relationships change over time? How are the relationships negotiated and maintained? What are the interfaces that mediate the relationships?

Figure 8.10. Inter-locale relationship dimensions.

8.2.2 Way-Finding in the Civic Sphere

Implicit in the previous discussions was the notion that people are able to find their way around the public sphere, otherwise how are they able to identify locales of interest, or access boundary information, or create new inter-locale relationships. The question then is, how does the civic sphere facilitate way-finding? Figure 8.11 captures some of the dimensions and issues to be considered.

We can talk about way-finding as the physical or virtual *navigation* between points. To a large extent, the inter-locale structure itself can determine how people navigate their way, what paths they are likely to take or able to take,

Way-finding in the civic sphere:
Typical Dimensions: physical ... virtual; focussed ... serendipitous; easy ... difficult; direct ... indirect; by location ... by features;
Typical Issues: How does the inter-locale structure facilitate movement and navigation? What representations or sources of information exist of other locales in the civic sphere? What are the signs or markers or search facilities to aid way-finding?

Figure 8.11. Civic sphere way-finding dimensions.

who they are likely to meet, and how they know where they are and where they can go.

In physical environments, this structure can take the form of the spatial configuration of the locale buildings and features. Hillier and Hanson(1984) discuss at length how spatial configurations, both within the home and in public spaces, influence paths travelled and hence opportunities for interaction. In computer-based environments, this structure can take the form of partitions in a network or explicit links in a hypertext document. Lynch's (1960) concepts of legibility and the role of paths, edges, districts, nodes, landmarks, can be interpreted for both physical and virtual domains.

The structure of the public sphere can be represented in some form, such as a map or a directory, that serves as a resource for way-finding. Other people or objects can be other sources of information about the inter-locale structure. Locale addresses, such as street addresses or network addresses, can also communicate structure information.

We can also talk about way-finding in terms of *discovery*, e.g., of people, objects, ideas, locales, etc., in which we might be interested. Discovery can happen via serendipitous encounters or focussed navigation, or even 'stumbling around in the dark'. Different searching mechanisms can be used. These can be facilitated by public resources, such as the telephone yellow pages or computer-based search engines.

There can also be options for different forms of movement, such as passing every point in between two points as must happen in bodily movement in the physical domain, or warping or 'teleporting' from one point to another without passing points in between (Benedikt, 1994) as can be facilitated in the virtual domain. Movement possibilities carry implications for how discovery can happen.

Because the members of CSG and the departmental staff all have offices in the same building, they are in relatively close physical proximity. They can find out the location of each other's office by looking up a departmental handbook, which is in both hard printed and soft electronic copy. They can ask other people. Similarly, they can find out who fulfils certain roles by looking up the staff directory. They can choose to physically walk to a different location, where they can happen to bump into people along the way. Alternatively, they can choose to navigate the virtual infrastructure of the department, where they can move directly from point to point.

8.2.3 Life-cycle Processes

The life-cycle processes for locales are concerned with the emergence and dissolution of locales, and by implication the emergence and dissolution of social worlds since locales only make sense in relation to a social world. An important aspect for the *emergence* of social worlds is that of discovery, mentioned in the previous section; discovery of other locales, people and resources that might lead to the emergence of a new social world and locale.

After the initial lab crisis was averted, Alan formed a new social world to devise an ongoing management plan. He was able to identify the people to be invited because of previous discussions with people and from seeing names on existing code in the system. He found out that two of the people who had previously worked in the labs were currently working elsewhere in the department. He sought these people out (via email and followup visit) and invited them to be part of his new group.

According to Strauss (1993), new social worlds can also emerge from 'arenas'. Arenas arise when different social worlds interact around some (often contentious) issue. New social worlds can arise out of these interactions as contentions are resolved and the worlds move closer together.

The *dissolution* of social worlds and their locales is also part of the locale life-cycle. When a social world no longer has a reason for being together, the members are likely to disband it, explicitly or implicitly. However, the output of a social world's work may need to be known or used beyond the life of that world. The term, *residual objects*, can refer to those objects which encapsulate the results of this work. Residual objects leave a trace of the locale after the social world has completed its collective task. These residual objects can then become incorporated into other locales where needed.

The new social world to put in place the student laboratory management plan disbanded once the plan was completed. The report they produced at the end became a residual object from their locale of work which then became incorporated into the CSG locale.

8.2.4 Civic Structure Summary

In summary, *civic structure* concerns the facilitation of interaction with the wider community within and beyond a person's known social worlds and locales. It encompasses issues of how to support the structuring of locales in the broader sphere, the relationships between locales, way-finding in the public sphere, and the emergence and dissolution of social world locales.

8.3. Individual Views

Individual view identifies the different perspectives that individuals who comprise a social world might hold of the one locale, together with an individual's aggregated view of the multiple locales in which they participate, as appropriate for the domain of interest.

Why is *individual view* important? While we are concerned with social worlds and their locales of work, it is important to remember that a social world is not a homogeneous group. It is comprised of individuals who each bring their own perspective, history, needs and agenda to the group.

By highlighting the perspectives of *individual-in-group*, rather than focussing on one or the other, the *Locales Framework* directly addresses the concern that Heath and Luff (1996a) have about the distinction between the individual and the collaborative:

> "With its emphasis on cooperation and, in particular, technical support for the "group" and cooperative activity, CSCW runs the risk of entrenching the distinction between the individual and the collaborative, allowing us to preserve a demarcation between particular tasks and their coordination. Observations of computer-supported cooperative work in real-world organizational environments suggest that it is both difficult and tenuous to delineate the individual from the collaborative." (Heath and Luff, 1996a, p. 125)

Many other studies of work have also indicated the subtle and complex interplays between individual and collaborative work and the relatively seamless transitions that people negotiate between different work contexts (Dourish and Bellotti, 1992; Heath and Luff, 1992; Ishii, 1990; Luff et al., 1992). In particular, Suchman (1996) and Goodwin and Goodwin (1996) describe in detail how individual perspectives contribute to a joint activity in an airline operations room, where:

> "The ability to see something is always tied to a particular position encompassing a range of phenomena including placement within a larger organization, a local task, and access to relevant material and cognitive tools." (Goodwin and Goodwin, 1996, p. 61)

If we were to explore a collaborative work environment solely from a group perspective, and ignore the individual's role in making the group 'happen', then we would fail to capture how this work is achieved moment-by-moment through the perspective of the contributing social world members.[3] Furthermore, each individual is likely to be a *member of multiple different social worlds* simultaneously, holding unique views of each of those worlds. Salvador and Bly (1997), for example, use the concept of 'constellations' to describe the dynamic individual-centric views of people and information from multiple work contexts that are held simultaneously.

Systems design needs to take greater account of the individuals' perspectives of, and engagement with, different locales. *Individual view* draws attention to the individual-in-groups' concerns by looking at the different individual views that can be held of the same locale and at the individual's view over multiple locales.

The notion of *centre* is an important organising principle for understanding *individual view*. Just as the group acts as a centre to attract and relate as locale the 'things' it needs from the broader environment, here it is the individual who acts as a centre of attraction, drawing from the locales in which they participate the spaces and things relevant to their social world roles or needs at any point in time.

8.3.1 Different Individual Views of One Locale

While there may be a group definition of the locale, the individuals in the social world rarely see the same things all the time in exactly the same way. Each individual will have their own idiosyncratic view of the locale reflecting their current level of involvement and focussed on those parts of the locale that are most relevant for them. This level of involvement is often associated with their current responsibilities, roles, activities, or interests.

Different views of the same locale can be held by different people because they have different interests or different levels of commitment or participation in the locale. Further, as the individuals' interest or level of participation in the social world changes, so their view of the locale will also change. Also, each individual could hold different views over the one locale depending on their own different roles or interests in the locale. This aggregation of views is called a *view set*. We can begin to characterise individual view and view sets of the one locale with the properties and dimensions outlined in Figure 8.12.

View, the aggregation of what is of interest from the locale for a particular person:
Typical Dimensions: all ... subset ... none; full ... peripheral ... none; imposed ... self-selected; implicit ... explicit; static, persistent ... dynamically changing; predictable ... unpredictable; high level ... in detail;
Typical Issues: where there are other people who share a similar view, it may be possible to define a *sub-locale* of interest.

View set, the different views that a person may hold over the one locale:
Typical Dimensions: single view ... multiple views; stable ... changing infrequently ... changing frequently; ad hoc switching between views ... planned or phased switching between views;
Typical Issues: how does the person manage the different views in the set; are there relationships between various views.

Figure 8.12. View properties of *individual view*.

At any point in time in relation to a particular view, we can ask about the individual's level of focus and participation in the locale reflected in their locale view (Figure 8.13). By focus, we mean the degree to which the individuals are attending to the locale view. By participation, we mean their level of actual engagement in the locale.

Focus, the degree to which the locale view is attended to:
Typical Dimensions: all ... subset ... none; intense/full ... peripheral; foreground ... background; coarse granularity, high-level ... fine granularity, detail; one-off ... intermittent ... continuous;

Participation, the level of actual engagement in the locale:
Typical Dimensions: all ... subset ... none; peripheral ... intense; active ... passive; direct ... indirect; restricted ... open; isolated event ... intermittent ... ongoing;

Figure 8.13. Focus and participation properties of *individual view*.

Frances, Helen and Tex all hold different views over the elock locale. Frances, as the person assigned with primary responsibility, is closely involved in the day-to-day running of the elock application and interactions with the users of the application. Helen has a background view of the locale that is less detailed and involved than Frances' view. This view changed significantly to a more focussed and detailed view when she was actively participating in the locale with Frances to overcome the elock problem. Tex's view of elock is very much focussed on the application code and associated tools, although the details of this view will change depending on whether he is engaged in maintaining or upgrading the application.

In physical environments, individual perspectives can sometimes be both facilitated, and potentially made visible to others in the group, by the physical orientation and positioning of objects and people in relationship to one another. In virtual environments, more pro-active steps have to be taken to make this perspective information mutually available, if at all.

The two hardware engineers might be working together in the machine room, but they can be focussed on different areas. Where they are positioned, where their body is facing, and the machine, tools, parts, and manuals they have close to hand indicates their current individual perspective on their shared locale of work.

Spatial positioning and orientation are key features used in the maintenance of separate work spaces, and in the production of joint activity in Suchman's (1996) analysis of an Operations room event and in Heath and Luff's (1996a) study of a London Underground control room.

Each person who is a member of the locale's social world will potentially hold their own unique set of views over the same locale. This can be a source of potential conflict within the group. A significant amount of work in collaborative groups therefore has to do with the continual re-alignment and re-orientation of individual perspectives to the shared common purpose (Suchman, 1996) and workspace(s).

In working together to fix the elock problem, Helen and Frances had to engage in communication work to align their individual views of the locale so that they could work on the problem together.

Mutuality mechanisms, to be discussed later in this chapter, play an important role here. *Mutuality* can be seen as the mechanisms by which individuals can update their view of the locale, its members and objects, according to their interactional needs. For example, Robinson's (1993) common artefacts and Schmidt and Simone's (1996) coordination mechanisms can be seen as supporting the coordination of individual views; they provide common reference points of group activity and the state of the shared place of work, against which the individual's view can be updated.

8.3.2 Individual View over Multiple Locales

> "A major set of conditions for actors' perspectives, and thus their interactions, is their memberships in social worlds and subworlds. In contemporary society, these memberships are often complex, overlapping, contrasting, conflicting, and not always apparent to other interactants."(Strauss, 1993, p. 41)

People usually belong to multiple social worlds simultaneously and work on tasks from different social worlds at once, with varying degrees of focus and participation. Rather than work with a fixed group view of each locale, and attending to each locale in turn, people will often work with a view composed from *multiple locale views* — their workaday world. Into their workaday view will be drawn the things they need as they need them from whatever locales are relevant locales at the time. This aggregation of views from multiple locales is a different type of view set to the one described in the previous section where an individual can hold multiple views of the one locale; here the *view set* is filtered and aggregated from the base locales, whereas in the previous discussion, the view is filtered from the one locale.

The workaday world of people involves continually negotiating and managing their individual views over multiple locales, sometimes focussing on one exclusively, more often though having multiple locale views at varying levels of focus at the one time. People are often able to move relatively seamlessly and unselfconsciously between these locale views with their different activities, maintaining dynamically varying levels of focus and participation in the other locales as well. Physical and virtual spaces support different ways of doing this.

In some instances, context switching between different social world activities can be associated with re-location from one physical space to another. This is particularly so when the activities of a social world are closely mapped to a particular space, such as the machine room for the hardware engineers or the squash courts for the squash team. We can also choose to map an activity to a space when we want exclusive focus, for example, when CSG members move from their offices to a closed meeting room for their weekly meeting.

There are many instances though where different activities are not necessarily associated with a distinguished physical space. For example, on my desktop are objects drawn from my activities in multiple different locales — part of my view over those locales. There might be a paper that I am co-authoring with a colleague, but there might also be the agenda for a departmental meeting, the squash court schedule that I have to review as the club secretary, and so on. Switching between these tasks can be seen as switching between different social world involvements and their different locales. The computer screen can be used to present an analogous view over multiple virtual locales of work. As discussed in Chapter 5, the workspace shown on page 56 represents Sue's filtered view of the virtual locales in which she participates. Such computer-based locales facilitate different forms of dynamic view configuration and context switching than is possible in a physical medium.

An obvious question at this point is why talk about involvement in multiple social worlds, why not just talk about people working on lots of different tasks at the one time?[4] While it is quite adequate at one level to describe this as multi-tasking, multi-tasking fails to capture the social and interactional contexts in which those tasks are undertaken. The explicit positioning of the tasks within the life and locales of the associated social worlds draws attention to these broader task contexts.

In summary, as well as the properties and dimensions suggested in Figure 8.12 for the individual's view(s) of each of the component locales, we can also consider the related process issues noted in Figure 8.14 to understand their view over multiple locales.

- What are the multiple locales that the individual has an interest in?
- What are the locale views that the individual requires of each locale?
- What, if any, are the relationships between the locales and/or locale entities?
- How does the individual manage their interactions with multiple locales?
- What are the mechanisms available to support involvement in multiple locales, e.g., periodicity, location change, carrying things around, gathering things around, etc.?
- How are common views of the locales supported, i.e., what are the processes by which a sense of shared workspace is maintained when the individual has a selected view of the locale?

Figure 8.14. Typical process issues for *individual view*.

8.3.3 Individual Views Summary

Individual view is essentially about meeting the needs of individuals in a social world, and the needs of an individual in multiple social worlds. The locale creates a view over the 'world' from a social world perspective. The individuals in the social world further filter their own views of the locale to facilitate their particular involvement in the social world. An individual also belongs to multiple social worlds at once, and so will likely have an aggregation of views of each the associated locales as part of their workaday world.

8.4. Interaction Trajectory

"Actions are embedded in interactions [and systems of meaning] — past, present and imagined future." (Strauss, 1993, p. 24).

So far the *Locales Framework* aspects have characterised the more structural or definitional elements of locales – the people, spaces, resources, and broader contexts. The *interaction trajectory* aspect captures all of the dynamic and temporal aspects of the living social world and its interactions within and across locales — past, present and future — and the co-evolution of action, locale, and social world as the trajectory unfolds.

Why is *interaction trajectory* important? Trajectory related concerns have figured prominently in CSCW literature to date, both in social and technical reports, though often from conflicting standpoints. Some of concepts discussed in Chapter 2, such as situated action, work-practice, work and 'work about the work', double-level language, and articulation work, motivate this aspect as do the sensitivities to action highlighted in the symbolic interactionist and ethnomethodological perspectives. Accounts of work *in situ* highlight the situated nature of work and the difficulty in accounting *a priori* for the local conditions that will prevail at the moment of action. Many technical systems designed to support such work, however, rely on the abstraction of idealised work schemes and decontextualised and disembodied actions as their underlying basis. These issues have been discussed more fully in Chapter 2.

Interaction trajectory can help unify the concerns of these different standpoints by accounting for the situated nature of work as well as for the situational and temporal order and routine that can emerge in work. *Interaction trajectory* considers actions in context. Action separated from interaction is an analytic artifact (Strauss, 1993, p. 25), as is action separated from its situated moment-by-moment achievement. A central premise, drawn from Strauss' theory of action, is that actions can only make sense in relation to interactions and the broader interactional context.

In collaborative work situations, this interactional context is likely to have significant prominence for people since, by definition, actions will tend to be more closely coupled and interdependent. For individuals working in multiple locales, the management of their interactions across locales adds a further layer of complexity.

A social world locale as the primary unit of analysis provides an organising framework to capture this interactional context in a more tractable way. It also provides a way of understanding how the trajectory takes place, e.g., the goal of the interaction, the role of artefacts and objects, the role of the locale media (to be explored more fully in the *mutuality* discussion), and so on.

8.4.1 Trajectory Overview

As will become evident, *interaction trajectory* is a rich multi-faceted, and, therefore, somewhat complex aspect. *Interaction trajectory* is about the living social world and its interactions in and with locales. It is about how people engage with the setting and with each other and, by their actions, evolve a new set of conditions for further actions. As such, *interaction trajectory* is not only concerned with the current action, but also with the past and with the future, together with the processes by which these evolve. It is also concerned with people as 'interactants' who carry out the actions, each bringing their own perspectives, histories, and so on, to the interaction. And it is concerned with the more general conditions that actions take place in relation to, e.g., material, social, political, etc., and how the locale of work supports trajectory.

We can talk about *interaction trajectory* from many different perspectives. For example, social worlds and locales have trajectories; people and the entities in a locale have trajectories; events have trajectories; and so on. We can also discuss trajectory at many different levels of scale and granularity. *Interaction trajectory* is rich enough to be useful in all these various ways. However, as for all the aspects, the way in which *interaction trajectory* is explored for any particular situation will depend on what is deemed to be relevant for the questions at hand, i.e., the perspective or point of view given by the study or design exercise. Therefore, the centres and perspective principles also apply to trajectories. The definition of what comprises a trajectory, and whose trajectory it is, is dependent on the point of view being considered. From this perspective, there will be some actions that are more central to the trajectory, and other actions that are peripheral to it. There will be other trajectories closely related to this trajectory, and other trajectories less related.

The following discussions pull apart some of the conceptual richness of *interaction trajectory*, based to a large extent on Strauss' (1993) work (these concepts are descriptive devices only; there are often no such distinctions, or very blurred distinctions, in the lived realities of trajectories). The purpose of doing this is to understand how actions are currently supported in and across locales, and ultimately how we might design systems to better support social world actions. The discussions will touch upon the following themes:

- People as interactants and the trajectory focus
- Actions as the building blocks of trajectory along with the conditions in which actions are performed
- Trajectory sub-components as a course of action, past, present and future
- Concepts of phases, rhythms, schedules and routines
- The role of artefacts to support trajectory

8.4.2 Focus and Interactant

As a starting point, a trajectory can be differentiated by the focus or entity to which it relates and on the type of interactants involved, as outlined in Figure 8.15. This enables trajectory to be looked at from many different perspectives and at many different levels of granularity. We can follow the trajectory of a particular artefact, e.g., a software application, or of a particular event, e.g., the celebration of Australia Day, or of a particular individual. We can focus on their interactions in one locale or look at their interactions across multiple locales.

Focus the entity or entities to which the trajectory primarily relates:
Typical Dimensions: single ... multiple; simple ... complex; tangible ... intangible; obvious ... obscure;
Typical Issues: What is the entity type: individual; social world; locale; object; event; concept or idea; and so on.

Interactant the agent(s) undertaking the actions/interactions that make up the trajectory:
Typical Dimensions: human (individual, social world, aggregations of individuals or social worlds) ... non-human; direct agency ... indirect agency;
Typical Issues: what role does the interactant play in relation to the focus (see also Figure 8.4); how do they carry out their role.

Figure 8.15. Focus and interactant properties of trajectory.

The interaction can involve a few people and take place over a very short time period. An example of a very fine-grained scale of interest is Suchman's (1996) detailed analysis of a few minutes of activity in an airline operations room, as is Heath and Luff's (1996a) analysis of a London Underground control room. At other levels of scale, we could be concerned with a large number of people over a long period of time, or with a very specific event, or with the pattern of events in general.

The elock trajectory primarily relates to the elock software application, and its maintenance and evolution. The primary interactants are Frances and Helen, and also Tex. The administration staff, academic staff and students also interact at the functional interface of the elock application and so are also part of the elock trajectory. In the Systems Engineers study, I could have focussed on a specific episode of repair of the elock system rather than the software group at large. This would have revealed very different stories.

8.4.3 Action, Work-Actions, Meta-Actions, and Processes

Interactants perform *actions* in relation to the focus of the trajectory. Actions can be richly characterised along many dimensions (Figure 8.16). Of particular importance is the degree to which actions are coupled or linked with other actions.

Actions as the components of trajectory:
Typical Dimensions: core ... peripheral; simple ... complex; spontaneous ... considered; routine ... non-routine; requiring specific skills ... requiring no specific skills; tightly coupled with other actions ... loosely coupled with other actions ... uncoupled from other actions; independent ... interdependent; narrow range of effect ... broad range of effect; short duration ... long duration;
Typical Issues: what is the type of action: work-action, meta-action, management-related action, articulation action; what are the relationships among actions; how do interactants learn, know about or choose an action; are there necessary pre- or post-conditions for an action.

Figure 8.16. The action property of trajectory.

In the scenario presented on page 58, Sue's actions on the printer queue program are closely coupled with Tom's future actions on the program. He cannot start his action until she is finished hers. The actions that he performs will be in the context of the actions Sue is performing. Sue's email to Tom is also coupled with Tom's response, but this coupling has a different temporal dimension to it than the coupling of her phone call to the professor — the actions in the telephone call are tightly coupled in time as well as in the work sense. There is a looser albeit critical coupling between the actions of whoever installed the C libraries and the professor's problem that Sue is trying to fix.

Trajectories as courses of actions can be made up of different types of actions: the performative *work-actions* and the *meta-actions* that take place around the work-actions, i.e., the work around the work. *Work-actions* are the performative actions directly related to the task at hand, e.g., the running of the printer queue job, or the coding of the elock changes. *Meta-actions* happen around the work actions. They are needed because work actions take place in relationship to a unique set of conditions that can only be known around the point of action. For discussion purposes, I distinguish between two types of meta-actions: trajectory management and articulation work.

Trajectory management actions are to do with managing or shaping the course of the interaction. With a single individual, this management might simply involve having to decide how to proceed. For a group of people, trajectory management is more complicated and could involve strategies such as negotiation or persuasion, for example, to align goals or perspectives, or to negotiate a revised course of action at a high level. Obviously issues such as power and influence have a role to play in the emergence of dominant management person(s) and style(s) (Strauss, 1993, p. 56).

An overlapping set of actions falls under the broad umbrella of *articulation work*. The need for articulation work arises when multiple people are involved in an interaction and their actions need to be coordinated and aligned — the overhead price of interdependency. Articulation work also involves dealing with unexpected contingencies that arise during the course of the interaction (though usually at a finer level of detail than management actions). There are also the issues of resourcing the activity (tools, technologies, supplies, information, other services, etc.), the dividing of work into tasks, then the deciding of what work gets done by whom, where, for how long, for what pay-back, for what purposes, and according to what standards (Strauss, 1993, p. 59, 87).

At a higher level, there are other process-related issues to consider, many of which have already been alluded to in previous discussions. Examples of these include: what are the processes by which social worlds evolve, members join and leave; how are roles decided upon; what are the processes that lead to certain routines or conventions emerging, e.g., for when to use the telephone versus email; and how do social-worlds and locales co-evolve.

The crisis in the student labs meant that a lot of people were suddenly co-opted to help resolve the problems. However, increasing the team size also increased the amount of meta-work that Helen had to take on to ensure that people's actions were going to contribute to the solution. Helen had already engaged in trajectory management work with Kate to plan the operating system upgrade. When the problems became apparent, she had to dynamically re-formulate this plan, and then engage in significant articulation work to allocate tasks to the co-opted people, communicate with staff about the ongoing progress, and so on.

8.4.4 Conditions for Action and Support for Action

The actions that constitute a trajectory take place in the context of particular circumstances or *conditions* at the moment of action. Many general conditions will have already been highlighted in the discussions on *locale foundations*, *civic structures* and *individual view*, for example the social, organisational and personal conditions. It might still be important, however, to identify the specific conditions at the time of action.

We've already talked in general about the makeup of the elock social world and civic structure. At the point where the elock application fails, however, knowing that Tex is on holidays becomes an important condition for how the problem comes to be solved.

The locales identified in *locale foundations* also capture some of the spatial and material conditions for actions, i.e., the site and means. The relationship of these site and means to the trajectory of concern are characterised in Figure 8.17. It is these sites and means as part of the conditions for action that we are particularly able to influence by the appropriate design and deployment of technology.

8.4.5 Past, Present and Future

Interaction trajectory can be further described according to subcomponents of past, present and future courses of action. For each, the questions of who are the interactants and what are the target entities will also be relevant.

Site and means as part of the conditions for action:
Typical Dimensions: available ... unavailable; accessible ... inaccessible; optimal ... sub-optimal; constraining ... enabling; affordable ... expensive; rare ... common; depleted with use ... no impact with use ... increased with use; reliable ... unreliable;
Typical Issues: how do these influence or shape trajectory; how are they used and evolved as part of trajectory.

Figure 8.17. The 'site and means' property of trajectory.

Ways of approaching the *past* history of trajectory to the current point in time are captured in Figure 8.18. Many of these are particularly relevant for thinking about knowledge management and organisational memory issues; a significant amount of work has been undertaken in the organisational memory community exploring how past histories are known about and communicated (Ackerman, 1994; Bannon and Kuutti, 1996; Fitzpatrick, 2002).

Past history what has been the course of action to this point in time:
Typical Dimensions: explicit history ... implicit history, needing to be unpacked; captured in an artefact or similar ... captured in memory; centralised history/memory ... distributed history/memory; knowable ... unknowable;
Typical Issues: how is the history captured, recorded and made available in the locale; also knowing/choosing how far back is appropriate to go;

Figure 8.18. Properties of trajectory past.

The history of the student labs up to the crisis point was very difficult to uncover. There was no central account or record of the history. In trying to understand what had happened leading up to the crisis point in the labs, the members of CSG had to engage in significant re-construction work, e.g., drawing on Kate's verbal accounts of past actions and their rationale, looking at minutes from previous meetings, even seeking out people who had worked in the labs some time previously.

The *present* of the trajectory (Figure 8.19) is concerned with current action. Issues of interest include the following: What is the guiding vision that frames this action? What are the conditions under which this action will be taken? What are the possible actions that could be undertaken at this point? And what are the expected consequences of the action?

The over-arching vision of having an operational laboratory as soon as possible for the students drove the choice of actions to rectify the problems. One of the actions that was taken by Alan, however, had the unexpected consequence of undoing the work that Frances had done on the previous weekend.

The *future* of the trajectory (Figure 8.20) is about the imagined or projected course of action. This will in part be determined by the vision for the interaction,

Present trajectory properties:

Guiding vision framing the current action, drawn from the social world goal:
Typical Dimensions: single ... multiple; explicit ... implicit; clearly enunciated ... unclear; detailed, specific ... abstract, not specific; contentious ... agreed upon; familiar ... unfamiliar;
Typical Issues: how is the vision negotiated and shared;

Other relevant conditions at the point of action:
Typical Dimensions: few ... many; knowable ... able to be approximately known ... unknowable; predictable ... able to be approximately predicted ... unpredictable;
Typical Issues: how are these accounted for;

The set of possible actions from which the action choice is made:
Typical Dimensions: single option ... limited range ... unlimited range; familiar ... unfamiliar; obvious ... obscure;
Typical Issues: how do people know about the possibilities; how do they make choices;

Consequences of the action:
Typical Dimensions: knowable ... able to be approximately known ... unknowable; predictable ... able to be approximately predicted ... unpredictable; easy to evaluate ... difficult to evaluate;
Typical Issues: how do the consequences play themselves out.

Figure 8.19. Properties of the trajectory present.

the plan or plans for how to achieve that vision, and who is involved in the planning activities.

Future trajectory properties:

Projected vision for the trajectory:
Typical Dimensions: single ... multiple; explicit ... implicit; clearly enunciated ... unclear; detailed ... abstract; specific ... not specific; contentious ... agreed upon; familiar ... unfamiliar;
Typical Issues: how is the vision communicated, how are disparate visions handled;

Plan/strategy for achieving vision:
Typical Dimensions: none ... partially formulated ... fully formulated; unable to be specified ... able to be specified for the short term ... able to be specified for the long term; changing ... unchanging; changeable ... unchangeable; explicit - implicit; detailed ... high level; in terms of sub goals ... in terms of specific actions; imposed ... agreed upon; guiding ... prescribing;
Typical Issues: what is the planning process;

Strategist/Planner of the future trajectory:
Typical Dimensions: individual ... group ... organisation ... other; autocrat ... democrat ... consensus seeking; knowledgeable ... little knowledge; experienced ... inexperienced; creative ... functional;
Typical Issues: who decides on the planner; what authority do they have.

Figure 8.20. Properties of the trajectory future.

After the immediate crisis was over, Alan was assigned as the strategist to devise a future plan of management for the labs.

Because the representation of past and future courses of action has been the focus of much work in the workflow and process support communities, as discussed in Chapter 2, there is a plethora of methodologies and techniques that can be used to represent courses of action. This work can also be drawn upon as appropriate.

When the Adminstration Branch decided to change the number format, it was Helen not Frances who interacted with Tex about the elock changes because Helen knew the history of the elock application and had worked with Tex previously. Tex implemented the changes, but he had misunderstood the revised number format. When Frances and Helen tried to fix the problem, some of the conditions impacting on their actions were that Tex was on holidays, they did not know the source of the problem, there were time pressures to get it fixed, and so on.

8.4.6 Phases, Rhythms and Schedules

Orthogonal to these trajectory sub-concepts are the temporal-related concepts of phase, rhythm, and schedule that we can also use to characterise trajectories, as outlined in Figure 8.21.

Phasing the conceptualisation of trajectories into sub-parts where the actions are usually related in some way, perhaps to some sub-goal:
Typical Dimensions: agreed upon phases ... individually-held notions of phase; explicitly noted ... implicit; short duration ... long duration; anticipated ... unanticipated; clear delineation of phases ... blurred delineation of phases;
Typical Issues: how is the phase known and understood within the group; how is the phase delineated; how do transitions between phases happen.

Rhythms or periodicity of actions.
Typical Dimensions: regularly occurring patterns of actions or phases; short cycle ... long cycle; scheduled ... emergent; widely known ... unknown; predictable ... unpredictable;
Typical Issues: are there factors that influence the regularity of the rhythm.

Scheduling the relating of actions to other actions in temporal or work order:
Typical Dimensions: able to be planned for the long term ... able to be planned for immediate short term ... emergent; precise timing required ... approximate timing sufficient ... order required rather than timing;
Typical Issues: how is the schedule negotiated, represented, and evolved.

Figure 8.21. The phase, rhythm and schedule properties of trajectory.

Trajectory *phase* structures trajectory into sub-parts of related action. Members of the social world often use the phase names to talk about an understood set of actions.

The phases of the elock trajectory include development, maintenance, upgrade, and repair. Our discussions of the elock trajectory have focussed on an upgrade phase, out of which problems arose, leading to a repair phase.

Many trajectories can be characterised by their *rhythms or cycles* of regularly occurring patterns of activity. Robertson (Robertson, 1996; Robertson, 1997), for example, discusses at length the way in which the designers in her study use time and periodicity of actions, e.g., the regular occurrence of weekly meetings, as a resource for getting their work done together.

All members of CSG work with particular rhythms, including the half-yearly semesters interrupted by holiday periods, regular weekly meetings, regular database downloads for the elock application, and so on.

The way in which actions are related together in temporal or work order is another defining characteristic of trajectory – the *scheduling* of actions.

Kate was not able to schedule appropriately the work that needed to be done to have the student labs operational by the start of semester. Frances' weekend repair work in the labs that had to be subsequently undone is a case of work order dependencies not being known about beforehand and not being properly scheduled.

Another relevant concept to consider is *coincident trajectories* and relationships between trajectories. For example, we could look at a particular meeting and follow the trajectories of each of the participants leading to the meeting place, of the development of the agenda, of the meeting room itself, and so on. All these trajectories coincide for the time of the meeting (at one level of interpretation of trajectory) and then move off again after the meeting along their individual trajectories. Hagerstrand (1975) and Giddens (1984) both discuss in some detail "the intersection of time-space trajectories in day-to-day activity" (Giddens, 1984, p. 132).

Trajectories inter-related with the elock trajectory in time-space include the trajectories for Helen, Frances, Tex, the semester cycle, the Adminstration Branch, and so on.

8.4.7 Routines

Not withstanding the fact that work is highly contingent and situated, routinised action and the patterning of interactions can emerge over time through repetition. *Routines* are another fundamental resource for getting work done. They provide a certain amount of predictability and knowability about the interaction. Routines can sometimes be codified or reified and made explicit in guidelines or rules or procedures. Routines can also arise from habit and tacit agreement. This distinction between routine and non-routine action, and what constitutes routine, is not always clear — routine for one person or group look like chaos for another.

As part of the 'taken for granted' or the invisible aspects of the locale, routines can contribute to both efficiency and effectiveness (Strauss, 1993) because they are 'tried and true' and because they require less conscious effort on the part of the participants. However, routines can also contribute to inefficiency and ineffectiveness when they overly constrain people from using their creativity, intelligence, and local knowledge to deal with the specific conditions that will still arise at the point of action.

Because actions can never be completely routinised, breakdowns in trajectories can occur. Repair of breakdowns can require significant effort (management actions and articulation work) from the people involved to get the trajectory back on course. Understanding how breakdowns have come about can be particularly instructive for uncovering issues that are usually rendered less visible when the trajectory is flowing smoothly. There are many examples where the study of breakdowns has been a useful resource for deriving design insights (Curtis et al., 1988; Rogers, 1992; Sharples, 1993).

The problems with the elock application and the crisis in the student labs are both examples of breakdowns in CSG trajectories.

Understanding routines, and the variability around routines, can therefore be an important resource for the design of computer-based support for work trajectories, so long as this understanding also encompasses the work to make the routine work, and to evolve it to keep it relevant, and the variable conditions that can happen around routines.

8.4.8 Role of Artefacts in Coordination

In exploring *interaction trajectory*, we can also ask how members of the social world make specific use of their locale and its resources in getting work done. What are their specific interactional needs at each stage of the trajectory? What means, including media and mechanisms, do they use to support these needs? What do they use to facilitate routine action, or the allocation of tasks, or the repair of breakdowns, or the negotiation of a revised course of action? How are past history and future plans represented?

Looking at the role of artefacts can be useful here. Schmidt and Simone (1996) identify a role for artefacts as Coordination Mechanisms (CM). A checklist is an example of a CM.

> "In cooperative work settings characterized by complex task interdependencies, the articulation of distributed activities requires specialized artifacts which ... are instrumental in *reducing the complexity of articulation work*" (p. 162) "[A CM then is a] construct consisting of *a coordinative protocol* (an integrated set of procedures and conventions stipulating the articulation of interdependent distributed activities) ... and ... *an artifact* (a permanent symbolic construct) in which the protocol is objectified" (Schmidt and Simone, 1996, p. 165) (emphasis in the original).

Hughes et al (1997) similarly talk about how coordination can be facilitated by specifically designed or evolved artefacts, e.g., standard forms, where descriptions of the task can be embedded along with other relevant information to perform particular tasks.

When the team was co-opted to deal with the student lab crisis, coordination problems arose because there was no known protocol for solving the problems, and therefore no 'symbolic construct' to guide people's actions. Once the situation was stabilised, Alan developed a calendar for the group outlining a schedule of jobs over the coming weeks, together with an attachment describing what each of the jobs entailed. The calendar and attachment were rudimentary yet effective CMs for the upgrade of the labs.

8.4.9 Interaction Trajectory Summary

In summary, *interaction trajectory* captures the dynamic temporal aspects of social world interactions in and across locales, i.e., the social world in action, the conditional context for this action, the various types of action that are undertaken, and the locale support for action.

8.5. Mutuality

Awareness of people, spaces and resources in a locale is an essential ingredient for communication, coordination, and the interactive life of the social world life. *Mutuality* is concerned with the resources available for both the provision and the perception (or reception) of information through which this awareness can be achieved.[5] Mutuality is the catalyst then for cooperative work and shared workplaces.

Why is mutuality important? Why not just talk of awareness? The critical role of awareness in collaborative work and technologies to better support awareness have been the subject of much research and design activity in the CSCW community (Benford and Fahlén, 1993; Dourish and Bellotti, 1992; Fuchs et al., 1995; Fuchs, 1999; Gaver et al., 1992; Gutwin and Greenberg, 1998; Gutwin et al., 1996a; Heath and Luff, 1996a; Hudson and Smith, 1996; McDaniel, 1996; Nomura et al., 1998; Prinz, 1999; Rodden, 1996). A problematic outcome of all this work though is the "bewildering array of usage of the term awareness" (Robertson, 2002).

Many workplace studies have explored the role of awareness as an achieved outcome in the conduct of co-located activities, often with a focus on how people use perceived information to coordinate their actions. This lack of emphasis on the provision of that information for perception is understandable since so much of the information is freely and unselfconsciously available by virtue of physical bodies being embedded in a physical world, and being made of the same stuff (Robertson, 2002). More recently however, Heath et al (2002) have argued for the importance of also understanding how people make information available for perception:

> "To unpack awareness we initially need to consider how actions are shaped with regard to the participation of others, and how particular activities implicate different forms of participation from those within 'perceptual range of event'." (Heath et al., 2002)

Many techno-centric approaches, on the other hand, focus on the representation of information for awareness, the provision side. The emphasis is often on producing computer mediated forms of the types of information that are taken for granted in co-located situations but which are lost when people are distributed and/or work in a shared virtual workspace yet still need to collaborate, as with the systems engineers. This is a necessary challenge for "designers of awareness resources for shared virtual spaces [because] if people are to be aware of anything, then it has to be explicitly made available to their perceptions within those spaces" (Robertson, 2002). Perception and the ability to use the information is implicitly assumed.

Use of the term 'mutuality' moves the emphasis away from either awareness as an achieved outcome or from technologies independent of an embodied perceiver. Instead the emphasis is on the *mutual communicative processes* through which awareness is achieved — the *provision and perception* of information. The key question then is what are the possibilities for provision and perception of information for awareness given the specific people, spaces and resources involved in the locale and their interactional needs (who/what needs to be aware of who/what, when and in what ways)?

The principle of the *mutuality* aspect is that, for interaction to happen in a locale, there are basic requirements for provision and perception. Firstly, the potential interactants (human or otherwise) need some way of *producing or making* information about themselves *present and available* in the locale. Secondly, the potential interactants need some way of being *able to access* (*perceive* for people or *receive* for objects) this information about the other.

Both provision and perception possibilities for the interactants are facilitated by *mechanisms* associated with different types of spaces and things. These mechanisms can be inherent, such as air in a physical space for the transmission of sound waves, or they can be embodied in the person, artefact or other entity, or they can be designed and encoded explicitly. For the purpose at hand, the interactants will make selective *choices*, consciously or unconsciously, about the use of such mechanisms according to their *capability* to do so.

The following discussion will pull apart the interplay of provision and perception of informational resources, mediated by capability and choice, through which awareness is achieved. Further, because of the possibilities enabled by technology to achieve similar outcomes in different ways or new outcomes altogether as seen in the systems engineers study, it is also useful to pull apart the nature of the taken-for-granted elements. While If we are to design systems that support people in the richness of their workaday worlds, all of these elements need to be considered.

8.5.1 Provision and Perception Information

Provision concerns the ways in which information as a resource for perception can be made available and accessible in a locale to support the social world interactions there.

For the interaction of interest, there is the question of what entity information is needed about and what *types of information* are needed. For example, information might be needed about a person or an object or an action or any other locale entity – giving the entity '*presence*' in the interactional context. The types of information needed can include identity, form, function, interactional possibilities, current activity, current state, past state, location, and others as appropriate for the interaction.

Another question is about how the information is *(re-)presented.* The presence of some entities can be represented by simple information, such as identity. Other entities can be represented by multiple, perhaps disconnected, fragments of information, e.g., an object with different roles in different situations. For yet other entities, presence information can be a composite of multiple pieces of information such as identity, location, current state, and so on.

Different *levels of effort* can be involved in producing and conveying presence information. Information can be intrinsically embodied in the entity itself, e.g., via physical form, or it can be extrinsically associated information, e.g., identity. The provision of information can happen unconsciously or implicitly, e.g., via my bodily presence when I enter a room, or it can happen consciously or explicitly, e.g., conveying identity when I give my name or wear a name tag, or unobtrusively drawing attention by the deliberate change in voice modulation (Heath et al., 2002).

There is also a limit to the *range* in which presence information can be communicated effectively. For example, direct perceptual information about my body location in my office is limited to those with visual access.

Frances and Helen can be present in their elock locale via their bodily form, and represented by their name, role, task list, office address, etc. Tex is unable to be bodily present because he is thousands of miles away. All three can be virtually present in the elock locale, represented by their system user identification. The elock application within the locale can be represented variously by its application name or lines of code or compiled byte codes or even its functionality.

Perception is the complement of provision for communication and interaction purposes. Awareness is enabled when an entity receives or perceives presence information provided by another entity. The receiver can gain information about who, what, when, where, why, and how relating to the other (McDaniel, 1996). For example, who is working on what task? What are they doing? Where are they doing it? What tools are they using? What is the current state of an object? When did it last change? And so on.

Helen and Frances only become aware that there is a problem with the elock application when the functionality fails; this functionality was the way they perceived the elock 'presence'. In fixing the problem, Helen can see Frances sitting at her computer terminal, can see and hear her typing in commands, and can hear her talk about what she is doing to fix the problem. Neither of them can 'see' Tex working on the code, though they might later notice some functional effect of his work. However, they can issue an explicit system command to detect whether he is currently logged into the system and running specific processes; this is using his system 'presence' of a username identity.

There is also the question of *reciprocity*. To what degree should the entities be equally present and/or aware of the other, and to what extent should an entity know about how and by whom its presence information is received?

When the elock system is functioning well, it is sufficient for Helen to be peripherally aware that Frances is maintaining the system. When the elock system fails, Frances and Helen need a more reciprocal and fine-grained awareness of each other's activities, and of the current state of the application.

Granularity of information:
Typical Dimensions: course grained ... fine grained; high level ... detailed;
Typical Issues: the type of entity the information is about; the type of information being communicated;

Provision/perception of information:
Typical Dimensions: passive ... active; implicit ... explicit; mediated ... direct; embodied ... disembodied;
Typical Issues: how the information is produced, projected or received;

Range of projection of presence and perception of information:
Typical Dimensions: *for presence:* directed ... general; *for perception:* peripheral ... intensely focussed;
Typical Issues: the *range(s)* within which information is projected, c.f., nimbus (Benford and Fahlen, 1993), or information is gathered, c.f., focus (Benford and Fahlen, 1993); the *dimension* along which range is meaningful and how it is to be measured, e.g., may be in geophysical space, Cartesian space, virtual space, interest space and so on (see (Rodden, 1996)).

Reciprocity i.e., the degree to which the entities involved have to be, or are able to be, aware of the other's presence and vice versa:
Typical Dimensions: equal ... unbalanced; whether the other is known ... whether the other is unknown;
Typical Issues: how reciprocity issues are negotiated, monitored, enforced, etc.

Figure 8.22. Properties and dimensions for provision and perception of information.

Further, how are people able to maintain a sense of awareness of their own presence and actions? While such *self-perception* is given for physical space interactions, it becomes a significant issue for interaction in virtual spaces where the effect of action in the virtual space is removed from the production of the action in physical space, e.g., through typing at a keyboard; actions here are mediated, indirect and disembodied.

Frances' coding activities in trying to fix the elock application are only available to her through the mediation of fingers tapping keyboards and seeing the the unix developers' representation of code text in a window on the screen.

Figure 8.22 captures some of these characterising properties of informational resources for awareness. These general concepts can be applied at many levels of scale, not just to the entities in locale, as previously mentioned. They are also relevant to aggregations of people, objects, information, actions and locales, and to the interactions between locales as discussed in *civic structures*.

8.5.2 Mechanisms Enabling Provision and Perception

Another question for the *mutuality* aspect is this: what are the *mechanisms* that enable the provision and perception of information in a locale?

There are four defining characteristics for mechanisms. The first three are: the *medium* or space in which the interaction takes place; the degree of *temporal coupling* of the interaction; and the degree of *spatial coupling*. The interplay of these characteristics will largely determine what mechanisms are available for use. A fourth characteristic, the degree of *work coupling*, is also an important issue; this has already been discussed under the *interaction trajectory* aspect.

These characteristics are outlined in Figure 8.23. By way of an example, a depiction of the mechanisms used by the systems engineers is presented in Figure 8.24 as a matrix involving the medium, time and space characteristics.

The medium or space in which the interaction takes place:
Typical Dimensions: physical ... virtual;

The degree of temporal coupling of the interaction:
Typical Dimensions: synchronous ... semi-synchronous ... asynchronous; continuous ... discontinuous;

The degree of spatial coupling of the interaction:
Typical Dimensions: co-located ... proximate ... distributed; also the spatial arrangement, and positioning and orientation in space.

The degree of work coupling of the interaction, i.e., the degree to which the presence and awareness events are inter-related from the perspective of the shared task:
Typical Dimensions: loosely coupled ... tightly-coupled; coupling at the process level ... coupling at the outcome level.

Figure 8.23. Defining characteristics for *mutuality* mechanisms.

The following discussions explore physical medium mechanisms and virtual medium mechanisms in more detail. These mechanisms are worth drawing explicit attention to because they provide fundamental resources for interaction: "not only do individuals produce actions with regard to material [and virtual] aspects of the local environment, [...] the environment provides a fundamental resource in making sense of the actions and activities of others" (Heath et al.,

2002, 'and virtual' my addition). Understanding the interactional needs that different mechanisms serve can help point to design opportunities for better support of those interactions.

	Synchronous		***Asynchronous***	
	Co-located	***Distributed***	***Co-located***	***Distributed***
Physical	Corporeality: size, shape, form eye contact voice gesture Embodied action (5 senses)	Assigned offices Use of office door Telephone, page Verbalise actions Shouting through walls (voice, hearing)	Leaving notes Evidence of action Up-to-date lists Traces: footprints perfume finger prints	Messages: answering machine voice mail postal mail Photos
Virtual	Disembodied action Constructed: user ID event streams System functionality	Chat tool	Email Event histories Configuration management	Event notification Email Configuration management

Figure 8.24. Table showing mutuality mechanisms available in CSG for different combinations of medium (physical, virtual), temporal (synchronous, asynchronous) and spatial (co-located, distributed) features.

Physical Medium Mechanisms

When people are *synchronously co-located* in a *physical* space there is a range of mechanisms they can use to structure or configure information, often with little conscious effort, because people and objects have bodily mass that is material and tangible. And because people are bodily immersed in the space, they can make implicit or explicit use of all the human senses to perceive that information. Specific features associated with physical space mechanisms make them useful resources. For example, there is a tight coupling of space and time resulting in almost simultaneous production and perception of information. There are a variety of ways for implicit information provision and perception to happen by virtue of physical embodiment in space. Rich aggregated or integrated information can be produced with minimal effort and often with redundancy, for example, using all of physical form, location, body posture, voice tone, words and gesticulations for the one communicative act. And it is possible to selectively target and use any combination of multiple sensory channels.

Robertson (1997) presents a taxonomy of embodied actions "as classes of cognitive practices" that perform communicative functions in co-located interactions because they are simultaneously and publicly available to all the interactants. She divides the taxonomy into individual embodied actions in relation to physical objects, other bodies and the physical workspace, as well as group activities constituted by individual embodied actions.

Many workplace studies provide rich examples of the mechanisms used by people to provide and perceive information for awareness. Suchman (1996), for example, notes that "work activities and workspaces are mutually constituted, in ways that are structured and available for detailed understanding" (p. 35). Similarly, Heath et al (2002) show through the detailed study of work in a control room that people are incredibly skilled in the ways they "design and produce actions to render features of their conduct selectively available to others", such as through raising the voice, or changing body or gaze orientation. In a similar vein, Hollan and Stornetta (1992) provide examples of types of mechanisms that can be used in physically proximate interactions, including "eye contact, body posture, stereotypical openings and closings in conversations, or even the strategy of going down to the lounge to see who's taking a break from work". Other mechanisms noted include encouraging others to look at or notice an action or event, producing talk in particular ways to make features audible, relying on being overheard, making use of artefacts, and so on (Heath et al., 2001).

In *distributed synchronous* interactions, embodied actions are not so readily available and opportunities for providing and perceiving information are more limited. Other mechanisms come into play. The telephone is one example of a mechanism affording verbal presence and auditory perception. The information is not as rich as in the co-located case, but there can also be advantages to reducing redundancy or irrelevant information.

Helen and Frances work in both a physical and a virtual medium, with mechanisms as depicted in Figure 8.24. They can be aware of each other's physical presence in a number of ways. They have assigned offices that happen to be next door to one another. These give a likely location for finding the other. As they work together, they come to know that Frances always leaves her door slightly ajar if she is in, but Helen always keeps hers closed. They can also hear activity in the office next door, they can see each other in the corridor, they can visit each other's office, they can see the activity that each other is physically engaged in, they can talk, they can shout through their shared office wall, and so on. They can also be present via pagers, email, telephone, notes, etc. Being thousands of miles away, Tex can only share a virtual medium with Helen and Frances for their elock work, including email and the telephone.

For *asynchronous* interactions, both *co-located* and *distributed*, mechanisms can provide resources for awareness and generally involve leaving 'traces' or 'footprints' that point to past activity. These traces or footprints are often mediated by artefacts in the locale. Such traces might include messages on bulletin boards, notes in a file, the rearrangement of artifacts, updated lists, voice recordings, etc. Postal mail in the physical domain or email in a virtual domain facilitate more directed targeting of information.

Virtual Medium Mechanisms

The lack of mechanisms inherent in the virtual environment for the provision and perception of information for awareness has already been discussed at length in Chapters 5 and 6.

As can be seen in Figure 8.24, the systems engineers have few mechanisms in the virtual medium to support their presence and perception needs. Instead, they make compensatory use of less than optimal mechanisms, removed from the medium in which the need arises. These include physical space mechanisms such as worklists and meeting discussions to create publicly available representations of the virtual workspace.

Virtual mechanisms to provide resources for awareness need to be explicitly designed and encoded in software. An obvious disadvantage of this is the effort required to anticipate what mechanisms might be useful and then to develop those mechanisms. A clear understanding of interactional needs will provide a good basis for deciding what might be useful. An advantage, however, is that the virtual space can be exploited to provide innovative mechanisms providing new types of informational resources that aren't available in physical spaces. For example, the relationships between time and space can be manipulated. Information can be disaggregated and more selectively targeted. Identities can be fragmented. The same entity can be provided with multiple simultaneous representations and locations. And so on.

Discussions in Chapter 2 have already pointed to specific technologies that are being designed to provide resources for awareness. Rodden's (1996) model of awareness can provide some useful concepts, compatible with the *Locales Framework*, for thinking of innovative solutions for different types of existing virtual spaces and applications. The model uses concepts of presence, position, proximity and awareness relative to a shared space of objects, not a spatial frame of reference. Shared space, distance and proximity are determined by the objects and relations in the application structure such as a file structure or hypertext links. Users are considered to inhabit a shared application and are able to project their presence and actions to be made publicly available through the objects forming the space.

Other Mechanism Issues

There are many other mechanisms that can be used to enable resources for awareness that do not have strong temporal and/or spatial mappings.

Role is one mechanism. Dourish and Belotti (1992) talk about role-restrictive awareness in some workflow systems where an individual's awareness of the shared work space is updated according to the role they play on a 'need to know' basis.

Artefacts or a *common field of work* can mediate the way in which information is projected and received. Robinson's (1993) common artefacts, such as the hotel key-rack, and Schmidt and Simone's (1996) coordination mechanisms, such as a checklist, can be seen as mediating group awareness of the shared place of work.

Mechanisms can be used to *amplify, dampen, augment or filter* information for awareness. In a physical environment, for example, walls, doors, and windows can be used to alter the projection and perception of information. Windows enable the transfer of visual information but hinder auditory forms of information. Partitions in an open plan office cut off a visual representation of presence but still allow potential auditory presence to be available beyond the partition. A microphone can extend the range to which voice presence can be projected. In their virtual reality tele-conferencing system, Greenhalgh and Benford (1995) designed adaptor objects to alter the presence and awareness scopes of virtual objects.

Using different representational forms in different media is another mechanism for changing the availability of information within the workspace. The same informational content, for example, can be represented through the mechanism of text on the medium of paper, or through drawings on a whiteboard and so on. Each representational mechanism offers quite different possibilities for visibility and interactional use.

The to-do lists that the engineers were asked to write is an example of an information entity. These lists were variously available in the locale as a computer-based file in a system directory, as printed hard-copy versions of the file, and as notes on a whiteboard in an office.

The inter-relationships and dynamics among various mechanisms for presence and perception also need to be considered. These include, for example, the potential interplay between media, temporality and spatiality and people's use of mechanisms to move around media, space and time to get their work done. Part of understanding *mutuality* is understanding this interplay for the particular situation at hand.

8.5.3 Capabilities and Choice

In any situation, there is likely to be a range of potential mechanisms to support the exchange of information for the purposes of interaction. The person's (or entity's) ability and preparedness to make use of these mechanisms, however, is mediated by a number of factors including capabilities and choice, which in turn are influenced by pragmatics, personal preference and cultural norms.

The *capabilities* factor has to do with the person's ability or entity's designed capability to utilise the available mechanism. For example, a mute person is not able to make use of the transmission of sound in air for the projection of an auditory presence in a physical medium. Nor does a deaf person have the capability of receiving auditory information. Similar capability issues apply to computers; a personal computer that does not have a sufficiently powerful video card, for example, will not be able to display video information. Likewise, bandwidth constraints might determine whether presence is projected across a network via the medium of text or via audio and video.

Physical objects can be designed in such a way as to encode information for awareness so that they can play a mediating role in mutuality among other interactants, such as the hotel key rack mentioned previously. Virtual objects can also be encoded to mediate and represent various types of projection and reception behaviour, e.g., through event detection mechanisms (Fitzpatrick et al., 2002).

The *choice* of which mechanisms to use in a particular interaction can reflect the *pragmatics* of the context in which the interaction is to take place. Choice can also reflect *personal preference*. Pragmatics helps answer the question of what form of production or perception is most appropriate for the task at hand.

If Helen wants to communicate with Tex who is thousands of miles away, she can choose from letter, telephone, email, or personal visit. Each provides different mechanisms for presenting self and content and has different temporal and cost implications and different possibilities for perception.

Personal preference can also play a role in choice of mechanism. Another influence on this choice may be *cultural norms* associated with the social world. Understanding the nature of the social world as part of locale foundations can help inform when such choices might be made.

To ask work-related questions, some members of CSG used the group mailing list while others would prefer to use direct email or face-to-face discussion with the person(s) they thought could best help them.

8.5.4 Mutuality Summary

In summary, *mutuality* is concerned with the *mutual communicative information processes* through which awareness is achieved – the *provision and perception* of information. It considers how spaces and resources are made available and accessible to people and how people and their activities are made available and accessible to others through the spaces and resources they use as locale. For the purposes of design, it is especially concerned with how mechanisms associated with the spaces and resources of the locale are being, or can be, used to support those information processes.

8.6. Summary

This chapter has provided a wide-ranging introduction to each of the *Locales Framework* aspects, providing motivation for why each is important and exploring some of the properties, dimensions and issues that can be used to characterise the aspect. This is not an exhaustive discussion by any means. The main aim has been to introduce initial thinking around the aspects as part of a tool for understanding and designing for complex socio-technical environments.

How this tool is used is up to the individuals involved and the situation at hand. The next chapter will consider how the *Locales Framework* can be applied to understanding and designing wicked problems, continuing the focus on CSCW by way of illustration.

Notes

1 While not within the scope of this book, it would be interesting to explore if and how these layers or similar layer concepts can be interpreted for the notion of locales, to help in both characterising current locales, and in the design of new or enhanced locales. For example, would there be similar layers for the virtual locales that will be the outcome of the design process? Could these layers provide a new way to think about dynamically reconfigurable software, i.e., in terms of what is made re-configurable and how the re-configuration processes are supported?

2 Many other forms of relationship diagrams could similarly be used. For example, we could also represent some of the relationships in Figure 8.9 as a configuration of a set of circles around the central locale, where distances between circles indicates the strength of the relationship and labelled connections indicate the nature of the relationship (different types of connections such as dotted lines or solid lines could differentiate relationships of influence versus more interactive relationships and so on, and could also show the directionality of effect).

3 This perspective is not often embodied in systems built to support group work. Most systems offer fixed group views of the world, e.g., MUDs and wOrlds (Fitzpatrick et al., 1995), where all participants see the same thing all the time. However, even where the actual display is the same, the individuals who use the information there do so with different purposes in mind and from different positions in both the physical space and the organisational/problem space. Other systems do attempt to account for individual perspectives. For example, e.g., the DIVE system with individual viewpoints and actionpoints within a common spatial frame (Benford and Fahlén, 1995), and more recently, selective workspaces in MILANO (Agostini and De Michelis, 1997).

4 This was a question raised by John Bowers (personal communication, 1996).

5 In the original thesis, I used the terms 'presence and awareness' as the mutual components in awareness but this was confusing since awareness was the outcome of perception of presence information. I've changed the terminology here to make the distinctions clearer.

Chapter 9

LOCALES FRAMEWORK APPROACH

The *Locales Framework* has grown out of my own journey with understanding and designing for the support of work. This journey has taken place in the context of the broader community journey where many other people are also grappling with issues around the wicked problem of design for complex human environments. Before going on to explore how to work with the framework, I want to highlight some of the other work going on in the community that was closely related to the *Locales Framework* at the time it was developed, specifically the Lancaster viewpoints and framework dimensions, Activity Theory, Soft Systems Methodology, ORDIT and Contextual Design.

9.1. Related Approaches

Lancaster Viewpoints and Framework: Closely related to the *Locales Framework* in both time of development and in conceptual content is the Lancaster viewpoints and framework dimensions work (Hughes et al., 2000; Hughes et al., 1997). At the same time that the *Locales Framework* was being evolved, ethnographers and computer scientists at Lancaster University were addressing the issue of how to present ethnography in the design process to help bridge the gap between ethnography and design. The resulting viewpoints and framework approaches identify many of the same concerns as the *Locales Framework* for the purposes of design. The three *viewpoints* — ecology, workflow, and egological organisation — represent generic features of workplaces that are used to structure ethnographic data. The three framework *dimensions* — distributed coordination, plans and procedures, and awareness of work — are used as presentational devices to communicate issues key to the design process.

The *Locales Framework* and Lancaster work evolved independently yet there are significant similarities. For example, 'ecology' addresses issues similar to the *locale foundations* and *mutuality* aspects by considering the spatial organisation of work, the affordances offered there, and the ways in which these support awareness. 'Awareness' also directly addresses *mutuality* aspect concerns. 'Workflow', 'distributed coordination', and 'plans and procedures' address *interaction trajectory*-related issues. 'Egological organisation', with its focus on the individual, addresses concerns similar to *individual view* aspect.

The relationship between viewpoints and (Lancaster) framework dimensions centres around the framework being able to offer "a more general examination of the nature of systems within a work context" (Hughes et al., 2000) and so being more specifically related to systems design. While it is not clear why there needs to be a distinction between data structuring categories and presentational categories, it is interesting that there is a such a significant overlap with the *Locales Framework* in common issues identified as important for the design process.

The main differences in the approaches stem from the theoretical starting points. The Lancaster work is primarily driven from an ethnomethodological perspective[1] involving sociologists and computer scientists, growing out of the lived experience of the wicked problem of using ethnography in design. e.g., for the support of air traffic controllers (Bentley et al., 1992). The locales work has been driven more from a systems design perspective, wanting to know how to incorporate the complexity and unpredictability of real world settings into the design process, and growing out of the practical experience of designing CSCW systems.

A shared concern of both approaches, however, is in "avoiding the 'over-formalisation' of this process as this risks entering into some kind of prescriptive analytic agenda that serves to obscure the phenomenon under investigation" (John O'Brien, personal communication, Sept. 1997). This is coincident with the positioning of the framework as a broad sensitising framework to be intelligently interpreted for the situation at hand. Despite all hopes or efforts though, there is always the chance that any such framework will be used in unintended ways because of the different ways in which abstractions are viewed within the various disciplines, as previously discussed in Chapter 2.

Activity Theory: The *Locales Framework* also shares some similarities with Activity Theory. As overviewed in Chapter 2, Activity Theory has been promoted with the CSCW (and HCI) communities as providing an appropriate conceptualisation of cooperative work that can take account of the emergent features of work and also give good design metaphors; see, for example, (Kuutti, 1992; Kuutti, 1995; Redmiles, 2002).

Fundamental to both Activity Theory and the *Locales Framework* is the notion that actions are continually evolving. Activity, as the primary unit of analysis in Activity Theory, is congruent to some extent with locale, the unit of analysis in the *Locales Framework*, in that activity not only captures "a minimum meaningful context for individual actions" (Kuutti, 1995, p. 26) but that this "context is constituted through the enactment of an activity involving people and artifacts" (Nardi, 1995b). By including such context, Kuutti (1995) argues that the notion of activity is also "essentially collective even if [the] main interest is in individual actions", although I have argued in Chapter 2 that the notion of the collective as 'community' is yet to be fully developed.

Another point in common between Activity Theory and the *Locales Framework* is the explicit recognition that "an individual can and usually does participate in several activities simultaneously" [*op.cit.*]. Also, in emphasising the mediating role of artefacts in an activity, there is similarity with the characterisation of the means or things through which people accomplish their activities. Further, both Activity Theory and the *Locales Framework* lend themselves not only to describing how an activity is currently performed, but also how it can be evolved and improved. This is an emphasis missing in other approaches such as ethnomethodology.

Like other social science approaches adopted into CSCW and HCI, however, Activity Theory is being asked to do a job for design that it was never intended to do when developed in its home discipline of Soviet psychology. I have already discussed the complexity and diversity of Activity Theory and how this complexity and diversity makes it difficult for newcomers to learn. It is not clear though how much of this complexity is actually relevant for the pragmatic agenda of understanding work and designing support technologies.

Despite this, Activity Theory is becoming more widely used, as evidenced by a 2002 special edition of the CSCW Journal on Activity Theory and the Practice of Design (Redmiles, 2002). Perhaps this collective experience will result in a pared-down version of Activity Theory that captures essential concepts and relationships for the purposes of design, otherwise Activity Theory is likely to remain a tool for specialists.

Unlike Activity Theory, I do not set out to define a theory of collaborative work, nor is the framework dependent on an in-depth knowledge of Strauss' theory to be useful, even though the language of Strauss' theory of action is used in the description of the *Locales Framework*. By not requiring engagement with Strauss' theory, *Locales Framework* can be more quickly accessible for both researchers and designers regardless of background. On the other hand, it is still possible to engage at deeper theoretical levels for those who want to do so.

The *Locales Framework* concepts are not as richly or completely developed as those in Activity Theory, and hence not as circumscriptive. Instead, the *Locales Framework* is presented as a set of broad-brush open-ended categories and concepts that can provide different perspectives for understanding work, but that still allow for the situation itself and the focus of the exercise to dominate the analysis.

SSM, ORDIT, Contextual Design: It is interesting that within the Information Systems (IS) and HCI disciplines, various pragmatic methodologies have been developed by systems designers with similar motivations to the *Locales Framework* — to account for the broader socio-technical context of computer systems design, and to help envision what could be as well as describe what is the current situation.

Within the IS area, Checkland (1981) developed *Soft Systems Methodology* (SSM) in the 1970s. This was a methodology for managers who needed to design systems to address 'soft' problem situations. By 'soft' problems he meant those that were fuzzy and unstructured, involving interacting human beings, where the features of the problem are not easily understood or quantifiable, not unlike Rittel and Webber's (1973) notion of a wicked problem. The practice of SSM involves a series of (iterative) steps: acquiring a general understanding of the problem domain and the various stakeholders, e.g., via 'rich pictures', mind maps, organisational models etc.; formulating concise definitions of various domain elements; developing conceptual models from these definitions; comparing the models with reality; defining the possible improvements and changes to bring about the improvements; and taking action to implement the changes.

Drawing together experiences with SSM along with other systems analysis techniques, and with requirements capture and prototyping techniques, Eason and Olphert (1996) have developed a different methodology called *ORDIT*, an acronym for 'Organisational Requirements Definition for Information Technology Systems'. ORDIT includes the following constructs: a method for modelling the socio-technical system based on roles, responsibilities, and role relations; techniques for generating alternative models based on statements of user requirements; ways of representing alternative models so that users can gain experience with them; and evaluation techniques.

Another user-centred design technique for requirements elicitation, developed within the HCI discipline, is Contextual Inquiry, latterly called *Contextual Design* (CD) (Beyer and Holtzblatt, 1998). CD was developed as a method to bring usability studies out of the laboratory and into the users' own work context. Its methods draw on techniques from ethnography, field experiments and participatory design. A contextual inquiry is usually carried out by an inter-disciplinary team of people who interview and observe the users in context over a period of a couple of hours. They analyse the collected data by clustering related issues into 'affinity diagrams', and then order and label the affinity diagram into an 'index of understandings'. This has similarities with a grounded theory approach. Other techniques that are used include artefact walk-throughs, future scenario workshops, and prototype test drives.

As part of the analysis, CD uses different types of graphical work models to represent work practices. These models map closely to subsets of issues for different *Locales Framework* aspects. A *flow* model captures communication and coordination patterns, and a *sequence* model shows detailed ordering of steps to accomplish some task; these are similar to some *interaction trajectory* concerns. A *cultural* model represents the cultural and policy constraints on work, capturing some of the concerns of *civic structures*. A *physical* model depicts the physical environment of work, and an *artefact* model captures the structure and intent of the physical things used in work; both of these models address *locale foundations* concerns. *Individual view* issues are captured by the fact that work models are drawn up for each of the individuals observed; a single common view of the work is derived out of these models.

Like the *Locales Framework*, all three approaches are motivated to address the broader socio-technical context of systems design, However, the *Locales Framework* is the one that most explicitly seeks to address the *interactive* and *collaborative* needs of the individuals involved. The *Locales Framework* also places more emphasis than SSM and ORDIT on individual perspectives and on the role of spaces and things in the life of the domain under consideration. CD also does this to some extent.

SSM and ORDIT are more concerned with gaining consolidated, high-level overviews of the socio-technical context of work. Such overviews tend to suffer the same weaknesses as other high-level abstractions and methodologies such as workflow modelling; they render invisible the practical accomplishment of work and the 'work about the work'. The *Locales Framework* on the other hand, while accounting for similar high-level features, is also concerned with how individuals practically accomplish their work. It is this level of analysis that can be most informative for the functional details in design.

Compared to the *Locales Framework*, both ORDIT and CD have well-developed techniques for engaging user participation in the design process. ORDIT's main focus is on facilitating change through design using an *a priori* set of abstractions. CD's main focus is on contextually grounded requirements analysis techniques. Since the *Locales Framework*, as currently articulated, is mainly about developing a set of high-level concepts rather than a methodology, it would be interesting to explore if and how the techniques of CD, and to a lesser extent ORDIT, could be applied to engage users more directly with the understanding and designing phases of the *Locales Framework*. Conversely, the broad aspects of the *Locales Framework* could be used to augment existing CD observations and data structuring exercises.

The convergence to such similar solutions for all these related approaches are encouraging signs of collective engagement and learning and are entirely in line with 'wicked problem' characterisation of design for socio-technical systems – the iterative process of learning more about both the problem and the solution over time.

9.2. Using the Locales Framework

I return now to the *Locales Framework* itself and outline a two-phase approach to working with the framework for the purposes of understanding locale(s) as they happen now, and exploring possibilities for how the spaces and resources can be evolved (or brand new spaces and resources can be created) as locales to better support social world interactions, and to also provide a language that can be used by both researchers and designers.

This will be not so much a discussion on methodology of use as on purposes of use. The actual processes by which the framework is applied in practice, and how the mapping is made between the analysis of work and the design of systems, is beyond the scope of this book. This is partly because of scale, but mostly because this understanding will need to grow through use. I flag possibilities for this work when I reflect in Chapter 13 on methodological issues that arise from use of the framework thus far.

9.2.1 Phase 1 — Understanding Current Locales

The aim in the first phase is to understand the locales of interest in their current state and how the interactional needs of the social world(s) are met (or not met). The framework can play different roles for different people in helping to facilitate this understanding.

The framework aspects can be used to *organise* and *make sense of existing* ethnographic or other user-centred data. This can be useful for researchers who do not necessarily have a technical background as the framework can help structure study data around themes relevant to the purposes of design. Alternatively, the framework aspects can be used as *heuristics* to help motivate initial questions and observations in the data gathering process. This can be useful for designers who do not have a research or social science background yet want to understand user needs first hand. The framework can also give people a way of thinking about and *articulating their own locales* of work and how these are used. This can be useful for participants as stakeholders engaged directly in the design process.

The usefulness of the framework for all these 'understanding' purposes will always be situation-specific (some aspects will be more relevant than others for understanding for different situations) and researcher-specific (people will bring different backgrounds and experiences to the understanding process). The framework can guide the researcher to look for the facilitating and constraining features potentially important for the practical accomplishment of work. At the same time, the uniqueness of each situation can still emerge in the account of the workplace since the framework is general enough so as not to prescribe nor circumscribe all that could be of interest.

While the *Locales Framework* evolved to address the communication gap between ethnography and design, it is not, in the end, dependent on ethnography as the only approach to data collection. For the pragmatic needs of system design, a variety of tools, techniques or theories can be used as appropriate to shed light on the issues at hand.[2] For example, a Distributed Cognition (Hutchins, 1995) approach could be used to explore in more detail the role of artefacts in mediating information flow within the workspace. Various workflow/process modelling techniques could be useful for uncovering the generic features of interaction. Participatory design techniques could be used to gain greater involvement of users in exploring their own locales of work.

9.2.2 Phase 2 — Evolving New Locales

The aim of the second phase is to explore possibilities for how existing spaces and resources could be enhanced as locales to better support the activities that take place there, or how altogether new spaces and resources could be evolved.

This moves the focus beyond the emergent situated nature of work *per se* to the features and mechanisms of the spaces and resources that support, or have the potential to support, that work as locale. The process is driven by interactional needs and understanding the broader context(s) in which those interaction(s) happen, not by *a priori* assumptions of technological solutions or by idealised abstractions of action.

The design options can then be explored but they are always grounded in an understanding of the actual or potential needs they should be supporting. The types of questions that would drive this process would be domain specific, and guided by the purposes for engaging in this exercise in the first place.

Examples of typical questions might include the following: What interactional needs does the social world have that are poorly or inadequately supported in their current locale(s)? How can the existing locale(s) of a social world be augmented or enhanced to better support mutuality, or individual views, or civic structures, or interaction trajectory? Can technology enable new ways of working? Can new social worlds be facilitated if computer-based spaces and resources were provided to be used as locale?

In answering these questions, the design phase could entail computer-based affordances to augment existing physical or virtual locales. Alternatively it could entail the creation of new virtual locales where none had previously existed. It could also involve the design, or better use, of physical affordances.

The second phase, then, is about exploiting the strengths of any available medium, physical or computational, and the synergy among them, to better meet the social world needs identified in the first phase. Note that the focus here is not on how to re-create physical domains in the virtual realm, nor how to make virtual interactions 'just like' face-to-face interactions.

The *Locales Framework* provides a language for identifying the features that can be designed and built as hard-coded stable systems, while also embracing the fact that situated cooperative work cannot itself be hard coded.

9.2.3 Preamble to Framework Use

This two-phase approach outlines how the *Locales Framework* – with its five aspects of locale foundations, civic structures, individual views, interaction trajectories, and mutuality – can provide a core set of concepts to promote a *principled approach* and *common language*, embracing both social and technical concerns and mediating both. While it draws on qualitative research methods for understanding, it is specifically motivated by the needs of systems design. While it is moving towards systems design, design decisions are grounded in an understanding of the group's needs.

The framework can embrace and mediate both concerns because it is based on a metaphor of place with locale as the unit of analysis. Locale is constituted in the relationship between a social world and the space and resources people in the social world use to meet their interactional needs. As such, understanding activities can focus on the accomplishment of work within the space, while designing activities can focus on providing computer-based spaces and resources to better support the accomplishment of work. Each focus, though, is necessarily with a fish-eye effect, maintaining the relationships to the broader locale context.

While this is not a discussion about methodology (although it is easy to see where methodologies associated with many of the related approaches previously discussed could be equally well adapted and applied here) there are some basic orientations to the use of the framework that are important to highlight here. The key point is understanding that the framework is a *tool* to be used as a resource for engaging with wicked problem design situations. Being a resource, it needs the creativity and skill of the people involved to intelligently interpret the framework for the situation at hand in light of the framing questions.

Given the way in which the aspects were defined in Chapter 8, it could be tempting to list each and every property and characterising dimension of each aspect. While such lists might create the initial appearance of some rigour or method, they would trivialise the richness and complexity of the domains under study. They would also ignore the primacy of the story itself and the dialogue that is needed between the various aspects to tell the story. As stated by Button and Harper (1996), analytic abstractions need to be grounded in analytic explanations of work that reveal how members handle contingencies.

The very point of laying out the property and dimension possibilities for understanding each aspect is so that the researcher/designer can *begin* to engage in a critical understanding of how the members of the social world accomplish their work within the possibilities and constraints of their locales, and how these locales could be enhanced or new ones created to better meet their needs.

The *Locales Framework* should be seen as a sensitising device, giving *'social thinking' pointers* or heuristics for key elements of a collaborative work environment. It can also help to give *'technical thinking' pointers* on the affordances of space and resources for support of interaction. It is a *shared abstraction* in the sense of being a common background against which domain-specific concepts and abstractions can be drawn, and design solutions can be explored.

The following quote is paraphrased from Strauss (1993) where he talks about his theory of action (my paraphrasing in square brackets). He could just as easily have been talking about how the *Locales Framework* should be viewed for the purposes of understanding requirements and designing systems:

> "... the principle function [of the locales framework] is not at all to supply or directly develop concepts that will constitute the [requirements analysis] about the particular phenomenon under study. Rather, what the [framework] is capable of doing is ... to inform [key aspects of a collaborative environment]. It is not that thinking in this way requires you to keep looking over your shoulder ...: Did I get this in? What have I forgotten? To use the [framework] in this way would be unreal, unworkable, and deadly for [systems design]. ... One of the striking paradoxes of this [framework] is that just because it has been expressed explicitly and systematically, in these pages, it can function implicitly during the course of [design] itself, rendering systematic the [analyst's] ordering of explanations." (Strauss, 1993, p. 67, 68)

9.3. Summary

In summary, the *Locales Framework* can provide the following for understanding and designing:

- A common language for describing what is as well as envisioning what could be

- A flexible unit of analysis applicable to different levels of scale (from local setting to global context, micro detail to macro patterns) and to different types of spaces (physical, virtual or mixed)

- A rich unit of analysis that can provide contextual connections even with a narrow focus (for example, the focus might be on a particular artefact but the artefact is necessarily understood within its broader locale context)

- A set of aspects encompassing diverse perspectives (from group to individual, structure to process, inside and outside views)

- A conceptual framework independent of any one theoretical orientation (albeit more closely connected to Strauss' theory of action)

- A framework rich enough to be sensitising to key elements of a collaborative environment but sufficiently generic, open and incomplete so as not to prescribe nor circumscribe all that is of interest

Does the framework capture the 'right' aspects or the only possible aspects for the support of collaborative work? Surely not. The five aspects are interdependent and overlapping in their concerns. suggestive of different perspectives, not absolute views. Different aspects might be more important than others for different domains and new aspects altogether might be needed to explain the phenomena at hand. As with all wicked problems, a robust dialogue between exploration of frameworks and their use in practice is essential if either is to be advanced. As such, this is an early working framework that will be evolved with use for the purposes of both analysing work domains and designing, building, deploying, and evolving systems within those domains.

The following chapters begin some of this reflective dialogue through my own experiences applying the framework for understanding and designing. The first study of a group of distributed researchers (Chapter 10) tests the usefulness of the framework for structuring data about the domain of interest. The second study applies the *Locales Framework* to systems design in a telehealth situation between the intensive care units of three hospitals (Chapter 11). The implications of the framework are then explored for the design of basic infrastructure for computer-based collaborative environments, as interpreted in the Orbit system (Chapter 12).

Notes

1 The commitment to an ethnomethodological position might explain why the developers feel that both viewpoints and framework are needed.

2 While this suggestion will upset many theoretical purists, my concerns here are more pragmatic, driven by what an approach can offer for design than by any theoretical allegiance.

PART IV

WORKING WITH THE LOCALES FRAMEWORK

Chapter 10

DISTRIBUTED RESEARCH WORK: A TALE OF TWO GROUPS

In this first study, I wanted to explore using the *Locales Framework* for sensitising observations of work and structuring data. I started off focussing on one research group called the Internet Exploration Unit (IEU). IEU was a distributed collaborative research unit with members from five organisations spread across four sites located in three cities. I thought the group would be interesting to study because they had recently been given a directive by management to develop more closely coupled collaborations across sites and organisations; this directive was driven by their funding body requirements.

The primary purpose of this study, then, was not systems design *per se* but as an exercise in using the *Locales Framework* to provide a structure for explaining if and how this closer collaboration came about, and what locales might be evolved to support this work. As it happened though, these closer collaborations failed to emerge. In contrast, a new cross-unit project involving some of the same IEU members emerged over the same period of time. Called Romany, this project demonstrated the very types of collaboration that management had hoped would happen in IEU. This will be the story of why these different situations emerged.

Interaction with the people of IEU and Romany occurred over a nine month period soon after the directive for closer collaboration was given. Study data was gathered from a number of sources using various qualitative techniques. These included observation, frequent unstructured discussions with all members of the group (some face-to-face, some via telephone), regular attendance at weekly video-conferencing meetings between sites, attendance at other ad hoc meetings including a workshop where all members were present, membership of group mailing lists and access to internal group documentation. Most of the data collection was conducted from one site, Site 1, where the majority of people were located; this will necessarily give some people more voice in the study than others, although everyone was included in observation or interviews at some time. Apart from interacting with other sites over video-conferencing, telephone and email, I visited Site 2 for a period of two days. I also met with people individually whenever they visited Site 1. As is usual with these studies, fictitious names have been used for all the people and groups involved; to make it easier to follow who is from where, the first letters of people's names and their parent institution will be the same.

A grounded theory approach was used for working with the data; the *Locales Framework* provided a way of organising the emergent themes. A *Locales Framework* lens helped with looking at the structure and dynamics of the IEU and Romany groups, drawing particular attention to issues of organisational coherence and support (civic structure), the motivation of the people involved (individual perspectives), and their accessibility to one another afforded or hindered by their physical locations (mutuality).

To tell the story of IEU and Romany, this chapter is structured as follows. After outlining the study method, I introduce IEU and overview what happened with IEU collaborations, and then do the same with the Romany initiative. The major part of the chapter analyses the key features of the successful Romany collaboration and discusses these in relation to IEU. It concludes with consideration of how the work of IEU may be evolved and on the use of the framework overall.

10.1. Introducing the Internet Exploration Unit (IEU)

Social world: The Internet Exploration Unit (IEU) had been established approximately three years previously with government and commercial funding as a non-profit cooperative research project. Its charter was to develop tools, technologies, and processes to manage distributed information.

Because of the contractual arrangements in place, the membership and management of IEU were relatively well defined, albeit complex. IEU consisted of thirteen core full-time and part-time researchers, although this number fluctuated because of summer students and visiting researchers. The core people were drawn from five different academic, government, commercial and research organisations, as shown in Figure 10.1, and were physically distributed across four sites in three cities spanning approximately sixteen hundred kilometers.

Frank, Fred and Fergus were from the Future Generation Systems research centre (FGS) and were located at Site 1. Also at the FGS site were Gail from the State Government, and Adrian from Acme Computing Company; Adrian was working on a rotating six month Acme secondment to IEU. Chris and Coby were from the Central University but came to the FGS site for their part-time IEU work to avoid student interruptions. Sam, Scott, Sue and Sandy were from the Scientific Research Group (SRG); Sam, Scott and Sue were at Site 2 while Sandy was in a different city altogether.

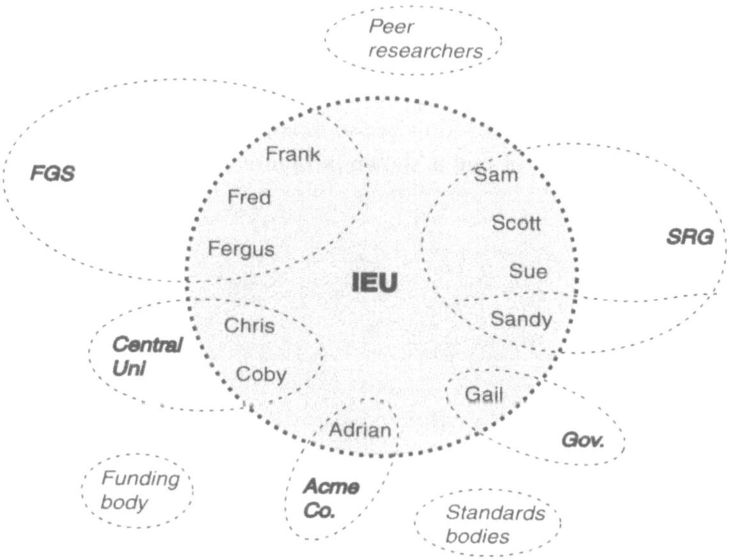

Figure 10.1. Distributed members of the IEU distributed research group, also showing related social worlds forming part of the civic structure for IEU.

The FGS and SRG personnel of IEU were all technically fully devoted to IEU; their positions were funded by the IEU via the host organisation that employed them. The other members had concurrent ongoing responsibilities with their parent organisations who also funded their involvement.

The FGS Board had direct responsibility for the management of IEU including IEU funds. Frank was the project leader, while day-to-day leadership of the group was jointly handled by both Frank from FGS and Sam from SRG.

To contain the scope of the IEU discussion, I will be focussing primarily on the IEU members from FGS and SRG at Sites 1 and 2.

Civic structure: The parent organisations of each of the members, as just mentioned, formed the major part of the civic structure for IEU. The FGS had five other research units, apart from its IEU association, looking at different aspects of future generation distributed systems. These units were spread over a number of sites in different cities. SRG had a large number of other researchers who were opportunistically formed into research teams when a commercial research contract arose; SRG had offices across a number of cities.

IEU itself was one of five sub-projects of a larger Cooperative Research Project (CRP) through which funding was channeled; members of IEU had to regularly report against quite specific CRP performance indicators covering research, education, and commercialisation. There were a number of other 'social worlds' that IEU related to: these included various standards bodies, professional and peer communities, international mailing lists and so on.

The civic structures for IEU ultimately played a significant role in fostering certain collaborations and discouraging others.

Sites and means: Physical space was at a premium for people at FGS Site 1. Two small open-plan rooms accommodated the permanent and visiting researchers; an example of one is shown in Figure 10.2.

Figure 10.2. One of the shared offices for IEU members at Site 1.

Each person's space included a desk, computer, bookshelf, notice-board, and a telephone. There were also shared bookshelves and a shared white-board. SRG offered more spacious accommodation; at Site 2, each person had their own partitioned office space.

Shared virtual spaces both within and across sites, were constituted from a number of different technologies. As well as the telephone, each full-time person had access to email, including from the group mailing lists. A full range of group information was available via group web pages which Frank was diligent in maintaining. Here, work in progress could be posted, archives of mailing lists stored, activity-tracking forms filled, and so on. All sites also recently acquired dedicated video-conferencing machines. These were located in Fergus and Fred's room at FGS Site 1, and in a separate meeting room at SRG Site 2.

When all the members gathered for a workshop, the workshop location becomes a shared physical locale for the duration of the gathering.

It will become evident that the physical separation of people across different cities had a significant impact on mutual availability, in turn hindering the emergence of new collaborations.

10.1.1 What Happened with IEU Collaborations?

Historically, the imperative that held IEU members together as a unit was their shared funding, reporting and management avenues rather than any interdependencies in work. The directive that the members of IEU needed to develop more closely inter-related research programmes was particularly aimed at FGS and SRG who, for political reasons, needed to demonstrate a relationship beyond shared funding and reporting.

Following the directive, Frank and Sam decided that a useful starting point in getting people more familiar with each other's work across sites might be to establish a weekly cross-site meeting. Rather than wait for the long-promised broadband network to be established, they set up a video-conferencing link between sites using $PictureTel^{TM}$ systems connected by an Integrated Services Digital Network (ISDN) line. Weekly conferencing sessions were scheduled between FGS-based people in Site 1 and SRG-based people in Site 2 (fortnightly sessions were also held between Site 1 and the second SRG site but will be included in the following discussions).

They also organised a two-day workshop attended by everyone in the group. The goal of the workshop was to plan a strategy for 12-24 months ahead that would foster closer working relationships and the possible merging of the main FGS and SRG sub-projects. From the workshop, the group produced an abstract system architecture that was used as the basis of their next report; each person also gave a verbal indication to the group of where they wanted to work in relation to the architecture. While useful to some extent, little more evolved in the way of concrete plans for closely coupled work between the researchers at a strategic level. The researchers returned to their separate work sites and continued working on their own projects. The workshop did, however, lay the foundations for exploiting future opportunities and for members moving their work in line with the architecture.

A Potential Collaboration

Two months later, a promising opportunity was identified for cross-site collaboration around a key component of their architecture. Frank was visiting the SRG people at Site 2 to discuss the details of the project charter he was writing for the next year's work. When he outlined the work Fred was hoping to do, Sam realised that he was wanting to work on essentially the same issue but from a different angle. Sam had already known from the video-conferences that Fred was looking at a particular standard but until now had never understood why. Frank and Sam agreed that Sam should talk to Fred about sharing aspects of their work.

Over the next few months there were various contacts between Fred and Sam. They started working on a document together to outline a common abstract model of the problem domain, revising drafts through email and phone discussions and the occasional face-to-face meeting. They were also planning to co-locate for a period of time to advance the work further. As it happened however, just as they were gaining some momentum, SRG management abruptly moved Sam onto a different SRG project that was in direct competition with IEU. The collaboration came to a sudden halt; a promising opportunity was lost.

Collaboration in Practice

While collaborations at the level of strategic importance wanted by management were slow to emerge, or failed to progress when they did emerge, there were some smaller, shorter-term, or less-strategic collaborations that took place within IEU. Frank and Sam worked closely together, producing management-facing documents reporting progress and outlining future work plans. People working at different SRG sites co-authored a paper together. Frank, Fred and Fergus organised a national conference. A prototype web-based tool was developed at one site, and was taken up and used at another site.

Most frequently, collaborations came about when people were on the one site, or when working on a very specific well-defined task where distinct parcels of work could be allocated. The collaboration around the use of the prototype was an example of the most typical inter-group collaboration – loosely coupled interaction at the interface of shared prototypes rather than closely coupled work on a shared problem.

10.2. Introducing the Romany Initiative

An interesting contrast to the IEU collaborations was an emergent collaboration called Romany, itself part of a larger international initiative about trying to produce a standard interface for performing information retrieval over the Internet. Romany evolved over the same period in which the FGS and SRG members of IEU were supposed to be finding ways to work together more closely. Some of the people in FGS were part of both IEU and Romany.

FGS was another complex organisation like CRP, mentioned earlier. It was a government and industry funded cooperative research centre involving dedicated research staff as well partners from academia, industry and government bodies. While located over a number of sites, the focus here was Site 1 where the FGS IEU people were located. FGS was structured into a number of different research units, each addressing different aspects of future generation distributed systems, including the Database Unit (DU) and the Middleware Unit (MU).

Romany involved people from the IEU, the DU, the MU and one of the participating universities, West University, as shown in Figure 10.3. All were located on the same campus, though the university people were in a different building.

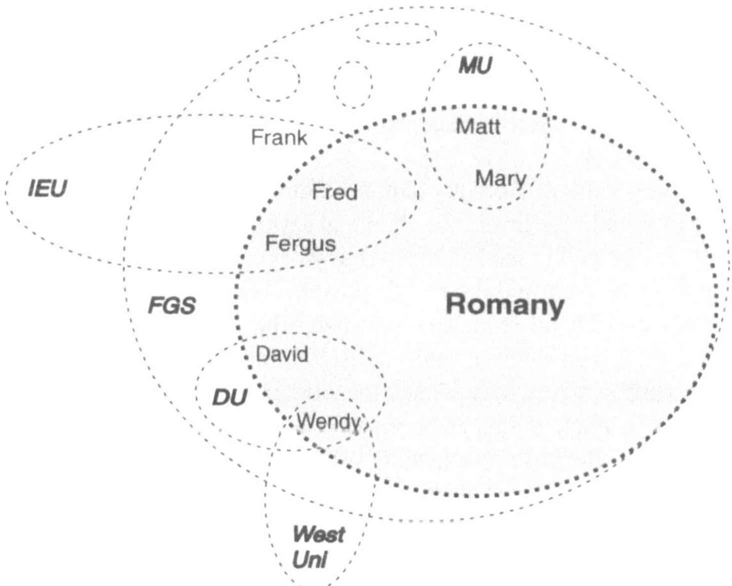

Figure 10.3. Members of the Romany group and related social worlds (civic structure)

10.2.1 What Happened with Romany Collaborations?

To some extent, the emergence of Romany was due to the happy coincidence of a number of trajectories. A lecturer at the West University and his researcher, Wendy, both associated with the FGS Database Unit (DU), had taken on a Masters student to look at writing a distributed object interface to a particular database protocol. For some time previously, Fergus from IEU had also been thinking about using a distributed object approach to address a similar problem but associated with the Internet rather than with databases. His ideas had grown out of discussions with colleagues in the Middleware Unit (MU).

It was only when Wendy was visiting FGS Site 1 and happened to mention her Masters project to some IEU people at FGS that Fergus and Wendy started to talk together about their shared interests. Realising that they were essentially dealing with the same issue, they decided to evolve a more generalised definition of both the problem and its potential solution than either of their technology-specific positions.

Around the same time, there was also a growing awareness in the larger international research community of the potential role for this kind of approach. Wendy posted a description of the student project to an international mailing list and was inundated with expressions of interest. Not long after, Wendy, Fergus and some other members of IEU attended an International Workshop at which many of the key people from the broader research community (and the mailing list) were present. Wendy and Fergus spent a lot of time talking to people, during which they decided to set up a new international mailing list for more focussed discussion. At this stage, Romany was yet to be formally-recognised as a project at FGS.

The ongoing work of Romany happened through interactions at a local level and at an international level. At the local level, Fergus was the only person nominally designated in the IEU charter as working on the problem. In practice he was part of an informal cross-unit project: Fergus worked with Fred from IEU, Wendy and David from DU, and two other colleagues from MU. They established their own internal mailing list and intranet page. They also held a one day workshop where they scoped the work they wanted to undertake. From this, they set in place some plans to write a 'strawman' Interface Definition Language (IDL). Because people were very busy with their other work, most of the ideas for the IDL were exchanged at ongoing meetings, usually held weekly or fortnightly. After each meeting, either Fergus or David would write up what had been discussed, and post it to the internal web page. This summary would form the basis for ongoing thought and would seed the discussions at the next meeting.

At an international level, many people were working on the same problem. For reasons such as commercial advantage, intellectual property rights, and friendly competition, no-one discussed their approach on the international mailing list until they had established work to present. Despite this, the Romany group knew a lot about what other groups were doing largely due to Wendy's interpersonal skills and the relationships she built up with international contacts; Wendy became the effective focal point for international research in this area and many people would often phone her from overseas to discuss issues.

As the work progressed, Romany was given formal recognition within the FGS project structure as a designated project in its own right.

10.3. Key Features of Collaboration

Why was the Romany initiative within FGS apparently so successful at forging cross-unit collaborations while deliberate IEU attempts to establish cross-participant collaboration were so unsuccessful? In this section, I draw out the key features of the Romany initiative and discuss them in relation to IEU: grass roots evolution, defined goals, stable core membership, organisational culture and support, individual differences and motivation, long lead time, understanding the details of work, key advances face-to-face, exploiting physical availability and accessibility, and the use of mediating technologies. These features are organised and presented here in relationship to relevant *Locales Framework* aspects.

10.3.1 Social World (Foundations) Features

Grass roots evolution: The Romany initiative was a self-selected group of people who found they had complementary research interests. Their collaboration and the emergence of a new social world, Romany, with its international connections, evolved from the *grass roots* via the interactions of the researchers themselves, not from any explicit management directive.

In contrast, IEU's drive for closer collaboration came about via a top-down management directive rather than from the grass-roots. While the regular video-conferencing sessions were established in part to foster opportunities for collaboration, the motivation for the effort was externally generated and contrived rather than internally generated and spontaneous.

Defined goals: The Romany group had a series of relatively well-articulated short-term *goals* for their shared work, such as setting up the mailing list and writing the IDL. These goals were discussed and owned by all the members of the group and were continually refined and revised as the project advanced.

IEU shared the high level goal of undertaking research in the same general domain of distributed information management but the work of IEU was largely carried out by individuals or small groups of two or three people at the same site working on largely autonomous projects. As stated by one IEU person: "Everyone was going in their own direction. There was no coherent view of what the group did." Activities such as the workshop and regular video-conferences were aimed at trying to evolve more specific work-related goals across sites, goals that could potentially tie together or evolve some of the existing sub-goals. The work involving Sam and Fred had the greatest potential for developing a new shared goal with the strategic impact sought by management but this was never realised.

Stable core membership: There was a relatively *stable core membership* in the FGS units from which Romany emerged. A stable core membership is necessary where emergent collaborations have a long lead time (as will be discussed below) during which relationships between people, and a shared history and deeper understanding of work can evolve.

The core membership of IEU was not stable. As stated previously, it was not uncommon for SRG management to divert IEU personnel to other non-IEU work, despite contractual arrangements. In the case of the potential collaboration between Sam and Fred, SRG decided unilaterally, according to their own agenda, to completely remove Sam from the IEU project. This effectively ended their common research work. Months later, IEU were still waiting for SRG to replace Sam on the project.

10.3.2 Civic Structure Features

Organisational culture and support: Organisational support was a key factor in the emergence of Romany. Even though, initially, the group was not formally recognised in the same way as IEU within the FGS structure, the management of FGS *actively supported* the Romany work by allowing the diversion of personnel and resources as requested; the Romany work was seen as synergistic with IEU work. This was in line with the *culture* at FGS which encouraged and rewarded closely aligned groups, creative research initiatives, cross-unit and external collaborations, and participation in international standards work, all of which were critical to the longer-term survival of the centre and meeting its requirements as a cooperative research group.

IEU on the other hand, operated in an environment of significantly different and often competing organisational cultures of FGS and SRG. This resulted in a dissonance between sites in the cultural and organisational support for IEU as a whole. Members also experienced the conflict of working under two sets of managers, one through the IEU structure and the other through their parent SRG or FGS structures.

In the SRG social world, there was an emphasis on commercial activities over research activities, and on the individual over the group. A diverse range of people were employed on the strength of their individual skills and interests. One of SRG's selling points was its ability to assemble the right team of people from this mix of skills and interests to exploit a commercial opportunity when it arose. Participation in IEU was regarded as such an opportunity and various personnel were designated to be involved.

However, the meeting of CRP objectives was secondary to its own objectives (whereas FGS and CRP shared similar objectives). Even though the SRG people were contracted to work full-time on IEU activities, they were frequently and opportunistically re-directed to work on an external commercial contract, often to the detriment of, or in direct competition to IEU. Despite using their IEU-acquired skills, IEU would be excluded from even noting the work among its achievements in the annual report. In one instance, an SRG person, Sue, did not want to do the external work because of the interruption to her own IEU work but she was told that she had no choice. From a contractual point of view, this was an issue of ongoing concern for FGS management who handled IEU funds.

In summary, a source of many of Frank's management problems within IEU arose from the conflicting organisational and political cultures in FGS and SRG, especially in their relative commitments to meeting group outcomes defined by their CRP funding body.[1]

10.3.3 Individual View Features

Individual differences and motivation: Each of the Romany researchers, especially Fergus, David and Wendy, were *personally motivated* to be involved in the group and benefited from that involvement. Some of the benefit was in identifying future research directions for their own work. Other benefits were more pragmatic but nonetheless critical in that they created possibilities for gaining ongoing funding for the centre and hence ongoing funding for their own jobs: organisation, group and individual benefits, in this case, were closely aligned.

Within IEU, there was no such alignment. In line with the dissonance between the major organisational cultures in IEU, there was a dissonance between FGS and SRG personal reward structures. For the FGS members of IEU, the ongoing funding of their jobs was intricately tied up with the ongoing success of IEU. The SRG people did not have the same level of motivation for involvement in IEU. They were already employed by SRG prior to their engagement with IEU and their jobs were relatively secure regardless of the outcome of IEU. Their motivation therefore had to come from different sources, e.g., from a management directive that they were designated to work with IEU, or from personal reward being able to conduct interesting research.

Less contentious but nonetheless important issues of *personalities* and *preferences* also played a role in the Romany and IEU collaborations. Not surprisingly, the more people liked each other, the better they were able to work together. In IEU, it was harder for people to build up these inter-personal relationships when they were physically separated.

10.3.4 Interaction Trajectory Features

Long lead time: The foundations for the Romany initiative were laid over a *long period of time* through activities such as 'happening' to find out what others were working on, sharing ideas, daydreaming about possibilities, participating in international mailing lists and workshops, and so on. Many of the corporate activities of FGS also provided mechanisms through which people became aware of other work going on in the centre. These activities included an annual Symposium, regular meetings for unit leaders, regular lunches for all FGS people where each subgroup reported on their work, and so on.

The potential collaborations within IEU also demonstrated tendencies for long lead times, with groundwork being laid through activities such as the regular video-conferencing sessions, the workshop and the process of writing the project charter. Ultimately though, a long lead time is a necessary but not sufficient factor in the success or otherwise of emergent collaborations as seen in the case with Fred and Sam.

Understanding the details of work: In the Romany initiative, it was only when people discussed the *rationale and detail* of work, rather than the high level overview, that they began to understand each other's perspective and the possibilities for collaboration.

This was also the case for the emergent collaborations that were observed in IEU. For example, it was only after Frank explained to Sam what Fred was doing and why, that Sam realised they were essentially working on a similar problem. This was despite months of video-conferencing sessions between their two sites at which Fred frequently reported that he had been doing this work. Because there had never been any discussion about why he was doing what he was doing or how it fitted into a larger agenda of research, Sam and Fred had no awareness of their common interests.

Key advances face-to-face: While the Romany group used a variety of communication media, most of the major advances happened when people were together *face-to-face*, exploiting the affordances of physical embodiment and co-location for intensive focussed discussions. This was just as true for their involvement with other international researchers; the new international mailing list was decided upon, not via discussions on existing mailing lists, but during discussions among various attendees at the International Workshop.

Face-to-face discussions were also pivotal in generating key advances for IEU. One important cross-site opportunity was the IEU workshop. While not generating the strategically-important collaborations they had hoped for, they were able to agree upon a common architecture against which they could each individually position their work. Frank had tried previously to facilitate the same sort of architectural discussions on the group mailing list by posting drafts of the project charter to the internal web page but was unsuccessful.

However, the distances between the SRG and FGS sites meant that face-to-face opportunities were not very common. Because of costs, individual travel was more common than group travel, Frank and Sam being the most frequent cross-site travellers to discuss management issues; they tended to make major decisions during these visits rather than in their weekly management phone-calls. It was during one such visit that Frank was also able to facilitate the potential collaboration between Fred and Sam.

10.3.5 Sites, Means (Foundations) and Mutuality Features

Exploiting physical availability and accessibility: For the people in the Romany initiative then, being *physically available and accessible* to one another was an important part of how their collaboration emerged over time, increasing the opportunities for face-to-face interactions.[2] While Wendy worked in a different building on the same campus as the rest of FGS, and while the IEU and MU people worked at opposite ends of the FGS building, they were all physically close enough to be easily accessible to one another. They could take advantage of chance meetings in the corridor or around the coffee machine or in the campus cafe. They could call meetings at which all were easily and quickly able to attend. They could drop in to each other's offices. Because such interactions could happen with minimal effort, e.g., walking a short distance to meet someone, or engaging in a burst of email exchange to decide on a meeting time, the members of Romany were able to respond in a focussed and timely fashion when opportunities arose.

Similar features were noted in same-site IEU collaborations. Sharing an office made it easy for Fergus and Fred to turn around and ask a question or to work together on a problem when they needed to. They could also take advantage of shared access to resources such as the whiteboard for writing up their 'to-do' list and being able to overhear discussions. In fact, they gained considerable awareness about the work of others just by being in the same physical space.

A significant but understandable problem then in trying to establish closer ties between FGS and SRG IEU members was the fact that they were not easily available and accessible to one another across sites — a case of *out of sight and out of mind.* They did not see each other around. They could not overhear conversations or oversee workspaces. They did not have opportunities for serendipitous interactions.

Use of mediating technologies: The Romany group used a variety of *technology in a secondary capacity* to support their easy physical interactions. The telephone, email, both direct and via their internal mailing list, and the web, provided additional media for communication and information sharing. The case was similar for the co-located members of IEU. Having a rich variety of communication media enables more appropriate choices about using different media for different purposes (Heeren and Lewis, 1997).

For the distributed members of IEU, technology provided their *primary* media of interaction across sites. Often the nature of the technology, or the nature of the group's use of the technology, did not support rich or serendipitous interactions, or facilitate group awareness.

The internal IEU *web* pages were used to store common documents, however people rarely accessed this information on a day-to-day basis. The web was also supposed to be used for tracking activities for the annual report. This activity tracking system had the potential for being a resource for awareness among the group of the activities being undertaken by other members but this was always of secondary importance to the reporting function. While Frank promoted use of the tool for his annual reporting activities, the others in the group found it a burden to use and activities were rarely kept up-to-date; an opportunity for shared awareness lost.

Other supporting technologies were *email* and the *telephone*. The group mailing list tended to be used infrequently, mostly by Frank, to relay management information to the group. Personal email was used more often but the group had no visibility into such discussions. Frank and Sam used the phone for weekly group management discussions, but rarely made major decisions over the phone.

While useful, the telephone and email only partly solved the availability and accessibility problem mentioned previously. For example, because of time-zone differences and individual commitments, Frank and Sam only had a small window during each day in which to phone each other. While email did not depend on the synchronous availability of each person, it introduced significant time lags in the flow of interaction that could otherwise have been solved by a quick visit to another's office.

Video-conferencing, too, supported interactions but its value was limited by both technology and use reasons. The technology-related reasons are generally well-understood and the IEU sessions were no different, suffering from technical problems, video delays, loss of eye contact and so on. As stated by Fergus, there was still a feeling of distance and separation that the technology could not overcome.

Use factors, however, were the major reason why video was not able achieve the effect of easy availability to one another. The sessions needed to be pre-booked rather than spontaneous. People did not use the system in-between the sessions because it wasn't part of their working environment and was disruptive to use (in FGS, because the machine was in a shared office space, and in SRG, because the machine was in a special meeting room that had to be pre-booked).

The format chosen for the sessions was relatively structured rather than free-flowing, focussed on reporting activities in terms of *what* had been done, rather than encouraging any explanation or discussion about *why* things were being done, what the outstanding challenges were, and so on. Such discussions, as we have seen were critical for the identification of potential collaborations.

10.4. Conclusions and Reflections

This study was undertaken as an exercise in using the *Locales Framework* to provide a structure for explaining if and how closer collaborations came about in IEU and what locales might be evolved to support this work. As it transpired, more tightly-coupled cross-site collaborations failed to emerge. This was in sharp contrast to the Romany initiative.

The *Locales Framework* analysis provided different perspectives on the comparative structure and dynamics of the IEU and Romany groups, highlighting issues concerned with the emergence of collaboration and/or the support of on-going collaboration. In summary, the key differences between the Romany initiative and the cross-site interactions within IEU appear to be concerned with organisational coherence and support (civic structure), the strong motivation of the people involved (individual views), and their accessibility to one another afforded or hindered by their physical locations and use of mediating technology (mutuality).

While it is beyond the scope of this book, and indeed the original purpose of the study, to fully explore the implications of these findings for future system support, there were some obvious social and technical issues that needed to be addressed if IEU were to have a chance of meeting its closer collaboration challenge (some of these issues are discussed in more detail in Fitzpatrick et al., (1998b)).

First, and most critically, there were complex organisational issues of competing cultures and different individual motivations that needed to be addressed. If these were not dealt with, then the value of any other approaches to improving interactions among the group would be severely hampered.

Second, there were the availability and accessibility issues. It was unlikely that all members of IEU would be physically co-located in the future. Hence a primary goal of other efforts should be to increase and improve interactional opportunities. More travel between sites by members other than Frank and Sam could be encouraged, as could the temporary secondment of staff to other sites to work on specific projects. Existing technologies could be used in different ways; for example, the video-conferencing sessions could be less structured, and could focus on the presentation and discussion of a piece of work rather than just the reporting of past activities. New locales of work could be created between sites, affording richer media for communication, providing more opportunities for serendipitous interactions, e.g., through video portholes (Dourish and Bly, 1992), increasing awareness of the actions of others, e.g., through use of tool such as tickertape, to be discussed in the next chapter, and bringing shared information spaces more into the foreground of work.

It is difficult to say how the outcomes of this study might have been different without use of the *Locales Framework*. The framework did allow for the uniqueness of the IEU and, as it transpired, the Romany situations to be paramount. While the framework aspects shaped the sorts of issues that initially took my attention, the story of the domains were predominant not the framework. The framework helped to make sense of the collected data, and encouraged exploration of phenomena from different angles. The civic structure aspect of the framework was particularly important in this situation for drawing attention beyond technical reasons and solutions for the group's problems. This might not have been the case had a more technologically-focussed requirements analysis been undertaken.

The processes for creatively and intelligently applying the framework to the situation were at times difficult because of the multi-faceted exploration approach. On the one hand, this allowed more of the richness and complexity of the 'wicked' situation to emerge; this was most evident in the various discussions of the potential IEU collaboration that never eventuated. On the other hand, this richness and complexity did not easily lend itself to the sequential style of reporting as in this chapter. It would have felt far more comfortable writing a hypertext document to explore the issues. There are obviously many links and interdependencies in the features I pulled out for discussion here, but for consideration of space, I've left these implicit. Doing more work to explore where some of these interdependencies were might point to the best opportunities for design interventions.

Further, the processes of using the framework could have actively involved the participants themselves. While I did report findings back to the group with implications for how they might move forward, they could have been engaged more directly in this process to understand if and how they might evolve their own locales.

Notes

1 This is similar to the conflicting social dynamics observed by Sanderson (1994) in his study of organisations participating in a collaborative research project.

2 This is in line with Kraut and Egido's (1988) findings from a study of research collaboration — physical proximity increases the likelihood of informal communication, and facilitates higher quality, lower cost communication than in the case of physical distribution. This in turn increases the likelihood for common interests to be identified and collaborations to emerge.

Chapter 11

DESIGNING FOR TELEHEALTH

In the IEU study, I wanted to explore the usefulness of the *Locales Framework* for focussing observations of work. In this study of a telehealth situation, I wanted to explore the usefulness of the framework for guiding solution design.

In a vast, sparsely populated states of Australia, it is not unusual to find regional hospitals without the range of specialist services or equipment that are available to people in the major centres. This can result in a poorer management of some patients because of a lack of expertise. It can also result in a large number of patients being transferred at great expense to the major centre, sometimes inappropriately, and sometimes with delays in the initiation of appropriate treatment, all because the receiving doctors are not sufficiently aware of the patient's state.

Intensive care telehealth is concerned with making clinical expertise, usually sited in a metropolitan tertiary hospital, more widely available to less well resourced regional hospitals, with the aims of transferring patients more appropriately or supporting better regional management of those patients who do not need to be transferred.

The telehealth situation in this study involved the intensive care units (ICUs) at three hospitals - one was a tertiary centre in a metropolitan city, the other two regional hospitals were at sites hundreds of kilometers away from the tertiary centre. All three hospitals were involved in a government-sponsored telehealth project looking at providing telecommunications support for remote consultations.[1] A unique feature of this project was that it was initiated, owned and driven by the clinicians themselves. Our wOrlds research group was a member of the project team along with clinicians from each of the hospitals involved, commercial vendors, and, in the initial stage, a socio-technical researcher.

Data was gathered over an 18-month period that covered both the early stages of the project and the post-deployment period. Various qualitative techniques were used in understanding consultation practices, including a series of discussions with clinicians from the three sites, analysis of audio and video tapes of role plays of remote consultations conducted by the clinicians themselves, and direct observation of ICU and consultation work practices.

Post-implementation, data was gathered through site visits involving observations and interviews. Usage log data collected by the project officers at each site for each consultation was also reviewed. My own health-care background necessarily came into play in my interpretation and understanding of the work involved, although I did make every effort to be as objective as possible by recognising biases and *a priori* assumptions.

For the purposes of the discussion here, I will call the tertiary hospital City General Hospital (CGH) and the regional hospitals West Districts Hospital (WDH) and North Districts Hospital (NDH) respectively. Each of the junior doctors and the doctor at the regional site will be referred to as a male 'doctor' and each of the senior doctors and experts at the tertiary site will be referred to as a female 'consultant'.

The ICU at CGH was a state-run tertiary training centre, 'tertiary' meaning that it was a major referral centre, and 'training' meaning that doctors wanting to specialise as intensivists (doctors who specialise in Intensive Care work) worked as registrars under the direction of a consultant intensivist. The ICU at WDH was also a state-run training hospital, with its own intensivists but with registrars drawn from non-intensivist specialties. It was a smaller unit than CGH with less access to resources and expertise, e.g., there was no neurosurgical expertise at WDH. The NDH ICU was an even smaller unit, run by anaesthetists rather than intensivists, and staffed mainly by senior medical officers, i.e., doctors who were not in any training program but who had at least one or two years experience since graduation. Many of these doctors were recruited from overseas on one-year contracts.

I will tell the story of these ICUs by first introducing some of the key features of current intra-ICU practice by way of background. I then discuss existing remote inter-ICU consultation practices, using the *Locales Framework* as an organising device to characterise current consultation practices and to motivate requirements for a richer and more persistent remote consultation locale. The telehealth solution decided upon by the project team is described and I use the language of the *Locales Framework* to explore how consultation practices have changed as a result and why some unexpected consequences happened.

11.1. Current Intra-ICU Practice

Before describing inter-ICU consultation practices, it will be useful to first overview intra-ICU practices. While this is mainly drawn from observations in

CGH, the overall patterns were similar in NDH and WDH. The Intensive Care Unit was a busy, noisy, high stress, unpredictable environment in which to work. Work patterns and patient loads were variable and unpredictable, depending on the moment-by-moment progress of a patient's condition and the unplanned arrival of new patients in varying life-critical states.

The Staff: Because of the intensive nature of care, each patient was assigned a primary nurse who cared exclusively for that patient during their shift. Each patient also had at least one doctor who was in charge of managing their treatment. One of the intensivists described his role, and by implication the role of other ICU doctors, as being the "GP (General Practitioner) of the hospital." Just like GPs in the community, they needed to call on, and coordinate, the expertise of other medical and ancillary specialties as needed.

The Patient: Almost by definition, ICU patients were critically ill. They were often unconscious and ventilated and were unable to actively participate in their own care, e.g., in the ways identified by Strauss in (Strauss et al., 1985). The were invariably connected to a plethora of technologically sophisticated equipment, all of which required a high degree of expertise to interpret and manage.

The Patient Record: Central to the practice of patient care was the patient record. The record was comprised of a number of different documents, including the observations of vital signs, printouts from machines, fluid sheets, drug sheets, surgical records, pathology results, radiological images (X-rays) and their reports, clinical notes by medical, nursing and allied health staff, and so forth.

While the content was basically the same, the form of the patient record was different across sites. At CGH, they used an electronic patient record, having recently moved to a networked clinical information system (CIS). At both WDH and NDH, the record was predominantly paper-based, bound together in folders called *charts*, although current in-use observation and medication sheets were kept temporarily on a clip-board at the patient's bedside.

Whether electronic or paper-based, the record was not a homogeneous document. There were no state-wide guidelines nor standard forms so each site had their own local practices about how the chart was formatted and organised. The form of the written content could vary as well. Nurses and doctors had their own (local) practices which were reflected in the chart, such as ways of drawing sketches, or using differentiating pen colours and stamps, their notes often written in almost illegible scrawl. Other clinicians, once they became familiar with these practices, used them as cues to filter and structure the information.

The sum of information constituting the patient record was thus contextualised, distributed, fragmented, and non-sequential. Interesting discussions of how such features impact upon, and are used in medical work can be found in

(Berg, 1997; Berg, 1999; Fitzpatrick, 2000b; Heath and Luff, 1996b; Schneider and Wagner, 1993).

Consultations: The clinicians in ICU engaged in a continual practice of consultation and presentation of patient cases.

Routine morning consultation rounds, for example, generally consisted of the group of doctors walking from bed to bed, listening to the night duty doctor present each patient's 'story'. Because of the fragmented and distributed nature of the patient record, significant effort was required to reconstruct and interpret the patient's story (Heath and Luff, 1996b) as part of the presentation process. The story was usually told using a common format of giving the patient's name, basic demographic information, the history leading up to the patient's admission to the unit, then using the systems of the body, e.g., respiratory, circulatory, etc., to go through the patient's more recent management and current status.

As well as his own notes, the presenting doctor often drew on many other sources of information in his story-telling, especially to answer questions from the listening group. He might involve the primary care nurse or other clinicians or the patient's family. He might draw people's attention by pointing to some aspect of the patient, e.g., the girth of their abdomen or a lesion on a limb. He might demonstrate the patient's responses by performing tests for all to see. He might point to bedside monitors or show various portions of the patient record. And so on.

For their part, the people in the round were not simply passive listeners. Their interactions depended on their role in the patient's care, their level of trust in what the doctor was presenting, their prior knowledge of the case, and how critically ill the patient was.[2] The more senior clinicians often engaged in their own concurrent discovery and interpretation of patient information; while the doctor was talking, they might flick through the patient notes or move to visually examine the patient themselves.

In the spirit of intensivists being the 'GP' of the hospital, consultations and interactions with peers in other specialties were also common place and followed similar reporting patterns. Thus, consultations were an integral part of a clinician's daily working life. They formed the basis for ongoing education, networking, and continual checking to engage relevant expertise as needed, and to ensure optimal patient management. They were a norm of clinicians' workaday lives, not exceptional events in any way.

11.2. Current Remote Consultation Practice

For smaller, less well resourced regional hospitals such as WDH and NDH, consultations with doctors at another institution were frequently necessary when they did not have access to particular medical expertise locally. As CGH was a major tertiary hospital in the state, the intensivists there handled a regular stream of phone calls from colleagues at remote sites, requesting opinions and input on the management of a case, or requesting patient transfer when the regional hospital was not able to provide adequate care for any number of reasons.

The current medium of communication was the telephone. When supporting documents such as X-rays or test results needed to be shared, they were transported between sites by courier. Ultimately, the success of the call depended on both clinicians building a shared understanding of the patient's condition. This in turn relied on the remote doctor's ability to verbally paint the patient's condition from complex clinical information.

The clinicians were remarkably skilled at this, but even so difficulties, breakdowns and uncertainties arose. This could result in both clinical and logistical problems in patient care management. The seriousness of the patient's condition was sometimes not appreciated and the patient was not transferred with the appropriate urgency. More appropriate care was not started early enough. Sometimes patients were transferred unnecessarily.

This telehealth project had its origins in just such a case, when ICU staff were discussing how to avoid what turned out to be an unnecessary patient transfer to CGH. As stated by one of the consultants involved, "the case had been discussed over the telephone, but this had not provided enough information (or confidence) to leave the patient in their local ICU." The clinicians decided that a richer form of telecommunications-based support might help alleviate these problems.

11.2.1 Locales Framework Analysis

The design of support for inter-ICU consultations could be technology-driven, focussing on the telecommunications aspect of the desired solution. Technological considerations alone, however, were not sufficient to meet the goals of better patient care and better use of health care resources. The *Locales Framework* offered a way of considering the total environment in which remote consultations took place and to motivate a solution grounded in work terms rather than purely technical terms, providing a language for ongoing evolution of practice and technology use. Articulating a set of requirements for systems design using the *Locales Framework* was a two phase process. The first phase involved the characterisation of the locale of work and the work trajectory as it currently existed. The next phase explored possible new locales and work trajectories.

Inter-ICU Locale Foundations

A remote consultation can be characterised as a transient social world formed around the need to access expertise about the management of a critically ill patient, as represented in Figure 11.1. The two central participants were the regional doctor and the tertiary consultant doctor who were drawn from the separate ICU worlds. There were also others who participated in a more peripheral way, e.g., the regional nurse who was looking after the patient, the nurses at the tertiary unit who would be taking over the care of the patient if he was transferred, the family who anxiously awaited the outcome of the call, any family or staff member from whom the regional doctor sought information in response to questioning from the tertiary doctor, and so on. Even more peripheral were the medivac team who might be involved in the transfer of the patient between facilities, the hospital administration concerned for the resource implications of care decisions, and so on.

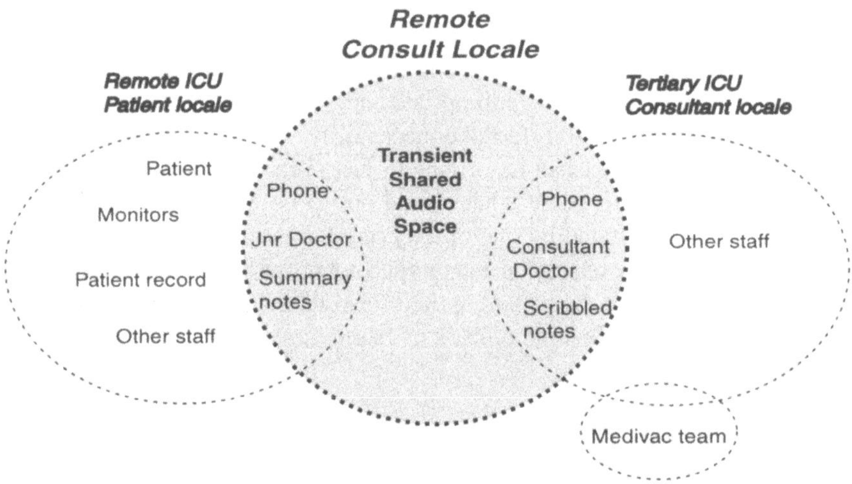

Figure 11.1. Existing remote consult locale between the remote and tertiary ICUs.

The *locale* for the consultation existed as a discontinuous audio space for the duration of the telephone call. The consultation social world, however transient, could be formed because the medium of the telephone facilitated the merging of the peripheries of the participating ICU worlds for a period of time, setting up a context for sharing information. In this way it could also be called an example of Engeström et al's (1999) knotworking.

The consultation locale did not necessarily end when the telephone call ends; the doctors could return to it, possibly several times and with some changes in membership, until the case resolved itself. But the residue of the locale outside of the telephone calls was very weak, providing no awareness of activity or shared information. It existed, in effect, only in the minds of the participants and the pieces of note paper carried in their pockets, and was reactivated only when one of the participants made the effort to do so.

As stated earlier, this form of remote consultation sometimes resulted in misdiagnosis, mismanagement, or inappropriate transfer of patients.

Inter-ICU Interaction Trajectory

While care of a patient in an intensive care unit was a continuous process requiring a large group of people highly focused on the patient, the inter-ICU consultations were by contrast unpredictable, transient and discontinuous.

There were several different *interaction trajectory* perspectives that could have been considered — the trajectory of the consultation, the trajectory of patient management, object trajectories, e.g., of the patient record, trajectories of the individuals involved, e.g., doctors, nurses, transfer teams, and so on. The confluence of all these different trajectories is obviously important for the consultation. In one consultation, for example, the expert radiologist had not yet interpreted the patient's X-ray, so the doctor had to rely instead on his interpretation when talking with the consultant (a confluence of the trajectories of the radiologist, the X-ray, doctor, and consultation). Full discussion of each of the trajectory types is not possible here. Instead, I will focus on the consultation trajectory.

The consultation trajectory was usually initiated by the regional doctor's call to the consultant in response to some critical patient-related event, where management advice and/or patient transfer was needed. Usually it occurred as an unscheduled event and depended on the availability of the participating doctors. The remote doctor usually had to remove himself from the patient bedside and from other care providers to go to the ward desk or unit office where the telephone was located. Consultations tended to be short, seldom more than 15-20 minutes.

Following brief introductions, the format of the consultation closely followed the form of the intra-unit consultation, where the patient's basic demographic information was given, followed by their admission history, followed by a body-systems style of reporting the current condition. The outcome of a consultation was usually a collection of suggestions for patient management, or a decision to proceed with a patient transfer.

In some cases the consultation was a one-off event. If the decision was to transfer the patient, one of the clinicians, usually the consultant, would then coordinate with the medivac transfer team who would be physically retrieving the patient. In other cases there were follow-up discussions when more data became available. These were often difficult to predict or plan precisely. Some consultations were spread over several telephone conversations over several hours or in some cases several days, each building on previous interactions. When consultations involved different personnel, e.g., because of shift changes or the need to involve others, additional effort was required to familiarise new participants with the patient and the work of constructing a shared understanding of the patient's conditions had to be repeated from scratch.

Inter-ICU Individual Views

In the remote consultation case, the individual views of the two clinicians could not be more different. The doctor had a detailed knowledge of the patient who was the reason for the consultation, as well as the state of affairs in his hospital.

However the consultant's whole view onto the shared locale was via the the doctor's voice. She could see nothing at all and usually had limited or no knowledge of the remote site and the local practices there. Thus she constructed in her head and on her note sheet a view of the patient's case that contained the 'high points' that the doctor chose to relay, building a highly contextualised and personalised substitute for the patient record. At the end of the call, this paper would be duly 'filed' in her pocket or in the closest rubbish bin. Once the call was terminated, the consultant had no view of ongoing events in the remote ICU until a follow-up call took place.

Another point to note about the view constructed in the consultation is that it was focussed almost exclusively on medical information. There were many other views which would potentially be created if others (nurses, therapists, administrators, etc.) were participants in the conversations as they were in intra-ICU consultations. Such conversations happened too infrequently as part of the process of transferring patients and important non-medical information was often not conveyed. For examples, in nursing hand-overs, the nurses would often mention how the relatives were coping, whether the social worker or chaplain had been contacted, whether accommodation arrangements had been made for the relatives, and so on.

Inter-ICU Mutuality

In the bedside consultation, all the participating doctors were physically immersed in the ICU; they had shared access to the rich environment of the patient, patient record, associated machines, other care providers and the general milieu of the ward. They could annotate the chart, write management notes, order tests, and so on. They also shared the tacit understandings relating to many local 'in-house' aspects of the unit and hospital operations.

The participants' experience of the remote consultation was significantly removed from this. The nature of telephone communication defined the limit of effective communication in the consultation locale. Firstly, only two people could participate directly and fully in the call at either end of the phone. Both needed to be available at the same time at specific locations. Others in the units who were physically co-present could potentially overhear one side of the call and participate indirectly. Yet others who were potentially impacted upon by the call had to rely on the participating doctors to pass on the necessary information after the call.

Secondly, the narrow bandwidth limits the exchange of information to that which could be characterised verbally. Consequently, the effectiveness of the consultation was largely reliant on the ability of the regional doctor to paint rich word pictures of the patient's condition. The patient was particularly reliant on the doctor to speak on their behalf, their corporeal presence in the unit reduced to clinical labels, laboratory figures and medical jargon.

At the other end of the call, the consultant had no direct or shared access to the doctor's information sources or to the patient. She could not flick through the chart, or glance at the patient or the bedside monitors etc. She had no awareness of what was going on in the unit or hospital more generally. She was totally reliant on what can be conveyed verbally to build up a picture of the patient's condition.

As happens with any call, issues of loss of status cues or misreading the level of confidence and competence could also arise when the doctor and consultant did not know each other prior to the phone call.

Inter-ICU Civic Structures

Figure 11.2 shows the *civic structures* in a conditional matrix format from the perspective of the patient in ICU. Similar *civic structures* were involved in the remote consultation social world, except the doctor and consultant were now at the centre of the social world.

Beyond this consultation core, there were a plethora of overlapping and intersecting social worlds of secondary/contingent interest. These included the participating hospitals, clinicians' peer groups within sites, professional groups across sites, State and Federal Government agencies (in relation to issues such as policies and funding), and the family of the patient. These secondary social worlds are of interest to the extent that they impacted upon the group of people involved in the remote consultation across sites.

The impact of *civic structure* peer groups and professional networks on this locale played a critical role in consultation practices. The locale was established when the remote doctor called the consultant, but deciding *who* to call was often contingent on who the remote doctor knew. Many of the doctors at CGH and WDH had trained or worked together over many years and had learnt to trust and respect each other — or not as the case may be. As one consultant noted:

> *Consultant:* "I've worked with Jim [remote doctor] for years, so I trust his judgement. So I didn't press him about the pictures, I trusted his interpretation ... but for a junior doctor I would have pressed him far more ... I would have liked to see the pictures [X-rays] ..."

Conversely, some of the NDH doctors were recruited from overseas and did not have these networks; one of them remarked that they had been loath to call CGH for help because they did not know anyone there. This is in line with an observation by Cicourel (1990) in relation to collaborative medical diagnosis:

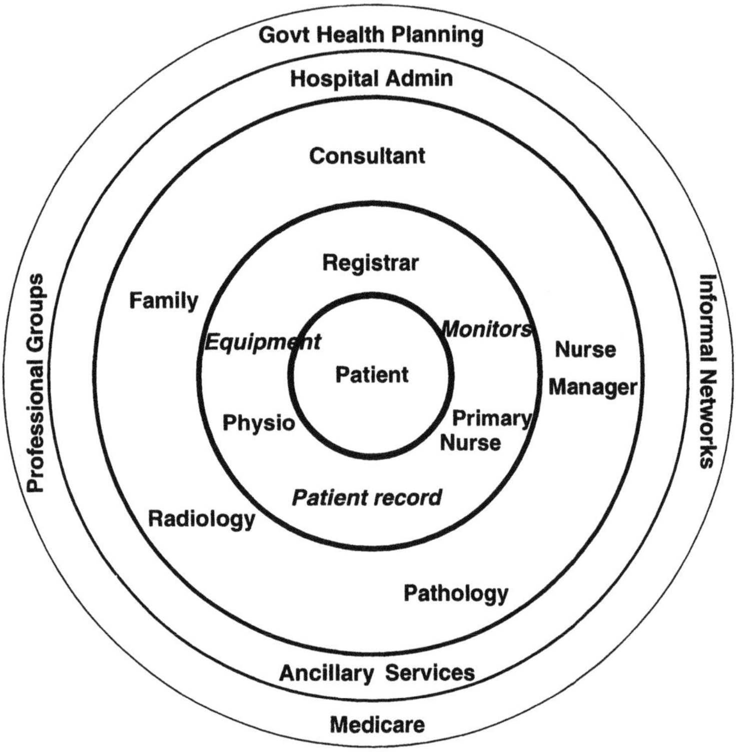

Figure 11.2. Conditional matrix representation of civic structures from the perspective of the patient, involving a single hospital. The first concentric ring encapsulates those most closely involved in the patient's locale. Consecutive circles indicate increasingly distant aspects of the civic structure.

> "Interpersonal relations and the credibility of experts, technicians and patients can both facilitate and block effective collaborative work relationships." (Cicourel, 1990, p. 241)

Another important aspect of *civic structure* for our locale of interest was the larger hospital complex of which the ICU was a part. Each hospital was evolving its own set of practices, procedures and policies within the constraints imposed by the state health department under which they were funded, and the structural rules and regulations governing the hospitals. Hence, local knowledge of standard operations, procedures, budgetary constraints, bed usage patterns, etc., all impacted on the ways in which the consultations proceeded.

There were other less well defined yet contentious issues that also need to be considered at this level. For example, complex medico-legal issues arose around privacy and security of patient information, and ownership of the physical patient record.

While all these issues were not going to be directly accounted for in the design of a system to support inter-ICU consultations, decisions certainly needed to take into account the potential impact of these structures on the remote consultation locale.

11.2.2 Motivating Systems Design

By using the *Locales Framework* to characterise existing inter-ICU consultation practices in this way, it was possible to identify problems and engage in the second-phase discussion, drawing out a set of requirements based on interactional needs for an improved consultation locale.

Bearing in mind that a consultation was the creation (however briefly) of a social world, the question then was how to ensure that the players in this social world had the richest possible site and means with which to communicate and share information about the patient of interest. An initial set of requirements could be summarised as a persistent shared workspace, providing richer communication channels, making information objects available across sites, and extending the participation in the consultation world. I will discuss each in turn. The primary characteristics of a proposed new locale are depicted in Figure 11.3.

On the ICU floor, the combination of bed, patient, monitors and record provided a persistent available and accessible 'place' to focus discussion about a patient. In the remote consultation, there was no such persistent 'place for interaction'. The provision of some kind of *persistent shared workspace* that could evolve over time would make it easier for clinicians to interact together, to re-orient themselves to a case on follow-up interactions, and to facilitate membership changes when new clinicians need to get involved.

Similarly, in bedside consultations the clinicians had access to the full range of modalities of communication — vision, voice, gesture, etc. In the remote consultation all they had was voice. The provision of *richer communications channels*, for example adding video, shared objects, and gesturing capabilities, would broaden the ways in which clinicians could interact during a consultation and facilitate more information sharing than was currently feasible — extending the limits of effective communication and opportunities for mutuality.

In the bedside consultation, the objects, tools and resources used included the patient, patient record, bedside monitors and other clinical staff. In the remote consultation, only a verbal summary of the patient record survived from this set. The doctor's inability to directly portray patient data, particularly radiological images, came through clearly as a major point of breakdown in current remote practices. A persistent locale could be *more richly furnished* by enhancing

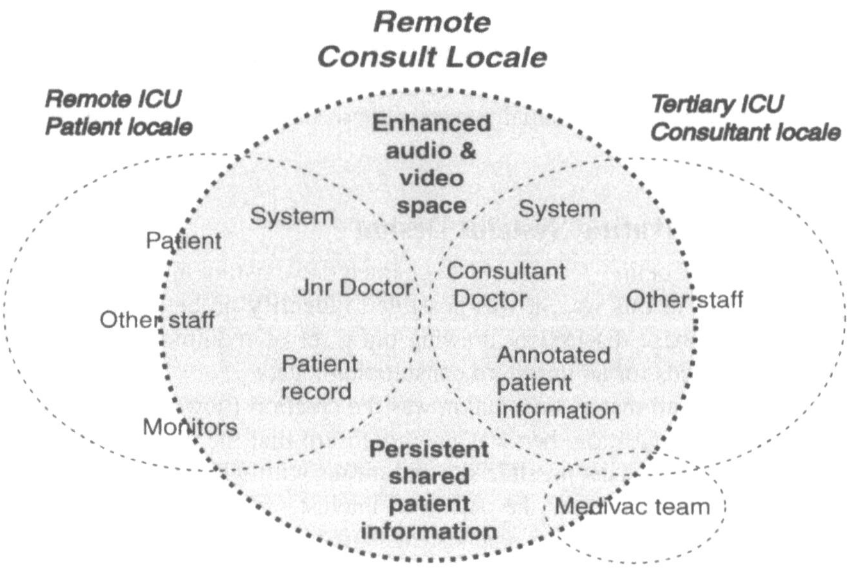

Figure 11.3. New remote consult locale between the remote and tertiary ICUs. The locale can now include persistent shared information. Participation can now include the patient and other staff at both ends, as well as the medivac team.

this set, for example to include (parts of) the patient record, video access to the patient, or networked access to bedside monitors. In particular, since the trajectory of patient condition and management was encapsulated in the patient record, improved access to the record could be the fundamental stepping-stone to improving remote awareness and management of the patient's trajectory.

The mode of access to this information also needed to be carefully considered. For example simply making radiological images available would be useful, but interaction around such images have a family of associated practices that include gesturing (Kuutti and Karasti, 1995). Ideally, these would also need to be accounted for.

Currently, only the doctor and consultant have any direct, meaningful participation in the telephone-based locale. With more persistent shared places and richer communication channels, the *social world could be extended* to involve others directly as needed in the ways they were involved in current inter-ICU practices. Extended participation could include other medical specialists, the nursing staff, the medivac transfer team and the patient's family. When it was feasible, the patient could also be directly involved rather than being indirectly represented by the doctor.

11.3. Evolving a Telehealth System in Practice

In this case study, the *Locales Framework* motivated the design space for a telehealth system rather than suggesting specific pieces of technology. These choices were made in the context of the inevitable budget constraints, involving users in a participative and iterative design cycle in which ownership of the system and responsibility for its evolution lay with the clinicians.[3]

Choices also had to be made in light of current practices and operational constraints. The regional hospital was entirely paper-based, thus coping with the existing paper record and plastic film-based imaging systems was an important factor. Another important factor was that remote consultations were already an established part of the lives of both remote doctors and consultants. The clinicians had evolved a rich set of practices to work within the limitations of a telephone call – it worked well enough most of the time. Any system we introduced must therefore take account of these practices (Fitzpatrick and Welsh, 1994).

Within these constraints, the project team decided to establish a capability for video-conferencing and data sharing between sites using ISDN and off-the-shelf hardware and software technologies. Appropriately configured personal computers, video and still digital cameras and a flat-bed scanner were installed on mobile trolleys in each unit so that they could be used from the patient's bedside when needed. Intel ProShare^{TM} was installed for video-conferencing. It also enabled sharing and manipulation of objects such as images, scanned X-rays and patient record notes via a multi-page whiteboard facility; these objects could also be saved at the local sites for later reference. A basic system configuration is shown in Figure 11.4.

11.3.1 Changing Consultation Practices

In the spirit of wicked problems, and the co-evolution of problem-solution understanding, the deployment of this system across the three ICUs has had significant impacts on the nature of consultation practices, some anticipated in line with requirements but others not so.

By extending the limits of communication, *participation in the consultation world* was extended. The regional doctor who initiated the consultation and the tertiary doctor being consulted were still the key participants in the call but now they could directly involve others as needed. For example, other staff members were co-opted to provide different areas of expertise. The patient's family were involved, for example, to answer questions about the patient's lifestyle or to meet the staff at the tertiary unit who would be taking over the care of their loved one. Patients themselves have also participated in the call.

Use of the system *changed the trajectory of care* for some patients. Some patients were able to be cared for in the regional unit with continued consul-

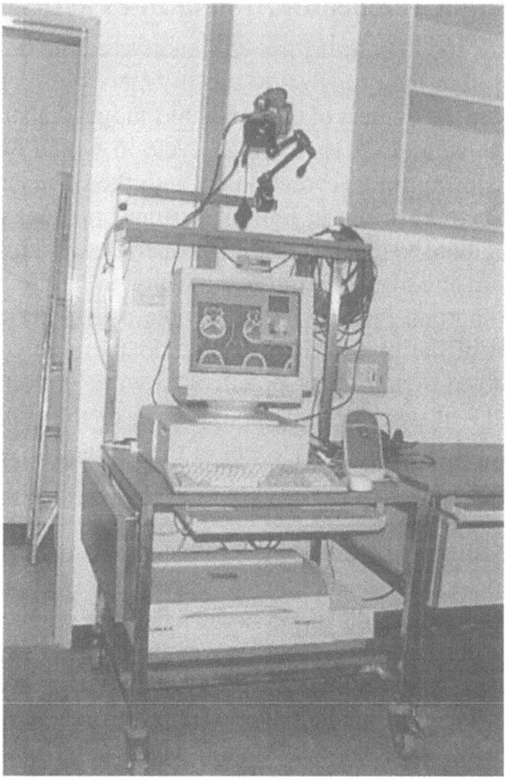

Figure 11.4. The mobile set-up for the prototype telehealth system at CGH. The set up includes a mobile trolley with PC, flat-bed scanner, call port, and digital video camera.

tant support when normally they would have been transferred (with budget, resource and skill implications for the regional unit). Another patient had a tracheostomy[4] performed prior to transfer because the medivac team were able to conduct a remote assessment of the patient beforehand (when normally they would only see the patient for the first time when they arrived for transfer when it is too late for such a procedure).

The network, video-conferencing and data-sharing capabilities increased the available bandwidth and *enriched the quality and quantity of information* that was shared within the consultation. Data including X-rays, scanned images, pathology results, indeed almost any relevant information, have been scanned prior to the video-conference, and then viewed and manipulated simultaneously by all participants. The tertiary consultant no longer had to rely entirely on the ability of the regional doctor to relay the patient's condition because she could now see for herself. As one of the doctors stated in an interview about using the system, "seeing is believing" and another, "you know that what you're seeing is what you will be getting."

The relationship of the consultation locale to *physical space* was no longer bound to the physical location of the telephone (the units did not have use of mobile phones at the time of the study). The consultation could take place from any location within distance of power point and network connections. The physical boundary of the consultation locale became flexible and the trolley was often wheeled to the bedside to show live video of the patient or their monitors.

The consultation locale was also been *extended across time* with a decreased reliance on strictly synchronous interaction. Now that shared source data could be saved, all the relevant people no longer had to be available at the same time since they could access the data at a later time. In one post-implementation survey, asynchronous access to data happened in nine out of thirteen consultations. This was particularly useful in an event-driven hospital environment where, for example, the consultant was urgently called to the operating theatre just as she was about to participate in a consultation. Other people could also make use of the information; a charge nurse at the tertiary unit accessed the stored patient information after a call had taken place to see how he needed to re-organise staff and equipment to care for the patient after transfer.

The *phases* of the consultation trajectory across time were also significantly shortened. Previously, it was not unusual for a consultation cycle to take days by the time a call was made, X-rays couriered to the tertiary clinician, further tests requested and undertaken, the new results couriered again to the tertiary centre, a decision made, and a patient transferred. This was now reduced to a matter of hours.

Clinicians also demonstrated their focus on getting their work done in spite of the technology, showing yet again that interactional needs are paramount and people will make *creative use* of any available 'site and mean' features. During one consultation in the middle of the night, the staff at WDH did not know how to use the scanning equipment but they wanted to show an image to the consultant at the other end. So they used the video camera to capture the image as someone stood on a chair to hold it in front of the ceiling light. In this case, the quality was sufficient to make a clinical judgement.

11.3.2 Unexpected Effects

The easiest part of the ICU telehealth project was setting up the hardware and software. The more significant and critical challenge was how to integrate the technologies into the everyday work practices of clinicians who were extremely busy, dealing with multiple competing demands, and wanting to focus on time-critical patient care, not the tools to deliver that care. To help the clinicians become familiar with the technology, a number of new educational and peer support activities were established across sites, including ward rounds, inservice education sessions and management meetings. This resulted in some unexpected effects, both across units and within professional groups.

The video-conferencing technology facilitated the *emergence of new transient social worlds* drawn from the participating ICUs for the above sessions. The most obvious benefit from such interactions was the sharing of expertise and resources, with particular advantages for the regional units through better educated staff.

A less obvious benefit was the strengthening and growth of *peer networks* across the units. Previously, the ICUs operated independently from each other. Interaction between the units was limited to occasional encounters between senior clinicians. Now the interactions were between whole ranges of clinicians, often at weekly intervals, who were getting to know about each other's strengths and areas of expertise. One junior doctor summed it up as "You get used to talking to them (in the education sessions) and build up a rapport. You gain a respect for their opinion." Another typical comment was "One of the values of the (inservice) sessions is that now we have no real hesitation to phone someone (for advice)."

As a result, relationships *between the ICUs* changed (improved civic structure networks) and new consultation and transfer patterns started to emerge. As people across sites came to know each other, they no longer call the tertiary CGH centre by default. Consultations were now taking place between NDH and WDH to draw on specific expertise. This never occurred prior to the system, and was changing the very nature of the relationship between all the ICU worlds.

There was also a significant strengthening of collegial ties within other *professional* groupings, with *impacts far beyond the sites involved.* The nurse educators were a case in point. They all belonged to a state professional association, the Critical Care Nurse Educators Association (CCNEA) but did not know each other. After deciding to conduct education sessions across sites, the nurse educators from the three ICUs started to meet together over the system to plan sessions. The meetings quickly evolved into far more general discussions and they soon realised how much practical and moral support they were deriving from each other. They discussed their experiences at the next annual meeting of the CCNEA, and also spoke of how they could see the association exploiting the technology. As a result, they established a network of small groups of critical care nurse educators throughout the state who met by fortnightly video-conferencing sessions; the social world relationships of a whole professional group were changed.

11.4. Conclusions and Reflections

The focus of this chapter has been the use of the *Locales Framework* for solution design and, as it happened, for understanding the co-evolution of technology and practice post-deployment. I have used the language of the *Locales*

Framework to describe current inter-ICU consultation practices, to motive requirements for better consultation locales enabled by technology, and for exploring how consultation practices have evolved through deployment and use of a specific technical solution, also exploring other unexpected effects from the system in use.

The *Locales Framework* was particularly useful for highlighting the transient audio-only nature of the locale and the comparative problems of such limited communication channels compared to rich co-present intra-ICU practices. It also enabled a focus on the interactional needs for conducting better remote consultations, taking account of the total context of those interactions — it was about designing a solution not implementing a technology. Because requirements were framed as needs, these needs can be met in a variety of ways, the current solution being just one example. This will make it easier to evolve the technical system to meet those interactional needs in even better ways as the clinicians become more comfortable with technology and as the general health infrastructure and network bandwidth improves.

Furthermore, as the discussion of use of the system in practice shows, the *Locales Framework* can provide a language for understanding and interpreting effects in a way that can enable generalisation and focussed facilitation of similar effects in other situations. Only through further iteration through the problem-solution space will we be able to tell. Certainly, though, this discussion puts an emphasis on the role of technology as being part of the spaces and resources available to people, and that different social worlds can make different uses of the same technology for the creation of different locales; installation of a telehealth system is not an end in its own right.

Notes

1 More detailed and differently-focussed discussions of this project can be found in (Kaplan and Fitzpatrick, 1997; Whiting et al., 1999).

2 This was a particularly interesting phenomenon. While the practice was based on science and well-researched evidence to a certain degree, clinical decision making was ultimately based on many other factors, e.g., the clinician's prior experience, their knowledge and trust of the literature, the medical specialty from which they viewed the world etc.

3 Proceeding from design motivation to clinical ownership of a specific solution can be a difficult process, involving many powerful and conflicting egos, inter-professional (doctor/nurse) power relationships, intrusion of external politics, relationships among sponsors and partners in the project, and so on, full discussion of which is beyond scope here.

4 A tracheostomy involves the surgical insertion of an artificial airway into the trachea when the air passage is blocked.

Chapter 12

CSCW ENVIRONMENT DESIGN: ORBIT AND TICKERTAPE

One of the motivations for this work was to find a principled approach to the development of support systems that fit into the workaday world. The previous chapters show the use of the framework in describing and analysing specific work situations. The *Locales Framework* can also give a language to talk about systems design itself, that is, how computer-based locales can be built to support work, or how computer-based tools can be added to enhance an existing physical and/or virtual locale.

In this chapter, I give a brief overview of Orbit, the prototype system developed within our wOrlds research group[1] to explore some of the infrastructural implications of the *Locales Framework* for building computer-based locales as collaborative environments. While the development of Orbit never proceeded beyond this point, the point is to show one example of how some of the concepts of the *Locales Framework* changed the way we thought about technical requirements for collaborative environments. (To distinguish between the broad conceptual notion of locale as presented in Chapter 7 and this particular instantiation of a computer-based locale, I will call Orbit's locales '*group-zones*' from now on although the term 'locale' will still be seen in the prototype interface.)

I also discuss a tool called Tickertape as an example of how existing locales of work can be enhanced by computer-based tools.[2] The different development and adoption stories for Tickertape versus Orbit provide interesting lessons about the importance of computer-based support fitting in with broader contexts of use.

12.1. Evolving Orbit

Chapter 3 described a previous collaboration system called wOrlds. wOrlds was a very useful prototype for starting to explore an approach to collaborative support that moved beyond previous action-based systems and their resultant problems. Many of the ideas in wOrlds have been taken up and explored by others in the CSCW domain; see for example (Kindberg, 1996; Roseman and Greenberg, 1996; Spellam et al., 1997).

On the basis of our (the wOrlds project group's) experiences in trying to understand the work of a group of systems engineers in order to deploy a version of wOrlds for the group, we started to understand some of the potential problems with this new system, as discussed in Chapter 6. One of our main critiques was that wOrlds ended up being a space-based or room-based system, simulating features of physical space, even though that was not the original design intention. Another major critique was that it only provided a group focus onto the work; it did not support individuals participating in multiple groups simultaneously with varying levels of intensity.

These were some of the insights that led to the development of the *Locales Framework*. They were also the key issues we wanted to first explore in the new prototype system, Orbit: how do we go about supporting virtual group places, group-zones, in which people can participate at various levels of intensity simultaneously?

Orbit, like wOrlds, can be described as a collaborative environment. As stated in Mansfield et al., (1997), "The [long-term] intent of Orbit is to provide a 'ubiquitous collaborative desktop' through which users will perform all shared and individual tasks."[3]

The design of Orbit is based upon a three-layer model. The base object layer contains the 'world' of external distributed objects from which a group can potentially populate their group-zones. The middle group-zone layer is where subsets of these objects are defined together into group-zones as relevant for particular social world needs. The top views layer allows an individual to compose views over, and participate in, multiple group-zones in the one view. This is the layer that distinguishes Orbit from wOrlds and every other rooms-based system of which we are aware.

This three-layer model is translated into the architecture of Orbit as shown in Figure 12.1. The object layer is composed of a set of repositories including BSCW (Bentley et al., 1997) for documents, web pages, etc., Envy for Smalltalk code, and CVS for C, Java and Python code. The core of the system is the Locale Service in the middle layer. The Locale Service "manages user sessions, stores the definition of [group-zones] (members, furnishings, group views), user details and handles locale-related events" (Mansfield et al., 1997). The Orbit Client together with MBone-based video and audio clients provide the user with the capabilities to compose multiple views over multiple workspaces.

12.1.1 Interpreting Framework Aspects in Orbit

In this section, I will go through the different aspects of the *Locales Framework* and show if and how we interpreted them in the Orbit prototype. The

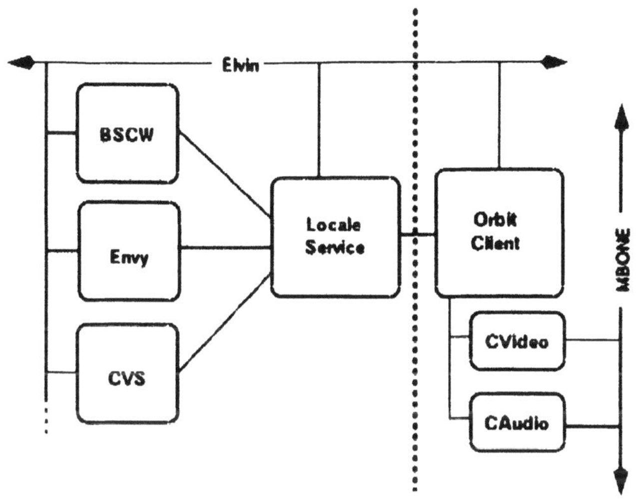

Figure 12.1. Three-layer architecture of the Orbit prototype. [Reproduced with permission from Tim Mansfield.]

reason for doing this is to show one iteration of trying to interpret the framework aspects so that others wanting to explore these concepts can learn from what we did here.

Locale Foundations

A group-zone is represented by a *locale control panel* in the Orbit navigator pane. Figure 12.2 shows a pane with seven different locale control panels. In each control panel, there is the locale name, a distinguishing colour chip, a current view level, three buttons for editing details, furnishings and views, and a 'presence' bar showing icons of people who are current members. The *details* button brings up a pane where the group-zone name, description, unique colour chip, and membership information can be changed.

Locale objects are called *furnishings* in Orbit. The furnishings button brings up a pane that allows members of the group-zone to add items. At the moment the only items are documents or folders; folders provide a primitive way of structuring the objects in a group-zone. When 'ticked', these objects will also be displayed in the workspace (to be discussed in the next section) with the same colour chip as the parent group-zone. Members can also select whether they are present, i.e., visible, in the group-zone, and how this *presence* is projected, e.g., via head icon, video and/or audio.

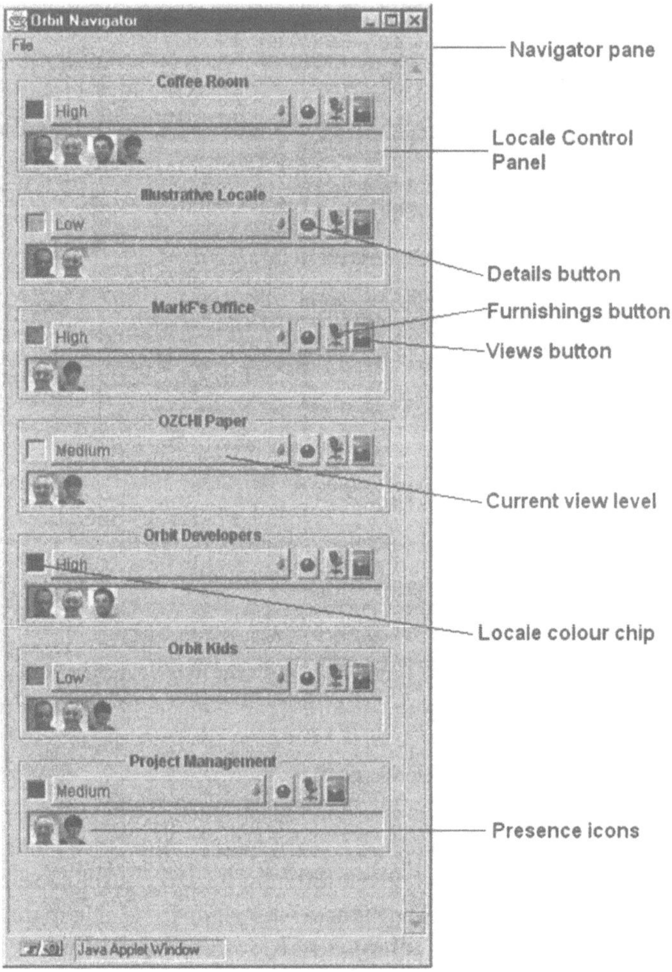

Figure 12.2. Orbit group-zones navigator.

The *views* button brings up a pane where both personal and shared group views of the group-zone can be defined. That is, having selected certain levels of presence for individuals and having selected certain objects to be visible, these can now be saved as a particular view with a defined view name.

Future work plans for *locale foundations* support included the following: a security model supporting different levels of access; different levels of membership; more support for asynchronous communication, and mediated communication; and more repositories as needs arise when new groups want to deploy Orbit.

Individual View

The *individual view* aspect is the key exploration undertaken in the Orbit prototype. As just explained, the views feature in the locale control panel of the navigator allows the user to define which objects from which group-zones they want to see at the current time. These objects are displayed together in the Orbit workspace as shown in Figure 12.3, with objects of different group-zones distinguished by different colour chips. In this way, the user is presented with a view over multiple group-zones simultaneously.

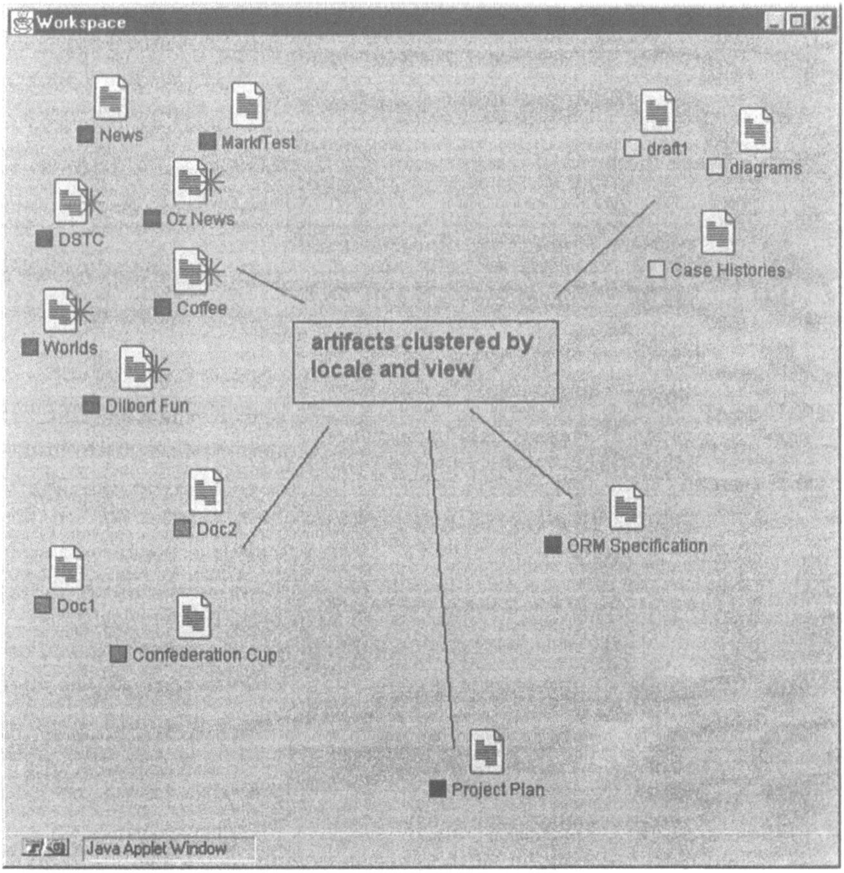

Figure 12.3. Orbit workspace showing simultaneous view over multiple group-zones as defined in the locale control panel.

Users generally follow a default naming scheme for the shared views in a group-zone, implying the level of intensity of involvement, e.g., HighVideo, High, LowVideo, Low, etc. However, the views can in fact be given any name.

The user can choose to activate one of these objects to work closely on it (all objects are representations of actual objects from one of the underlying repositories). The user can also choose at any time to re-define which group-zone objects to display. This allows the user to dynamically vary their view of the group-zone to enable different levels of interaction, from fully focussed to partial to peripheral.

These features enable many of the same features that we saw the systems engineers making use of in Chapter 5 for individual work. The difference is that these features are now enabled with explicit support for the group context of work as well as the individual context of work, allowing users to do the following:

- Easily represent aspects of their different locales in the one workspace
- Move relatively seamlessly from one locale's activities to another
- Easily change the level of involvement in different locales
- Engage in multiple locales simultaneously

In future work, we were also planning to further explore more dynamic view composition and better user interfaces for presenting and manipulating views.

Mutuality

Mutuality is supported to some degree for people, objects, and events through mechanisms that enable *presence* information to be made available in the group-zone. As already mentioned, users have various options for how they project their own presence information into a group-zone: via a presence icon of their head, or via full video and audio presence. Users can also choose how to make objects present in the group-zone; they can put an object into a folder, or they can select or de-select an object for display in a particular view.

To support awareness of events associated with a workspace-displayed object, Orbit uses a publish-and-subscribe event notification service based on Elvin (Segall and Arnold, 1997). When 'something' happens to an object, however 'something' has been defined, a red star appears at the right hand corner of the object icon.[4] The user can mouse-click on the star to display a menu showing the history of events associated with that object.

The same event notification service is used to support messaging between users within a group-zone via a Tickertape application, shown in Figure 12.4, that can be started from the navigator window. Both users and automated event watchers can send notifications via Tickertape directed to members of

Figure 12.4. Tickertape application where group-zone-specific messages can be displayed.

a particular group-zone. This mechanism can support both synchronous and limited asynchronous communication within the group-zone. I will return to Elvin and Tickertape later in this chapter. Fuller discussion on the range of uses for Tickertape can also be found in (Fitzpatrick et al., 2002; Fitzpatrick et al., 1999; Fitzpatrick et al., 1998c; Parsowith et al., 1998).

To better support mutuality aspects, future plans involved the development of user-tailorable event-notification widgets and of ways to support different policies related to the degree of reciprocity between presence and awareness requirements in a group-zone.

Interaction Trajectory

Because *interaction trajectory* was a central focus of previous ConversationBuilder and wOrlds prototypes (Bogia and Kaplan, 1995; Kaplan et al., 1992; Tolone et al., 1995), it was decided to explore other issues brought up by the *Locales Framework* that were more novel. As such, the current Orbit prototype offers little active support for trajectory management, apart from event histories associated with objects.

From previous experiences combined with the experience of Orbit, future work plans for interaction trajectory support included: support for work planning, e.g., by looking at different interpretations of workflow at different levels of group-zone granularity; better support for interaction histories, especially at the group level not just the object level; and support for shared action on group-zone objects.

Civic Structures

In the current prototype, *civic structures* was only minimally explored. The Orbit Navigator does provide a way of seeing all the group-zones together but thus far it is a relatively flat relationship. There have been some preliminary investigations, however, into a notion of courtyards between group-zones into which objects of shared interest can be placed. We were also wanting to explore more complexly structured group-zone relationships, e.g., neighbourhoods, sub-group-zones, and a hierarchy of group-zones, as well as looking at better support for user creation and dissolution of group-zones, including experimentation with a notion of residual group-zone objects when a group-zone is dissolved.

12.1.2 Orbit Summary

The *Locales Framework* challenges the activity-based or space/rooms-based infrastructure often used in the construction of CSCW environments. The Orbit prototype begins the exploration of some these infrastructural implications by providing a flexible toolkit environment to integrate essentially independent mechanisms within a common structure. These mechanisms implement different aspects of the *Locales Framework*; the framework provides the overarching template that enables the different mechanisms to cohere conceptually but without being overly prescriptive or circumscriptive.

In Orbit, a virtual locale is instantiated in a group-zone. Each group-zone is populated with objects and tools drawn from the underlying object repositories, and has mechanisms for controlling access and membership. View manipulation mechanisms enable the management of simultaneous views over multiple group-zones. To our knowledge, this was a novel approach to collapsing "the apparent duality, present in many older collaborative systems, between collaborative and individual work" (Mansfield et al., 1997). Mutuality is supported through the provision of various presence indicators and widgets. Users can tailor their environments to "mix-and-match different views, mutuality levels, over many group zones, according to the needs of the moment" (Fitzpatrick et al., 1998a).

12.2. The Coincidental Tickertape Lesson

For a variety of reasons (funding, resources, change of personnel), ongoing work with Orbit did not proceed past this initial prototype phase. It is difficult to know, therefore, whether these were better design directions for collaboration environments even if they were novel; we look forward to others learning from and building on this work. However, before development was stopped, we did attempt to deploy Orbit within our own and other workgroups in our organisation. In keeping with the nature of wicked problems, we were hoping to learn from these experiences and use the evaluation to progress the development of future versions of Orbit.

The deployment met with minimal success, largely because of its early prototype state (where the focus was primarily on testing individual features rather than providing a fully developed integrated suite of tools). We still learned two useful, though not unexpected, lessons. The Orbit environment would have to be robust and easy to use if people were to adopt it as their workaday computing environment, with careful thought given to the overhead of manipulating locale views in Orbit. It also had to support the information repositories and tools that people already used to get their work done.

These lessons were brought into sharp relief when compared with the parallel adoption of the Tickertape tool. While we were investing a lot of resources into developing Orbit, Tickertape was becoming a highly successful collaboration support tool in its own right yet without dedicated resources or management support.[5]

As discussed previously, Tickertape was one of the tools we integrated into the Orbit toolkit. Tickertape was a client interface (along with other clients such as Tickerchat) to a publish-and-subscribe event notification service called Elvin (Segall and Arnold, 1997). Messages that appeared in the Tickertape (or Tickerchat) window could be object-initiated notifications about changes or actions associated with that object or they could be chat messages (that act as user-initiated notifications) between users or groups of users (Fitzpatrick et al., 2002; Fitzpatrick et al., 1999; Fitzpatrick et al., 1998c; Parsowith et al., 1998).

As seen in Figure 12.4, Tickertape had a simple client interface; one of the Elvin developers had only written it so that they could demonstrate the underlying event notification service (the workings of which are normally hidden from view as part of the middleware technical infrastructure). As such, Tickertape was an incidental application around their core Elvin work; there was not a lot of 'design' thought put into making Tickertape highly usable or useful for wide deployment. Despite this, Tickertape came to be widely adopted by both technical and non-technical people at the grass-roots of our organisation, spreading through word of mouth and the enthusiasm of the developer team.

Why was it so successful at supporting many of the very things that we were hoping Orbit would support? The short answer is that Tickertape fitted in with people's existing locales of work (which consisted of a mix of physical and virtual tools and spaces) and met some core interactional needs around visibility of people and work, supporting coordination and communication. People were able to work around the basic usability features of the interface because they perceived the tool as being so useful in these regards.

A particular dialogue between two members of the Elvin developer group provided a good example to illustrate why Tickertape worked.

12.2.1 A Late Night Discussion around CVS

The dialogue, shown in Figure 12.5, was an actual interaction that took place between two of the developers of Elvin, Phelps and David.[6] It reflected a type of experience that happened many times per week. Phelps was at home, David was in the office. The dialogue started when one of them noticed a message that was initiated when the other checked in a file to their version control system, CVS:

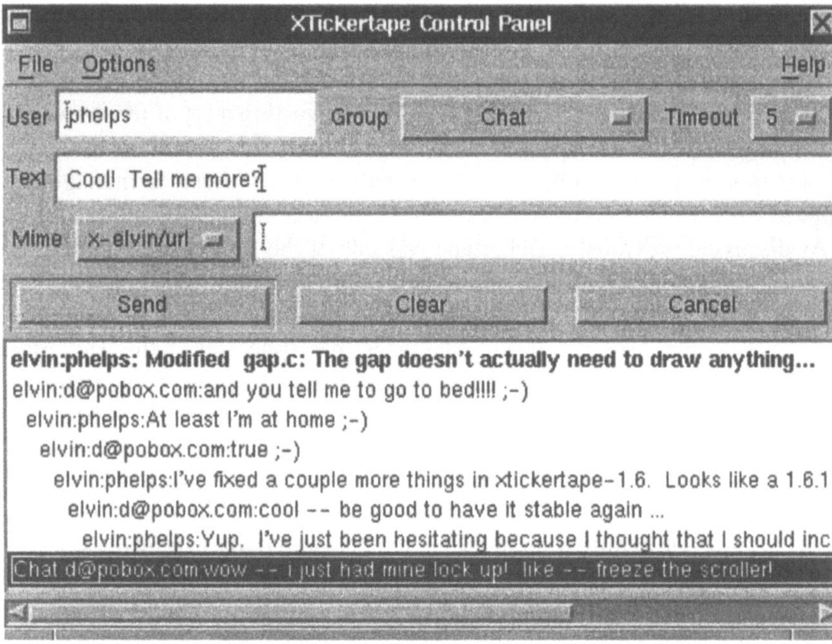

Figure 12.5. Control panel of Tickertape with threaded history dialogue showing a discussion generated by a file check-in to CVS. (Messages are truncated by control panel window size but would have been completely visible in the associated Tickertape window.

> It is late at night and Phelps is working from home fixing a bug in some Elvin code. When he is finished, he checks the file back into the code repository using the version control system, CVS. When prompted by CVS, Phelps enters the comment "The gap doesn't actually need to draw anything..." into the attached log file and completes the check-in.
>
> The developers have instrumented CVS so that this event causes an Elvin notification message stating the name of the modified file, in this case "gap.c", and the associated comment. The notification is then sent to people subscribed to the 'elvin' group (history line 1).
>
> David ('d') is working late back in the office and sees that Phelps has made some changes to the 'gap.c' file (line 1). He sends a message, joking "and you tell me to go to bed!!!!;-)" (line 2). Phelps and David then engage in some light-hearted banter about their working habits (lines 3-4). Phelps goes on to explain what he was doing for a new version of Tickertape and they have a short discussion around that work (lines 5-7). In the middle of the discussion, David has a problem with his Tickertape; it illustrates the bug Phelps has been trying to fix: "– i just had mine lock up! like – freeze the scroller!" (line 8) to which we see Phelps starting to respond in the dialogue text box "Cool! Tell me more?". And so they continued to discuss the new problem.

Like the systems engineers discussed earlier in this book, the Elvin developers formed a social world who worked in a mix of physical and virtual spaces that were populated with sophisticated hardware, software and other tools and resources. Their work on the Elvin code base was highly interdependent and collaborative but much of it took place in a virtual environment on virtual work objects where their presence and actions were largely intangible, disembodied and so not sensibly available to others. Communication and coordination was further limited when they worked from different physical spaces.

It was little wonder then that Tickertape became so quickly adopted and adapted by this group. Via the one interface, Phelps and David found out about computer-based events as they happened, engaged in social chit-chat, had a timely work discussion, and were both 'there' when a problem happened and could engage in collaborative diagnosis; all this even though they were not co-located, their actions were 'virtual' and their presence disembodied.

Tickertape provided a way for previously imperceptible actions in a virtual space to be given timely perceptible form and made available to others interested in such events; the CVS message sent to Tickertape provided David with resources he could make use of to become aware of what Phelps was doing. The integration of a chat-like facility with this event notification enabled these virtual actions to be re-connected to the embodied person producing that action, at least in the mind of the perceiver; David's response suggested that he clearly interpreted it as Phelps' action rather than simply a change of state of the CVS base. The coupling of actions and chat re-connected virtual activity to its broader social context and helped minimise the limitations of physical distribution.

The Elvin/Tickertape suite was more easily adopted than a tool like Orbit for a number of reasons. It integrated with, and augmented, the locales of the developers' workaday worlds to add a layer of information and communication support that was previously absent. The developers did not have to forgo their preferred work styles or change their sophisticated software development environment to take advantage of this support. They did not have to run separate tools for notification and for chat.[7]

Elvin/Tickertape was also easier to tailor to specific purposes, such as the instrumentation of CVS to generate the notifications, because of its technical simplicity. The overhead of tailoring Orbit for specific purposes was much greater; while the potential benefit could be greater in the long run, more careful consideration has to be given to the cost-benefit implications. As indicated by its rapid uptake beyond the developer group, Tickertape's user interface was also easy enough to learn and use despite the fact that was never 'properly' designed from a usability point of view with wide deployment in mind.

12.3. Summary

In the spirit of iterating through a wicked problem space to better solutions, I hope that better solutions will be evolved to support people working together as a result of our experiences with Orbit as a prototype computer-based locale environment and Tickertape as a tool to augment existing locales.

The development of the Orbit prototype was a technical exercise to explore how the concepts of the *Locales Framework* might provide new ways for thinking about infrastructural features that could be developed as part of a collaborative environment. While the interpretation of some of these features in the Orbit prototype were never able to be properly tested because development did not proceed to a fully integrated working environment, they still pointed to novel directions for collaboration support.

The simplicity yet success of Elvin/Tickertape suggests though that we should not always be looking for the most sophisticated solutions to meeting interactional needs, in this case *mutuality* needs. The Elvin developers already had well-developed work practices and generally functional locales of work. Tickertape was able to augment their workaday world to make available 'event-based' cues for use as perceptual resources for awareness, resources previously missing in distributed and computer-based activities. As an added benefit, it also facilitated lightweight informal interactions integrated closely with everyday tools and resources, enhancing social world communication and cohesion.

Notes

1 Ted Phelps, Mark Fitzpatrick, and Tim Mansfield have been the key developers and designers of the Orbit prototype. Other members of our group, including Simon Kaplan, Rik Taylor, Philip Johnson, Andrew Berry, Winnie Qui, Charles Herring, and Blaize Rhodes, have also made contributions to the prototype or to discussions around the prototype.

2 Bill Segall and David Arnold are the designers and developers of Elvin. Julian Boot, Ted Phelps, Blaize Rhodes, Michael Lawley and Shelina Gorain have all developed different versions of Elvin client interfaces.

3 Three versions of the Orbit prototype have already been developed—Mercury, Lite, and Gold—as presented in Mansfield et al., (1997). When I talk of the current version of Orbit in this chapter, I will be referring to Orbit-Gold. Orbit-Gold was built using state-of-the-art distributed object technology with persistent storage and CORBA-IIOP communications, deploying a Smalltalk server and a web-based Java client.

4 This is a very preliminary interface. More sophisticated icons were planned for later versions of Orbit.

5 This is not to say that Orbit was a bad idea. This was a minimal prototype, not a fully developed system. Also, in hindsight, we needed to do more thinking and analysis of if and how Orbit might have been used by any particular group and tailored Orbit appropriately for it to have any chance of successful adoption. We had expected that the developers would help put in the effort to tailor the system but there was insufficient initial benefit to encourage them to do this.

6 I am grateful to Ted Phelps and David Arnold for their permission to use this example.

7 More detailed discussion about how Tickertape via Elvin was used and why it worked can be found in (Fitzpatrick et al., 2002).

Chapter 13

CONCLUSIONS, REFLECTIONS AND FUTURE WORK

How to engage in understanding and designing for wicked problems has been the framing issue for the discussions in this book. I've looked at this issue specifically in relation to CSCW and the design of systems to support people who collaborate together for some shared purpose. Here, the issue was how to understand the nature of this workaday world of collaborative work for the purposes of design and how to design systems that take account of, and fit into the workaday world. I have characterised this issue as the CSCW design problem, an example of a wicked problem where there is no right or wrong answer, only better or worse solutions, and we only understand more about the problem as we work with different solutions.

I've conjectured that a significant part of what made the building of effective CSCW systems so difficult was the absence of a set of abstractions shared among the participating stakeholders — social scientists, computer scientists, and users. This resulted in a communications gap between how work was understood and how systems were designed. One reason for this was the multi-disciplinary nature of the CSCW community; those concerned with understanding and those concerned with designing tended to come from distinctly different backgrounds, neither of which fully prepared their proponents to work at the intersection of the two areas.

This book has been about continuing a dialogue between understanding and designing around these issues, both at the general (reflective) community level and at the specific (experiential) instance level, not to find *the* answer because, in the nature of wicked problems, there can be no definitive answer, but to evolve *better* understanding and do *better* designing.

The story told here has been about my own engagement in this dialogue, from reflecting on what I think we understand thus far from the general community experiences with understanding and designing, and then discussing our own experiences in building the wOrlds system and studying a group for whom the system was to be deployed.

The primary contribution from this dialogue has been the introduction of the *Locales Framework* as a core set of abstractions that can promote a *principled approach* to understanding the nature of work and designing systems to support this work, also providing a *common language* to facilitate communication between the two activities.

In engaging in this dialogue, I also expected to learn more about the design problem itself and will discuss some of these issues when I reflect critically on use of the framework in the two case studies and for Orbit design, leading to suggestions for future work. I will conclude with a postscript, reflecting more generally on the role of frameworks and on the role of people in the use of such frameworks. Before starting on this discussion, I first review the framework itself.

13.1. Review of the Locales Framework

The *Locales Framework* is based on a metaphor of place where the primary unit of analysis is *locale*. I defined locale as the place that arises from the use of space and resources (site and means) by members of a social world for their particular purpose, i.e., locale is constituted in the relationships between 'site and means' and a social world's interactional needs. Because locale arises in this relationship, it can be used as a shared abstraction to account for both the social world interactions and the 'site and means' and hence for both understanding and designing – the difference is a matter of perspective and focus on the relationship.

The *Locales Framework* comprises five aspects that characterise the nature of the workaday world from different perspectives. These aspects are interdependent and overlapping; they invite consideration of how the locale does, or could be evolved to, support the life of a social world and consideration of one aspect necessarily sheds light on other aspects:

- *Locale foundations* identifies the social world of interest and the spaces and resources (interchangeably called site and means) through which the people in the social world achieve their interaction.

- *Civic structure* identifies the relationship of this social world and its locales to the broader context, picking up on social, political, organisational, material, cultural, legislative, contractual, technological and other broader-sphere issues.

- *Individual view* identifies the different perspectives that individuals might hold of the one locale, together with an individual's aggregated view of the multiple locales in which they participate, as appropriate for the domain of interest.

- *Interaction trajectory* is concerned with actions and courses of actions, identifying the dynamic and temporal aspects of the living social world and its interactions within and across locales — past, present and future.
- *Mutuality* is concerned with awareness as an achieved outcome, identifying the mutual communicative processes through which awareness is achieved — the provision and perception of information for awareness. It considers how spaces and things are made available and accessible to people and how people and their activities are made available and accessible to others through the spaces and things they use as locale.

Together, these aspects can potentially capture a broad range of issues relevant to the life of a social world, from local setting to global context, from the individual to the group perspective, from static to dynamic features, and from informal to formal characteristics. Further, these aspects can be applied at any level of scale, from small to large groups, in short to long timeframes, in minute detail to high level overview, and for any type of space be it physical, virtual or mixed.

13.2. Reflections on Using the Framework

Having claimed that the *Locales Framework* could provide a principled approach to understanding and designing, as well providing a common language to facilitate communication between the two activities, it is worth reflecting on use of the framework for these purposes. I begin each discussion with a review of the proposed relationship of the framework to either understanding or designing.

13.2.1 Using the Framework for Understanding

Proposed relationship to understanding: The *Locales Framework* approach to understanding work has been specifically motivated by the *needs of systems design* rather than adherence to a particular theoretical stance. Although it draws heavily on Strauss' (1993) theory of action and on the more general ad hoc concepts emergent in the CSCW field, it is more about "[packaging] a set of sociological understandings so that they can be used to inform the analysis of working situations and the design of technologies to support cooperative work" (Dourish, 2001b, p. 94).

An important aim in the packaging of these understandings is for them to be rich enough to help sensitise people to key elements of a collaborative environment but also sufficiently general, open and incomplete so as not to prescribe nor circumscribe all that could be of interest. The aspects can be used as multi-faceted lenses to pass over the domain of interest. This lens is more like a fish-eye lens, not focussing on one aspect or domain element to the exclusion of everything, but with the focus necessarily in relationship with the whole locale context. It also encourages an emphasis on both interactions and the use of space and things in support of those interactions, space and things being the very targets of CSCW design activity.

For gathering an understanding of an environment first hand, the *Locales Framework* can serve as a set of heuristics to help motivate initial questions and observations as makes sense given the framing focus for the study; the focus helps determine what will constitute the locale of interest. For pre-existing study data, the framework aspects can be used as a basis for structuring and presenting data.

Either way, the *Locales Framework* is presented as a starting point to understanding the nature of work at hand. The spirit in which it can be used is similar to the way in which Strauss saw his theory of action being used. I repeat it here, paraphrased to talk about the *Locales Framework* (my paraphrasing in square brackets):

> "... the principle function [of the locales framework] is not at all to supply or directly develop concepts that will constitute the [requirements analysis] about the particular phenomenon under study. Rather, what the [framework] is capable of doing is ... to inform [key aspects of a collaborative environment]. It is not that thinking in this way requires you to keep looking over your shoulder ...: Did I get this in? What have I forgotten? To use the [framework] in this way would be unreal, unworkable, and deadly for [systems design]. ... One of the striking paradoxes of this [framework] is that just because it has been expressed explicitly and systematically, in these pages, it can function implicitly during the course of [design] itself, rendering systematic the [analyst's] ordering of explanations." (Strauss, 1993, pp. 67, 68)

Understanding use reflections: The two cases presented in Chapter 10 and Chapter 11 are examples of the *Locales Framework* being used to explore a situation at first hand. They involved different types of studies. The IEU distributed research study was exploratory, following emergent activity over a period of time. The telehealth study was undertaken with a specific goal in mind, the implementation of a telecommunications solution; the focus was on understanding more generally repeated patterns of work, i.e., remote consultations, then following through with implementation and post-deployment evaluation.

The discussions of the studies in the earlier chapters represented the outcomes of using the *Locales Framework*; here I reflect on some of the process issues in using the framework to arrive at those outcomes.

During data collection, I tended to use the *Locales Framework* in more implicit than explicit ways, e.g., I did not say "Today I'm looking at *individual view* issues." Rather, the framework aspects, with their properties and dimensions, were background resources that I used to both kick-start and augment my researcher's curiosity. Within the framing questions of the studies, they suggested issues to look at, questions to ask, and different ways to explore the same phenomena, particularly focussing on how spaces and things facilitated or constrained the phenomenon. In this way, the framework served as a sensitising device. This was particularly so for understanding why collaborations within the two distributed research groups evolved in the ways they did.

As would be expected in qualitative studies using observations, interviews, collection of artefacts, and so on, I gathered large amounts of rich data. During data analysis, I still used a grounded theory approach to work with the data, looking for emergent themes and patterns and coding the data with higher-order categories. The framework proved most useful as a way of structuring the data and organising these emergent themes and categories. Mind-maps (Buzan and Buzan, 1994) were useful for visualising these relationships around framework aspects. I also used matrices as a way, for example, to explore the commonalities and differences in the IEU and Romany collaborations against relevant framework aspects. The framework aspects were also helpful in encouraging deeper interrogation by applying different perspectives to the data.

While all of the aspects were useful for uncovering or telling the story of the study domains, some aspects were more important than others for a certain situation. In the IEU study, the *civic structures* aspect was particularly useful for drawing out the inter-organisational conflicts around which the individuals in the group had to negotiate their IEU involvement. For the telehealth study, the *mutuality* aspect was important for explaining some of the breakdowns that had occurred in telephone based remote consultations.

A *Locales Framework* analysis of breakdowns or critical problem areas, such as why significant IEU collaboration failed to evolve, or why inappropriate transfers sometimes happened with phone-based consultations, proved especially useful in understanding the accomplishment of work and providing focal points for envisioning how work could happen differently through the design of different or enhanced spaces to be used as place.

It is obviously difficult to say how the studies might have evolved differently without the framework. Still, despite being the 'originator' of the framework, it was no easy shortcut; qualitative research and analysis is a lot of hard work because ultimately the process is about letting the domain itself speak to what is important or relevant. The *Locales Framework* can be a useful resource but still requires creative and intelligent application on the part of the researcher. I will be returning to discuss the role of the researcher with respect to the framework in later discussions.

13.2.2 Using the Framework for Designing

Proposed relationship to design: The *Locales Framework* approach to designing systems is different from some of the more traditional computer-science approaches that focus quickly onto detailed specification of system behaviours.

Systems still need to be formulated as a tame set of requirements, as a space or resource, if they are to be built as software and hardware, but the framework can provide a way for design decisions to be motivated by the *group's interactional needs* in the practical accomplishment of their work, rather than by technical or simulation motivations alone or in isolation from contexts of use. This is a level of abstraction removed from the details of specific implementation choices.

Designers can use the *Locales Framework* aspects to help identify where features can be added to spaces and resources to enhance existing locales. Alternatively, new spaces and resources can be created out of which social worlds can create new locales, for example, to coalesce the distributed life of an existing group or to facilitate the emergence of a new group altogether. These enhanced or constructed locales can be physical, or computer-based ('virtual'), or a mix of both.

Design use reflections: The *Locales Framework* was used in two different ways for design: one based on specific workplace studies, to suggest possible directions for support of the IEU distributed research group and for a telehealth solution; and the other for design of a generic collaborative toolkit environment.

The framework did prove useful for promoting design decisions that took account of the total context of work. For example, the design suggestions for the IEU group not only touched upon new technologies to augment the existing locale, but also new ways of using existing technologies and, more critically, pointed to inter-organisational issues that had to be addressed. Design suggestions were also motivated by meeting particular interactional needs. This was particularly so in the telehealth study where the new remote consultation locale was designed to promote increased mutuality and access to shared information.

Overall though, using the *Locales Framework* for driving through to design solutions only took us a few steps on from the usual implications for design that I critiqued in Chapter 2. The *Locales Framework* proved more useful for motivating design than for moving on to the substance of design. The benefit that it offered over the ad hoc insights and implications previously reported was that we were able to tell a more complete and integrated design motivation story by using locale as the unit of presentation with its different framework perspectives. Further, the *Locales Framework* embraced both social and technical concerns whereas many study implications are more about counterpointing the 'social and the technical' to protect the social concerns from an onslaught of inappropriate technology.

From use of the framework, another type of gap in the design process became obvious. At the moment, the question of how to design better locales, or what even constitutes a better locale, is largely left to the intuition and skill of the designer. In one sense, this is not a problem since design is a creative process. The difficulty is related more to the relative newness of CSCW design as a field. Other creative design disciplines such as architecture have rich and well established traditions to draw upon[1]. Such design knowledge within the CSCW community is only beginning to evolve. As well as building upon a shared history of design, there is also a potential role for more principled guidelines to underpin the substance of design than intuition alone.

The second way that the *Locales Framework* was used for design was for the generic CSCW toolkit environment called Orbit. The framework facilitated a paradigm shift away from workflow or space as an underlying systems metaphor to a metaphor of place. The main contribution of this shift is that it encouraged an exploration of the strengths of the virtual medium in its own right for the creation of computer-based locales of work, rather than trying to replicate strengths from the medium of physical space into the virtual medium where they do not 'naturally' exist. The various framework aspects highlighted different locale mechanisms that could be created, or different ways in which mechanisms could be used, all within a coherent conceptual template. It also encouraged the exploration of mixed spaces as an integrated place or locale; the incidental experience with tickertape pointed to the ways in which collaboration support could be integrated into the workaday world.

13.2.3 Using the Framework — Other Experiences

Since the *Locales Framework* was first articulated, there are a number of other ways that it has been used. I highlight two of these here: workshops (for business development work with clients including issue identification, scenario planning and solutions architecture) and groupware heuristics.

Workshop activities: Prior to undertaking some consultancy research with a Government department, we held a workshop with all the members of the department to identify the main areas of concern for them. Facilitated by two colleagues[2] and myself, we used the *Locales Framework* as a vehicle to understand the scope of their work and to help the group collectively identify issues of concern. These issues then helped me focus the on-site observations and interviews and frame the subsequent report.

In this case, we applied the *Locales Framework* in the following way: After giving a brief introduction to the framework and its five aspects, we asked the participants to think about their own group and describe their role as a department (starting to understand shared purpose or what it is that defines them as a group) and the nature of their work. We also asked them to identify other social worlds (civic structures) that impacted on their work in some way.

From this high-level overview, we then moved the discussion to a specific activity from the past week that they thought 'typical' of their work – they chose the preparation of a Briefing Note for a government minister. The major part of the workshop was then spent walking through the trajectory of this Briefing Note preparation. We drew up a timeline representation of the activity, annotated it with notes at each point as suggested by different *Locales Framework* aspects, and highlighted areas where problems or breakdowns occurred. We probed with questions such as: who was involved at this stage, how did they find out about it, who did what, how did they know what to do, where was something put, why did something happen that way, how was this different to other times, and so on.

At the first pass, one person had reported the activity as a simple series of steps: "we received a Briefing Note request, we pulled out the previous Briefing Note and then we...". Two hours later, every person was amazed to see how complicated the activity actually was, and how many aspects were actually problematic when they had thought it a relatively routine case. While this is hardly surprising — Suchman's (1983) seminal study of office procedures shows there is nothing routine about 'routine' — the *Locales Framework* provided a language and a structure for the members of the group to appreciate this for themselves. In so doing, it also helped me better focus my limited on-site research time with them.[3]

In a completely different workshop exercise with different groups and facilitators, the *Locales Framework* was used to structure *future scenario planning* activities.[4] The perceived advantage for future scenario development was the multi-faceted perspective that it encouraged in thinking through future possibilities and the different levels of scale at which it could be applied, from what the world might look like, to how a fictional character would engage in this future activity.

The framework was also used with clients for *solutions architecture planning*, to brainstorm how various new technologies might come into play with the larger existing framework of customers, services and products. In this context, the framework was found to be particularly useful "for showing how the [client's] existing systems were insufficient to address certain customer needs highlighted by the *Locales Framework* 'lamps', and how various new technologies could be used to plug those gaps they didn't know they had." (Ralf Muhlberger, personal communication, Dec 2002).

Groupware heuristics: Greenberg et al (2000) used the *Locales Framework* to develop a set of heuristics for evaluating groupware. The heuristics were: provide locales; provide awareness within locales; allow individual views; allow people to manage and stay aware of their evolving interactions; and provide a way to organise and relate locales to one another. These heuristics were then applied to Teamwave Workplace, a commercial groupware product. Although two of the authors were very familiar with Teamwave, having been involved in early prototype development, the heuristics still proved useful in a number of ways. The language of the heuristics gave them a different way of characterising the system as supporting the basic idea of a locale. They also helped with identifying potential problems that the developers had otherwise not thought of. And they suggested ways of providing richer support for collaboration.

In the spirit of engagement with wicked problems, this was a first iteration of ongoing attempts to develop better heuristics for groupware evaluation building on the experiences gained here; see for example Baker et al., (2001). In applying a solution, more was learnt about the problem, for example, that groupware heuristics are likely to be harder to learn and harder to use in practice because of the subtle nuances of teamwork, and that different sets of heuristics are most likely needed for task-based groupware compared with groupware environments.

13.2.4 Using the Framework as a Shared Abstraction

The proposal here is that the *Locales Framework* can serve as a shared abstraction and communicative bridge between understanding and designing. This is because the primary unit of analysis is 'locale' and this unit arises in the relationship between 'social' concerns and 'technical' concerns. As such, the framework provides a base common language to account for both the wicked nature of the problem domain and the tame requirements of systems design. The framework can also help to describe current locales and work-practices, and to envision potentially new or enhanced locales to better support the life of a social world.

From experiences thus far, the *Locales Framework* has been able to play this bridging role to some extent. In the telehealth case, for example, the same *Locales Framework* language helped to describe the problems of the current situation, to position a design solution motivated by interactional needs, and to explain the impacts and changes arising from use of the system in practice. In the development of Orbit, the framework concepts, arising from the study of the systems engineers and other social science literature, became the focus for novel technical explorations. Subsequent uses of the framework in workshop contexts also show that it can be easily and quickly adopted by stakeholders as a lingua franca.

13.3. Moving Forward — Future Work

Drawing on these collective experiences, there are a number of potential avenues for evolving the *Locales Framework* and continuing the ongoing dialogue to address the wicked problem of design. Some of the suggestions below are more speculative than others but nonetheless might seed further thinking.

Methodological toolkit: To facilitate wider use, the processes for working with the framework need to be made more accessible, especially for people who are not traditionally comfortable with such an approach. This could take the form of a methodological toolkit that provides them with a collection of tools and techniques potentially useful for populating different aspects of the framework. For example, participatory design techniques could be included to involve the members of the social world in the articulation of their own locales and ways of working. Spatial layout maps could be used to map the flow of activity through a space and the relationships between objects, spaces and people. Process modelling techniques might be included as part of the tools for understanding trajectory. Design workshops could be used to help members of the social world or the design team evolve new or enhanced locales using the *Locales Framework* language.

Presentational toolkit: To support the communication of framework data, both the description of what is, and the design of what could be, better representational *techniques* and presentational *tools* are needed to convey the essence of findings in compelling and easily-accessible ways yet still be linked to the underlying data that grounds the finding. Some of the diagramming techniques used in Contextual Design (Beyer and Holtzblatt, 1998) and in the more recent MIME Grounded Innovation Map (Diggins et al., 2001) suggest ways of approaching the representational issues. Hypermedia tools might be useful for supporting different levels of presentation from high-level concepts to grounding data, and also for making more visible the different perspectives on the same phenomena, the connections between different framework aspects, and the moves from current to future locale possibilities.

Principled sharing and re-use approaches: In reporting on our own experiences with using the framework for design, one of the issues was knowing how to design better locales — are there principled approaches that could suggest *what constitutes a better locale* and that could help move the output from a *Locales Framework* analysis into more substantial systems design than is currently the case? Alexander's (1979, 1987) notions of patterns have potential here (Kaplan et al., 1998).

Many people are already exploring patterns to support interaction design using Alexander's approach of defining a pattern as the solution to a problem in a context (Erickson, 2000). More recently these are being applied to CSCW concerns (Martin et al., 2001; Crabtree et al., 2002). Martin et al (2001) use more of a descriptive approach rather than a problem-solution approach; they define patterns of cooperative interaction using a particular descriptive structure as a way of organising and presenting material from ethnographic studies to make them available as resources for CSCW design. A stated reason for doing this is to promote comparison across different pattern examples and to draw out generic pattern overviews. Many of the fields used in their pattern structure share concerns with different *Locales Framework* aspects. Crabtree et al (2002) extend the use of descriptive patterns in their work on domestic environments to support the "elaboration of a design space through the identification of discrete application areas." This is all work that can be built upon in trying to develop a more principled approach to sharing and re-using *Locales Framework* analyses for design, where the *Locales Framework* aspects are used as a structuring mechanism.

Technology toolkits: Since the outcome of the *Locales Framework* analysis might be suggestions for enhancement of existing locales, it would be useful to know what existing technologies are available, and how they are able to support various aspects of the framework. To this end, an analysis and *characterisation of technologies* in *Locales Framework* terms could be undertaken. Related work could also be the development of a systems *infrastructure toolkit* out of which new locales or locale components could be constructed for specific needs. The work on Orbit begins one such exploration. There could also be some merit, for example, in exploring more options for facilitating mutuality by investigating if and how Robertson's (1997) taxonomy of embodied actions could be supported, e.g., what computing infrastructure is needed to support gesturing around a shared locale object.

Application domains: More recently, there has been a significant growth of interest in the use of *mobile devices and pervasive computing*; see for example the IEEE journal "Pervasive computing: mobile and ubiquitous systems". Pervasive computing blurs the boundaries between virtual and physical spaces in interesting ways and changes the nature of interaction with both. The *Locales Framework* could be used to characterise the broader context of spaces, resources and interactions into which devices could be embedded — putting devices into their locale context. The very nature of mobile and pervasive computing, where the individual interacts with multiple devices embedded in an environment or interacts through one device but from multiple locations, suggests that the *individual view* aspect could be particularly useful for characterising how such environments will be experienced and interacted with. The *mutuality* aspect could also encourage different ways of thinking about the interactional needs that such devices and environments could support and how these would work in synergy with the rich array of physical and virtual space mechanisms that people already make use of.

There are also potential applications in the commercial software development world. *Personas* (Cooper, 1999) are becoming increasingly popular as a way of presenting and communicating information about different audience segments throughout the software development lifecycle; ideally this information is ethnographically-derived though not necessarily so. The *Locales Framework* could be used as a way of structuring persona stories to ensure a rich multi-faceted description of their contexts and interactions. This would be telling the story from the perspective of *individual view* where the persona is at the centre of the fish-eye lens but necessarily bringing in the relevant locales in which they interact.

Another use in commercial contexts could be as a heuristic tool to understand client situations in early project phases. Dealing with tight timeframes and limited resources, it often isn't possible to engage in in-depth background research about a client and their problem. The *Locales Framework* could be used as a *brainstorming tool*, with or without client and/or stakeholder involvement, to help map out as rich a picture as possible covering example areas of: their business, the stakeholders, the locations and 'tools' of trade (*locale foundations*), the markets they operate in (*civic structures*), the perspectives of different stakeholders (*individual view*), how they do business (*interaction trajectory*), and how all this is enabled or constrained by the spaces and resources they use (*mutuality*). A similar exercise could also be used to map out an initial understanding of the client's audience groups (internal or external). An outcome of such exercises might be the identification of questions, issues, conflicts in understanding, problem areas and so on, enabling a more focussed and targeted use of resources and time to deliver highest value. For example, it could help identify and frame the focus for in-depth user research to understand the needs of a particular audience group. It could point to critical organisational issues that need to be addressed among stakeholders concurrent with the development of a technical solution.

13.4. Postscript: Reflections from a Distance

Before concluding, I want to reflect more broadly on the *Locales Framework* as an approach to dealing with the wicked problem of design given the distance of time since it was first developed.

One of the central concerns for the CSCW community is the relationship between system design and the social sciences and how best to engage in this relationship for the better support of cooperative work arrangements. I have been presenting the *Locales Framework* as a set of shared abstractions for the CSCW community (and the socio-technical community more generally). I have argued that the framework can support both understanding and designing: it accounts for and is grounded in the sociality of work but still allows for the uniqueness of each workplace and work-practice to be uncovered; it also accounts for the pragmatic needs of design and systems building. I have further argued that the framework can serve a bridging role between understanding and designing because the same unit of analysis, locale, can be used by both, the different use a matter of emphasis and perspective but with locale always as the shared centre.

13.4.1 Converging to Better Solutions

On the one hand, I remain convinced that engaging at this interface of understanding and designing is important and that finding better ways to ground design in the sociality of work and to orient social understandings to the needs of systems design is still an open yet critical issue. Two recent developments suggest that we might be converging to solutions based on *shared frameworks* and focussed on *relationships* for moving forward on the wicked problem of design. One development is the experiences of the MIME project and their Grounded Innovation Map. The other is Dourish's proposal for embodied interaction as a foundation for interactive systems design.

Grounded Innovation Map

The European-funded project, Multiple Intimate Media Environments (MIME)[5] looked at the relationship between computer technology and people's experience of media collections around the home. The ethnomethodologists and designers working on the project provide an engaging account of the process of evolving innovative practices to enable them to work together, one outcome being a structured representation of fieldwork data, called a Grounded Innovation Map (Diggins et al., 2001).

What is most interesting is that the Grounded Innovation Map was developed sometime after the *Locales Framework*, and independent of it, yet it is very similar in both concepts and approach. As with the *Locales Framework*, the Grounded Innovation Map was developed as a bridge between ethnography and design, facilitating communication between the two, providing a "shared orientation", but not owned by either discipline. Also similar to the *Locales Framework*, the map is not intended to be self-sufficient, but is presented as a heuristic tool that can be helpful for organising data in way that is more oriented to design. The major map categories also share similarities with *Locales Framework* aspects, the categories being people, things (enablers), space and time, with sub categories to different levels of specificity, and often characterised by dimensions defined as continua. While the actual definition of the categories is specific to the context of the home, they are very similar to *locale foundations* and *interaction trajectory*.

What the map provides that the *Locales Framework* doesn't is a representational form for laying out the categories and overlaying the representation with indicators for potential innovation points. A similar approach would be very useful in representing *Locales Framework* findings. What the *Locales Framework* provides that the MIME map doesn't is a richer grounding in a metaphor of place and in the definition of locale as the unit of analysis that will enable the *Locales Framework* to be more generally applicable. The map categories, on the other hand, were only ever meant to be specific to the local practices of the team and the domestic environments they studied.

In summary, however, what the MIME work reinforces is that there is a potential role in practice for such *mediating frameworks* as the *Locales Framework* or the Grounded Innovation Map that can sit in-between understanding and design.

Embodied Interaction

Paul Dourish (2001b) has recently outlined a new foundational approach to the design of interactive systems called 'embodied interaction'. He develops the embodied interaction perspective by first observing that social computing (of which CSCW is an example) and tangible computing share a common basis: that we experience the world by engaging directly with it and so both consequently draw on the same set of human skills and abilities. From this, he explores the notion of embodiment as a form of participative status and discusses how embodiment is relevant to interactions with computers. Drawing on phenomenological understandings concerned with embodiment, Dourish goes on to propose how they can form a foundational approach to embodied interaction.

Of most interest here in relation to the *Locales Framework* work are some underlying themes they share, even though these themes are grounded in different philosophical and sociological traditions, and play out in very different ways.

The central shared theme is *relationship.* Dourish suggests that embodied interaction can "provide a new way of conceptualizing the relationship between technology and social settings" [*op.cit.,* p. 203]. This notion of relationship is also key to the definition of a locale, locale arising from the relationship between people and their use of space and things as place.

A sub-theme is to do with meaning. Dourish suggests that an embodied action conceptualisation of the relationship between people and technology puts a focus on practice, i.e., not just what people do, but "what they *mean* by what they do, and with how what they do is meaningful to them"[*op.cit.,* p. 204]. Strauss' theory of action, from which many *Locales Framework* concepts have been drawn, is based on the idea that the shared purpose of the social world (however that is understood), members' interactions and the conditions arising from past actions provide the meaningful context for actions; locale, then, can also be understood as a unit of meaning.

Appropriation is another core element of an embodied interaction perspective on the social-technical relationship. Appropriation is about "the emergence, establishment, and evolution of working practices and their relation to the settings — technical, organizational, physical, etc — in they they emerge and are worked out [. . . and] how special features of technical design support or interfere with appropriation" [*op.cit.,* p. 204]. Again, while not discussed in the same way, appropriation can be seen as the practice by which locale trajectories evolve over time and the way features of spaces and things are used: "*Interaction trajectory* is about the living social world and its interactions in and with locales. It is about how people engage with the setting and with each other and, by their actions, evolve a new set of conditions for further actions" (Chapter 8, this volume).

In summary, what the embodied interaction approach reinforces is that exciting possibilities lie in the *relationship* between the social and the technical. This relationship is more than just a collection of the constituent elements — something new is created at the nexus of the relationship. Nor is relationship a static thing — by definition it is a living dynamic ongoing engagement among all the parts, where both the participating elements and the relationship itself change over time. As stated for the embodied interaction perspective: "technology and practice cannot be separated from each other; they are coextensive and will coevolve" (Dourish, 2001b, p. 203).

No wonder then that the design of interactive systems is a wicked problem where the problem can never be fully specified and where we only learn more as we try out solutions; we are dealing with a continually changing relationship. However, the convergence to common themes and approaches suggest that as a community we are well able to engage in this ongoing dialogue about how to do design better. We could ask whether the Grounded Innovation Map is a better mediating framework than the *Locales Framework* or whether embodied interaction is a better characterisation of the relationship between the social and the technical than locale (however we want to define 'better' here). It would seem that the more interesting question to ask is what we can learn from each of these, along with many others, that will progress our understandings even further.

13.4.2 Does a Framework Lead to Better Solutions?

While on the one hand, I am excited about the possibilities of mediating frameworks and relationship-based foundations for design, I also have some open questions about an approach like the *Locales Framework*. My concerns are to do with the trade-offs we make in taking a pragmatic position and how we judge the balance between doing better applied work, when compared to our original discipline positions, versus losing core value through trying to do too much for too many people and losing deeper theoretical connections.

Role of frameworks (and theories): The *Locales Framework* is in the genre of frameworks rather than theories: "In an attempt to be more applied, many of the new approaches have sought to construct conceptual frameworks [. . . providing] a set of constructs for understanding the domain rather than producing testable hypotheses [as with theories]" (Rogers, 2004, to appear).

In a recent insightful article looking at Activity Theory and Distributed Cognition, Christine Halverson (2002) asks the more general question of "what does CSCW need to DO with theories?" She suggests that we want theories (Halverson also includes frameworks and approaches along with theories here) to provide the following four things: *descriptive* power in that they provide a conceptual framework to help make sense of the work; *rhetorical* power by providing conceptual structures that map to the world and help us name things in the world; *inferential* power enabling us to make inferences that will lead to design insights or enabling us to make predictions about consequences; and finally *application* power in that they enable us to describe the world at the right level of detail to bridge the gap to pragmatic design.

The *Locales Framework* can potentially provide all of these to some degree: it provides a coherent conceptual framework with locale as a unit of analysis, it names concepts, it enables inferences about what can make a better locale (framed in terms of interactional needs), and it deals with the spaces and things that are the focus of design activities. It can also provide a way to compare different domains and studies. But the questions to ask are: who is it providing these things to, what is actually being provided, and where does the work happen?

Rogers also points to another problem of applied frameworks, that they often do not "adhere to the epistemology of the original theory" resulting in "a dilution and oversimplification of concepts, that then become vulnerable to misinterpretation" (Rogers, 2004, to appear). This is certainly a potential problem for the *Locales Framework*; while Strauss' theory of action informed the development of much of the framework, I have argued that the framework can stand in its own right as a sensitising device independent of Strauss' theory. An advantage is that it saves people from having to be familiar with an incredibly dense and rich theory. But what is lost in doing this?

Role of an in-between framework: As just alluded to, my aims in developing the *Locales Framework* have been unashamedly pragmatic from the very beginning. I knew that many of the hard-core systems designers with whom I worked would never read the myriad of workplace studies reported in the CSCW literature or engage, for example, with Activity Theory or Strauss' Theory of Action. I wanted to package a set of social understandings about cooperative action and the workaday world so that they could be accessible to systems designers. I also saw many workplace studies that were rich with interesting insights but it wasn't clear how they might relate to design. I wanted to package a framework for thinking about the role of spaces and things in enabling interactions so that social scientists might have a better understanding where their findings might be relevant to design.

The *Locales Framework* sits in an in-between place. It attempts to mediate social and technical *concerns* through the concept of locale. It attempts to mediate social and technical *practice* through a common abstraction and a common language, helping to orient one practice towards the other. In so doing, it becomes a "different enterprise from either sociology of systems design, with different goals and methods" (Dourish, 2001b, p.9) and is owned by neither discipline (Diggins et al., 2001). It is also deliberately open and high-level so that it is not seen to prescribe or circumscribe concerns or practice. In the end though, is the framework so in-between, so high-level, and so open that it is of no use to anyone?

Role of concepts: In providing rhetorical power, the *Locales Framework* offers named concepts such as shared goal and role (in relation to social world foundations). Schmidt (2000) argues convincingly about the problems of presenting such rich notions as generalised common-sense constructs because they lead people to ignore the practical work in their ongoing accomplishment.

Even though I discuss, for example, that goals can be fuzzy and vague, that they might be the subject of contention or ongoing negotiation and that there are processes by which goals might be negotiated, shared, and evolved, I know that readers might choose to read 'goal' as having greater rhetorical power than intended (especially when it could take a level of social science sensitivity and effort to understand these issues). Presenting goal as part of a table of characterising properties and dimensions can reinforce this thinking. Indeed Rogers' survey of practitioners suggest that such ad hoc common-sense concepts are quickly and easily taken up "to provide a way of articulating current concerns and challenges" (Rogers, 2004, to appear).

So what to do? Do we take the attitude that getting practitioners and non-social scientists to even think about some of these common sense constructs is better than not thinking about them at all in design? Or do we lose too much of the deep understandings of the ongoing accomplishment of daily life to render them useless for design? There are significant trade-offs either way.

Effort, benefit and invisible work: As with all theories and frameworks, there is an overhead of time and effort involved in understanding them and knowing how to use them (Rogers, 2004, to appear). Even though one of the motivations for the *Locales Framework* was to make social thinking more accessible so that people didn't have to come to grips with dense theories or have a social science background, there is still a significant level of effort of required – I even found the framework hard work to use in the beginning and I was the developer of it.

Will hard core software developers be prepared to put in that effort? On the one hand, I could argue that the framework can be used at different levels of engagement, from knowing the broad definition of the aspects, to knowing some of the possible ways to think about an aspect, to using the more detailed tables of properties and dimensions to trigger thinking, to understanding more of the theoretical and ad hoc constructs underpinning the framework. But does the more critical and high-level uses of the framework lead us back to previous concerns about tradeoffs, about using the framework in more prescriptive ways than intended, and rendering invisible the richness and complexity of the actual accomplishment of work?

Will the *Locales Framework* be a useful and usable extension to software designers' requirements analysis toolkit for the design for complex social environments? And to what extent does the assumption that a toolkit such as the

Locales Framework could even be useful for software practitioners ignore the invisible work in the skilled practical accomplishment of social thinking and understanding itself (Forsythe, 1998)?

Will social scientists see any value in learning to understand it when they have much richer or very different constructs from their own traditions? Again, I've tried to make the concepts so high-level that they could be explored from any number of theoretical standpoints (e.g., a Distributed cognition approach might be useful for exploring the role of mediating artefacts in locales). But can they be useful in practice? Is there any added benefit from engaging in the effort to do so? Does it actually help them orient towards design any better than current approaches?

I have also talked about the framework becoming a shared abstraction mediating practice. But how does the framework become a shared abstraction in the first place? Sharing does not happen by decree but by active engagement and negotiation, but by whom and how is the sharing accomplished? What is actually shared? Is a shared abstraction an unrealistic or misguided notion in the first place?

In summary: I obviously have no answers here. I want to be fundamentally pragmatic, to improve solutions being designed for people so that they better fit into the workaday world, but I want to be aware of the points where such pragmatism stops delivering value. At its core, this boils down to a wicked problem issue. There is no right or wrong answer, only better or worse solutions; the judgement of better or worse is very subjective and we will all have different tradeoff points. How do we judge 'better' in these cases? Is it better to have some social thinking in software design practice, and vice versa, than none at all, or is there a minimum value point that we have yet to reach?

13.4.3 Shared People not Shared Abstractions?

Instead of looking for shared abstractions, I wonder whether it is really 'shared people' we should be developing and, in fact, are developing; people who can engage with both the understanding of social needs and the practice of software design, who can be edge dwellers of both communities, and who can facilitate and mediate dialogue between them.

The whole emphasis on the articulation of a framework that can be shared (and on asking what theories can do for CSCW) inadvertently gives primacy to the conceptual tool and not the people in the process. Many successful design outcomes are due more to the people involved and their sensitivities and creativity rather than to any particular framework or theory. It is likely they will have done just as good a job for understanding and designing whether they had used the *Locales Framework* or Activity Theory or Distributed Cognition; the foci might have been different, the language might have been different, the actual outcomes might have been different, but the ultimate solution could still be judged as providing better support. This is not to deny that frameworks and theories can play a role, but as resources for creative intelligent engagement with the domain and questions at hand; ultimately the work lies with the people involved not the framework.

13.5. Conclusion

I started this book by saying that it would a story of the evolution of the *Locales Framework*. I have gone on to describe the framework as if it were the outcome of this journey. By definition of the *Locales Framework* as a solution to a wicked problem, I make no claim that it is the 'right' solution but rather one iteration in arriving at better solutions to the problem of designing systems that fit into the workaday world of people.

The following quote from Schmidt (2000) is about the value of CSCW technology experiments. It highlights a wicked problem orientation to learning more by doing and reflecting:

> "... the [technology] experiments provide indispensable insights, not only in the advantages and problems with applying those technologies for CSCW purposes, but also often – when the experience is carefully documented – in the (perhaps unforeseen) problems that can arise when such technologies are introduced in the social organization of work." (Schmidt, 2000)

The reflections in this final chapter have been presented in the same spirit. I have reflected on some of the strengths and weaknesses of the *Locales Framework*, and on how it might be evolved to make it more accessible and facilitate more extensive use. I have also reflected more generally on the role of such frameworks and the tradeoffs inherent in their presentation and use.

Perhaps, though, what this book has really been about has not been the framework at all but has instead been describing my own journey towards becoming a 'shared person', an edge dweller, through a process of doing, reflecting, and learning that will be ongoing.

Notes

1 For example, most 'good' homes are designed with basic components of kitchen, bathroom, living room, bedroom. The creativity is in the detail of the components, how they are related together and how the facade of the home is presented.

2 Simon Kaplan from the University of Queensland and Tim Mansfield from the Distributed Systems Technology Centre were the co-facilitators of the workshop.

3 A report arising from this research, focussing on expertise sharing, can be found in (Fitzpatrick, 2002).

4 The scenario planning and solutions architecture uses of the *Locales Framework* were developed by Ralf Muhlberger when working at the Distributed Systems Technology Centre in Queensland, Australia.

5 This is a European Commission funded project involving Philips Design, Xerox Research Centre Europe and Nottingham University. Details can be found at http://www.mimeproject.org.

References

Abbott, K. R. and Sarin, S. K. (1994). Experiences with workflow management: Issues for the next generation. In *Proceedings of ACM Conference on Computer Supported Cooperative Work*, pages 113–120, Chapel Hill, North Carolina.

Abel, M. J. (1990). Experiences in an exploratory distributed organization. In Galegher, J., Kraut, R., and Egido, C., editors, *Intellectual Teamwork: Social and Technological Foundations of Cooperative Work*, pages 489–510. Lawrence Erlbaum, Hillsdale, NJ.

Ackerman, M. S. (1994). Augmenting the organizational memory: A field study of Answer Garden. In *Proceedings of Conference on Computer Supported Cooperative Work (CSCW'94)*, pages 243–252, Chapel Hill, NC. ACM Press.

Adler, A. and Henderson, A. (1994). A room of our own: Experiences from a direct office share. In *Proceedings of ACM CHI'94*, pages 138–144.

Agostini, A. and De Michelis, G. (1997). Rethinking CSCW systems: the architecture of Milano. In *Proceedings of the Fifth European Conference on Computer Supported Cooperative Work (ECSCW'97)*, pages 33–48, Lancaster. Kluwer Academic Publishers.

Alexander, C. (1979). *The Timeless Way of Building*. Oxford University Press, New York.

Alexander, C., Heis, H., Anninon, A., and King, I. (1987). *A New Theory of Urban Design*. Oxford University Press, New York.

Anderson, B., Button, G., and Sharrock, W. (1993). Supporting the design process within an organisational context. In *Proceedings of the Third European Conference on Computer-Supported Cooperative Work*, pages 47–59, Milan, Italy.

Anderson, R. J. (1994). Representations and requiremetns: The value of ethnography in system design. *Human-Computer Interaction*, 9(2):151–182.

Baecker, R. M. (1993). Media spaces. In Baecker, R. M., editor, *Readings in Groupware and Computer-Supported Cooperative Work*, chapter 13, pages 775–779. Morgan Kaufmann, San Mateo, CA.

Baker, K., Greenberg, S., and Gutwin, C. (2001). Heuristic evaluation of groupware based on the mechanics of collaboration. In Little, M. R. and Nigay, L., editors, *Engineering for Human-Computer Interaction (8th IFIP International Conference)*, volume 2254 of *Lecture Notes in Computer Science*, pages 123–139, Toronto, Canada. Springer-Verlag.

Bannon, L. and Kuutti, K. (1996). Shifting perspectives on organisational memory: From storage to active remembering. In *Proceedings of 29th Annual Hawaii International Conference on Systems Science*, volume III, pages 156–167, Los Alamitos. IEEE Computer Society Press.

Bannon, L. J. and Bödker, S. (1991). Beyond the interface: Encountering artifacts in use. In Carroll, J. M., editor, *Designing Interaction: Psychology at the Human-Computer Interface*, chapter 12, pages 227–253. Cambridge University Press.

Bannon, L. J. and Schmidt, K. (1991). CSCW: Four characters in search of a context. In Bowers, J. M. and Benford, S. D., editors, *Studies in Computer Supported Cooperative Work: Theory, Practice and Design*, pages 3–16. North-Holland, Amsterdam.

Bardram, J. E. (1997). Plans as situated action: An activity theory approach to workflow systems. In *Proceedings of the Fifth European Conference on Computer Supported Cooperative Work (ECSCW'97)*, pages 17–32, Lancaster. Kluwer Academic Publishers.

Bellotti, V. and Sellen, A. (1993). Design for privacy in ubiquitous computing environments. In *Proceedings of the Third European Conference on Computer-Supported Cooperative Work*, pages 77–92, Milan, Italy. Kluwer.

Benedikt, M. (1994). Cyberspace: Some proposals. In Benedikt, M., editor, *Cyberspace: First Steps*, chapter 7, pages 119–224. MIT Press, Cambridge, MA.

Benford, S., Bowers, J., Fahlén, L. E., Greenhalgh, C., Mariani, J., and Rodden, T. (1995). Networked virtual reality and cooperative work. *Presence: Teleoperators and Virtual Environments*, 4(4):364–386.

Benford, S., Bowers, J., Fahlén, L. E., Mariani, J., and Rodden, T. (1994). Supporting cooperative work in virtual environments. *The Computer Journal*, 37(8):653–668.

Benford, S., Bullock, A., Cook, N., Harvey, P., Ingram, R., and Lee, O. (1993). From rooms to cyberspace: models of interaction in large virtual computer spaces. *Interacting with Computers*, 5(2):217–237.

Benford, S. and Fahlén, L. (1993). A spatial model of interaction in large virtual environments. In *Proceedings of the Third European Conference on Computer-Supported Cooperative Work*, pages 109–124, Milan, Italy. Kluwer.

Benford, S. and Fahlén, L. E. (1995). Viewpoints, actionpoints and spatial frames for collaborative user interfaces. In *Proceedings HCI'94*, Glasgow, UK.

Benford, S. and Mariani, J., editors (1993). *Requirements and Metaphors of Shared Interaction, COMIC Deliverable 4.1*. COMIC Esprit Basic Research Action 6225. Available via ftp://ftp.comp.lancs.ac.uk/pub/comic/.

Bentley, R., Horstmann, T., and Trevor, J. (1997). The World Wide Web as enabling technology for CSCW: The case of BSCW. *Computer Supported Cooperative Work: The Journal of Collaborative Computing*, 6(2-3):111–134.

Bentley, R., Hughes, J. A., Randall, D., Rodden, T., Sawyer, P., Shapiro, D., and Sommerville, I. (1992). Ethnographically-informed systems design for air traffic control. In *Proceedings of the Conference on Computer-Supported Cooperative Work*, pages 123–129, Toronto, Canada. ACM Press.

Berg, M. (1997). On distribution drift and the electronic medical record: Some tools for a sociology of the formal. In *Proceedings of the Fifth European Conference on Computer Supported Cooperative Work (ECSCW'97)*, pages 141–156, Lancaster. Kluwer Academic Publishers.

Berg, M. (1999). Patient care information systems and healthcare work: A sociotechnical approach. *International Journal of Medical Informatics*, 55:87–101.

Bermann, T. and Thoresen, K. (1988). Can networks make an organization. In *Proceedings of the Conference on Computer-Supported Cooperative Work*, pages 153–166, Portland, Oregon. ACM Press.

Bernstein, A. (2000). How can cooperative work tools support dynamic group process? bridging the specificity frontier. In *Proceeding of the ACM 2000 Conference on Computer Supported Cooperative Work*, pages 279–288. ACM Press.

Beyer, H. and Holtzblatt, K. (1998). *Contextual Design: Defining Customer-Centered Systems*. Morgan Kaufmann, San Francisco.

Bignoli, C. and Simone, C. (191). AI techniques for supporting human to human communication in CHAOS. In Bowers, J. M. and Benford, S. D., editors, *Studies in Computer Supported Cooperative Work*, pages 103–118. Elsevier Science Publishers B. V.

Bjerknes, G. and Bratteteig, T. (1988). The memoirs of two survivors. In *Proceedings of the Conference on Computer-Supported Cooperative Work*, Portland, Oregon. ACM Press.

Blair, G. S. and Rodden, T. (1991). The Impact of CSCW on Open Distributed Processing. In *International Workshop on Open Distributed Processing*. IFIP.

Blomberg, J., Burrell, M., and Guest, G. (2003). An ethnographic approach to design. In Jacko, J. and Sears, A., editors, *Handbook of Human Computer Interaction*, pages 964–986. Lawrence Erlbaum Associates.

Bly, S. A., Harrison, S. R., and Irwin, S. (1991). Media spaces: Video, audio, and computing. *Communications of the ACM*, 36(1):29–47.

Bodker, K. and Pedersen, J. S. (1991). Workplace cultures: Looking at artifacts, symbols and practices. In Greenbaum, J. and Kyng, M., editors, *Design at Work: Cooperative Design of Computer Systems*, chapter 6, pages 121–136. Lawrence Erlbaum Ass., Hillsdale, NJ.

Bödker, S. (1991). *Through the Interface - A human activity approach to user interface design*. Lawrence Erlbaum Associates, Hillsdale, N.J.

Bödker, S., Knudsen, J. L., Kyng, M., Ehn, P., and Madsen, K. H. (1988). Computer support for cooperative design. In *Proceedings of the Conference on Computer-Supported Cooperative Work*, pages 377–394, Portland, Oregon. ACM Press.

Bogia, D. P. and Kaplan, S. M. (1995). Flexibility and control for dynamic workflows in the wOrlds environment. In *Proceedings ACM Conference on Organizational Computing Systems COOCS'95*, pages 148–159, Milpitas, CA.

Bogia, D. P., Tolone, W. J., Bignoli, C., and Kaplan, S. M. (1993). Issues in the design of collaborative systems: Lessons from ConversationBuilder. In *Proceedings Schaerding International Workshop on Task Analysis and CSCW*, Schaerding, Austria.

Bowers, J. (1995). The social logic of cyberspace or the interactional affordances of virtual brutalism. In Bullock, A. and Mariani, J., editors, *Assesment and refinement of models of interaction, COMIC Deliverable 4.3*, chapter 6, pages 91–147. Available via ftp (as at Dec 2002) ftp://ftp.comp.lancs.ac.uk/pub/comic/.

Bowers, J., Button, G., and Sharrock, W. (1995). Workflow from within and without: Technology and cooperative work on the print industry shopfloor. In *Proceedings of the Fourth European Conference on Computer-Supported Cooperative Work*, pages 51–66, Stockholm, Sweden. Kluwer.

Bowers, J. and Churcher, J. (1988). Local and global structuring of computer mediated communication: Developing linguistic perspectives on CSCW in COSMOS. In *Proceedings of the Conference on Computer-Supported Cooperative Work*, Portland, Oregon. ACM Press.

Bowers, J., Pycock, J., and O'Brien, J. (1996). Talk and embodiment in collaborative virtual environments. In *Proceedings CHI'96*, pages 58–65, Vancouver, BC Canada. ACM Press.

Brand, S. (1994). *How Buildings Learn: What happens after they're built*. Viking, London.

Brooks, R. (1991). Comparative task analysis: An alternative direction for human-computer interaction science. In Carroll, J. M., editor, *Designing Interaction: Psychology at the Human-Computer Interface*, chapter 4, pages 50–59. Cambridge University Press.

Bruckman, A. and Resnick, M. (1995). The MediaMOO project: Constructionism and professional community. *Convergence*, 1(1):94–109.

Büscher, M., Mogensen, P., and Shapiro, D. (2001). Spaces of practice. In *Proceedings of the Seventh European Conference on Computer Supported Cooperative Work*, pages 139–158, Bonn, Germany. Kluwer Academic Publishers.

Button, G. and Dourish, P. (1996). Technomethodology: Paradoxes and possibilities. In *Proceedings of the ACM Conference on Human Factors in Computing Systems (CHI'96)*, pages 19–26, Vancouver, BC Canada. ACM Press.

Button, G. and Harper, R. (1996). The relevance of 'work-practice' for design. *Computer Supported Cooperative Work*, 4:263–280.

Button, G. and Sharrock, W. (1995). The mundane work of writing and reading computer programs. In ten Have, P. and Psathas, G., editors, *Situated Order: studies in the social organization of talk and embodied activities*, chapter 12. University Press of America.

Buzan, T. and Buzan, B. (1994). *The Mind Map book: How to Use Radiant Thinking to Maximize Your Brain's Untapped Potential.* E. P. Dutton.

Carroll, A. M. (1993). *ConversationBuilder: A Collaborative Erector Set.* PhD thesis, University of Illinois at Urbana-Champaign.

Checkland, P. (1981). *Systems Thinking, Systems Practice.* J. Wiley & Sons, Chichester.

Cicourel, A. V. (1990). The integration of distributed knowledge in collaborative medical diagnosis. In Galegher, J., Kraut, R. E., and Egido, C., editors, *Intellectual Teamwork: Social and Technical Foundations of Cooperative Work*, pages 221–242. Lawrence Erlbaum Associates, New Jersey.

Clarke, A. E. (1991). Social worlds/arenas theory as organizational theory. In Maines, D. R., editor, *Social Organization and Social Processes: Essays in Honor of Anselm Strauss*, pages 119–158. Aldine De Gruyter, New York.

Conklin, J. and Begeman, M. L. (1988). gIBIS: A hypertext tool for exploratory policy discussion. In *Proceedings of the Conference on Computer-Supported Cooperative Work*, Portland, Oregon. ACM Press.

Cooper, A. (1999). *The Inmates are Running the Asylum: Why High-Tech Products Drive Us Crazy and How to Restore the Sanity.* SAMS.

Corbin, J. (1991). Anselm Strauss: An intellectual biography. In Maines, D. R., editor, *Social Organization and Social Processes: Essays in Honor of Anselm Strauss*, chapter 3, pages 17–42. Aldine De Gruyter, New York.

Crabtree, A., Hemmings, T., and Rodden, T. (2002). Pattern-based support for interactive design in domestic settings. In *Conference Proceedings on Designing Interactive Systems: Serious reflection on designing interactive systems*, pages 265–275. ACM Press.

Cuff, E. C. and Payne, G. C. F., editors (1984). *Perspectives in Sociology.* G. Allen & Unwin, London, 2nd edition.

Curtis, B., Krasner, H., and Iscoe, N. (1988). A field study of the software design process for large systems. *Communications of the ACM*, 31(11):1268–1287.

Curtis, P. (1992). Mudding: Social phenomena in text-based virtual realities. In *Proceedings of 1992 Conference on Directions and Implications of Advanced Computing*, Berkeley, CA. Also available as Xerox PARC Technical Report CSL-92-4.

Curtis, P. and Nichols, D. A. (1994). MUDs grow up: Social virtual reality in the real world. In *Proceedings of the 1994 IEEE Computer Conference*, pages 193–200.

Damer, B., Kekenes, C., and Hoffman, T. (1996). Inhabited digital spaces. In Tauber, M. J., editor, *CHI '96 Conference Companion*, pages 9–10, Vancouver, Canada. ACM Press.

Davenport, T. H. and Short, J. E. (1990). The new industrial engineering: Information technology and business process redesign. *Sloan Management Review*, 31(4):11–26.

de Michelis, G. (1991). A CSCW environment: Some requirements. In *Computer Supported Cooperative Work - the multimedia and networking paradigm*, Unicom Conference, London.

De Michelis, G. and Grasso, M. (1994). Situating conversations within the language / action perspective: The Milan conversation model. In *Proceedings of ACM Conference on Computer Supported Cooperative Work*, pages 89–100, Chapel Hill, North Carolina.

Derycke, A., Smith, C., and Hemery, L. (1995). Metaphors and interactions in virtual environments for open and distance education. In *Proceedings ED-media'95*, pages 181–186, Graz, Austria.

Derycke, A. C. and Kaye, A. R. (1993). Participative modelling and design of collaborative distance learning tools in the Co-Learn project. In Davies, G. and Samways, B., editors, *Proceedings of IFIP Teleteaching'93*, pages 191–200, Trondheim, Norway. North-Holland.

Desmond, M. (1995). The shape of things to come: Alpha World brings a 3-D virtual world to the internet. *Multimedia World*, pages 16–17.

Diggins, T., Tolmie, P., Tap, H., Pycock, J., MacLean, A., and Karsenty, A. (2001). The ongoing dialogue between ethnomethodology and design. XRCE Working Paper.

Dollimore, J., Roberts, T., and Coulouris, G. F. (1990). Towards a language for defining stucture in message-based cooperative working. In *Proceedings of the IFIP WG 8.4 Conference on Multi-User Interfaces and Applications*, pages 253–271, Amsterdam. IFIP, North Holland.

Dourish, P. (1996). *Open Implementation and Flexibility in CSCW Toolkits*. PhD thesis, Department of Computer Science, University College London.

Dourish, P. (2001a). Process descriptions as organisational accounting devices: the dual use of workflow technologies. In *Proceedings of the 2001 International ACM SIGGROUP Conference on Supporting Group Work*, pages 52–60. ACM Press.

Dourish, P. (2001b). *Where the Action Is: The Foundations of Embodied Interaction*. MIT Press, Cambridge, MA.

Dourish, P., Adler, A., Bellotti, V., and Henderson, A. (1996). Your place or mine? Learning from long-term use of video communication. *Computer Supported Cooperative Work*, 5(1):33–62.

Dourish, P. and Bellotti, V. (1992). Awareness and coordination in shared workspaces. In *Proceedings of the Conference on Computer-Supported Cooperative Work*, pages 107–114, Toronto, Canada. ACM Press.

Dourish, P. and Bly, S. (1992). Portholes: Supporting awareness in a distributed work group. In *Proceedings of ACM CHI'92*, pages 541–547.

Eason, K. D. and Olphert, C. W. (1996). Early evaluation of the organisational implications of CSCW systems. In Thomas, P., editor, *CSCW Requirements and Evaluation*, pages 75–89. Springer-Verlag, London.

Egger, E. and Wagner, I. (1993). Negotiating temporal orders: The case of collaborative time-management in a surgery clinic. *Computer Supported Cooperative Work*, 1(4).

Ellis, C., Gibbs, S., and Rein, G. (1991). Groupware: Some issues and experiences. *Communications of the ACM*, 34:38–58.

Engeström, Y. (1991). Developmental work research: Reconstructing expertise through expansive learning. In Nurminen, M. J. and Weir, G. R. S., editors, *Human Jobs and Computer Interfaces*. Elsevier Science Publishers, Amsterdam.

Engeström, Y., Engeström, R., and Vahaaho, T. (1999). When the center does not hold: The importance of knotworking. In Chaiklon, S., Hedegaard, M., and Jensen, U., editors, *Activity Theory and Social Practice: Cultural Historical Approaches*, Aarhus, Denmark. Aarhus University Press.

England, D. (1995). Critique of approaches to interaction and visualisation. In Bullock, A. and Mariani, J., editors, *Assesment and refinement of models of interaction, COMIC Deliverable 4.3*, chapter 9, pages 187–195. Available via ftp: //ftp.comp.lancs.ac.uk/pub/comic/.

Erickson, T. (2000). Lingua francas for design: sacred places and pattern languages. In *Conference Proceedings on Designing Interactive Systems: processes, practices, methods, and techniques*, pages 357–368. ACM Press.

Evard, R. (1993). Collaborative networked communication: MUDs as systems tools. In *Proceedings of the Seventh Systems Administration Conference (LISA VII)*, pages 1–8, Monterey, CA.

Fish, R. S., Kraut, R., and Chalfonte, B. (1990). The VideoWindow system in informal communications. In *Proceedings CSCW'90 Conference on Computer-Supported Cooperative Work*, pages 1–11, Los Angeles.

Fish, R. S., Kraut, R. E., Root, R. W., and Rice, R. E. (1993). Video as a technology for informal communication. *Communications of the ACM*, 36(1):48–61.

Fitzpatrick, G. (1996). Computers in work — work in computers: An ethnographic study of a systems administration group. Technical Report 356, The University of Queensland Department of Computer Science.

Fitzpatrick, G. (2000a). Centres, peripheries and electronic communication: changing work practice boundaries. *Scandinavian Journal of Information Systems*, 12:115–148.

Fitzpatrick, G. (2000b). Understanding the paper health record in practice: Implications for ehrs. In *Proceedings of Health Informatics Conference (HIC2000)*, Adelaide. HISA, ISBN 0 9585370 5 4.

Fitzpatrick, G. (2002). Emergent expertise sharing in a new community. In Ackerman, M., Pipek, V., and Wulf, V., editors, *Sharing Expertise: Beyond Knowledge Management*. MIT Press, Cambridge, MA.

Fitzpatrick, G., Kaplan, S., and Mansfield, T. (1996). Physical spaces, virtual places and social worlds: A study of work in the virtual. In *Proceedings of ACM 1996 Conference on Computer Supported Cooperative Work*, pages 334–343, Boston, MA. ACM Press.

Fitzpatrick, G., Kaplan, S., and Mansfield, T. (1998a). Applying the locales framework to understanding and designing. In Calder, P. and Thomas, B., editors, *Proceedings Australasian Computer Human Interaction Conference (OzCHI'98)*, pages 122–129, Adelaide, Australia. IEEE.

Fitzpatrick, G., Kaplan, S., Mansfield, T., Arnold, D., and Segall, B. (2002). Supporting public availability and accessibility with elvin: Experiences and reflections. *Computer Supported Cooperative Work: The Journal of Collaborative Computing*, 11(3-4).

Fitzpatrick, G., Kaplan, S., and Parsowith, S. (1998b). Experience in building a cooperative distributed organisation: Lessons for cooperative buildings. In *Cooperative Buildings: Integrating Information, Organization, and Architecture (CoBuild'98)*, number 1370 in Lecture Notes in Computer Science, pages 66–79, Heidelberg. Springer.

Fitzpatrick, G., Mansfield, T., Kaplan, S., Arnold, D., Phelps, T., and Segall, B. (1999). Augmenting the workaday world with elvin. In *Proceedings 6th European Conference on Computer-Supported Cooperative Work (ECSCW'99)*, pages 431–451, Copenhagen. Kluwer Academic Publishers.

Fitzpatrick, G., Parsowith, S., Segall, B., and Kaplan, S. (1998c). Tickertape: Awareness in a single line. In *Human Factors in Computing Systems: CHI 98 Summary*, pages 281–282, Los Angeles. ACM Press.

Fitzpatrick, G., Tolone, W. J., and Kaplan, S. M. (1995). Work, locales and distributed social wOrlds. In *Proceedings of the Fourth European Conference on Computer-Supported Cooperative Work*, pages 1–16. Kluwer Academic Publishers.

Fitzpatrick, G. and Welsh, J. (1994). Groupware: helping or hindering care processes? In Carter, B. and Walker, D., editors, *Proceedings of the 2nd National Health Informatics Conference(HIC94)*, pages 281–285, Gold Coast, Australia. HISA.

Fitzpatrick, G. and Welsh, J. (1995). Process support: inflexible imposition or chaotic composition? *Interacting with Computers*, 7(2):167–180.

Flor, N. V. and Hutchins, E. L. (1991). Analyzing distributed cognition in software teams: A case study of team programming during perfective software maintenance. In Joenemann-Belliveau, J., Moher, T. G., and Robertson, S. P., editors, *Empirical Studies of Programmers: Fourth Workshop*, pages 36–64. Ablex Publishing Corporation.

Forsythe, D. E. (1998). "it's just a matter of common sense": Ethnography as invisible work. *Computer Supported Cooperative Work: The Journal of Collaborative Computing*, 8(1-2):127–145.

Fuchs, L. (1999). AREA: a cross-application notification service for groupware. In *Proceedings 6th European Conference on Computer-Supported Cooperative Work (ECSCW'99)*, pages 61–80, Copenhagen. Kluwer Academic Publishers.

Fuchs, L., Pankoke-Babatz, U., and Prinz, W. (1995). Supporting cooperative awareness with local event mechanisms: The GroupDesk system. In *Proceedings of the Fourth European Conference on Computer-Supported Cooperative Work*, pages 247–262, Stockholm, Sweden. Kluwer.

Garfinkel, H. (1967). *Studies in Ethnomethodology*. Prentice Hall, Englewood Cliffs, N.J.

Gasparotti, P. and Simone, C. (1990). A user defined environment for handling conversations. In *Proceedings of the IFIP WG 8.4 Conference on Multi-User Interfaces and Applications*, pages 271–289, Amsterdam. IFIP, North Holland.

Gaver, W., Moran, T., MacLean, A., Lövstrand, L., Dourish, P., Carter, K., and Buxton, W. (1992). Realizing a video environment: EuroPARC's RAVE system. In *Proceedings of ACM CHI'92*, pages 27–35.

Gaver, W., Sellen, A., Heath, C., and Luff, P. (1993). One is not enough: Multiple views in a media space. In *Proceedings INTERCHI'93*, pages 335–341, Amsterdam, The Netherlands. ACM Press.

Gaver, W. W. (1992). The affordances of media spaces for collaboration. In *Proceedings of ACM Conference on Computer Supported Cooperative Work*, pages 17–24, Toronto, Canada.

Gaver, W. W., Smets, G., and Overbeeke, K. (1995). A virtual window on media space. In *Conference on Human Factors in Computing Systems CHI'95*, pages 257–264, Denver, Colorado.

Gerson, E. M. and Star, S. L. (1986). Analysing due process in the workplace. *ACM Transactions on Office Information Systems*, 4(3):257–270.

Geyer, W., Richter, H., Fuchs, L., Frauenhofer, T., Daijavad, S., and Poltrock, S. (2001). A team collaboration space supporting capture and access of virtual meetings. In *Proceedings of ACM SIGGROUP Conference on Supporting Group Work (Group'01)*, pages 188–196, Boulder, Colorado. ACM Press.

Giddens, A. (1984). *The Constitution of Society*. University of California Press, Berkeley.

Glaser, B. and Strauss, A. (1967). *The Discovery of Grounded Theory*. Aldine Publishing Co., Chicago.

Goldschlager, L. and Lister, A. (1988). *Computer Science: A Modern Introduction*. Prentice Hall International, London, 2nd edition.

Goodwin, C. and Goodwin, M. H. (1996). Seeing as a situated activity: Formulating planes. In Engeström, Y. and Middleton, D., editors, *Cognition and Communication at Work*, chapter 4, pages 61–95. Cambridge University Press.

Greenberg, S. (1996a). A fisheye text editor for relaxed-WYSIWIS groupware. In *Common Ground: CHI'96 Conference Companion*, pages 212–213, Vancouver, Canada.

Greenberg, S. (1996b). Peepholes: Low cost awareness of one's community. In *Common Ground: CHI'96 Conference Companion*, pages 206–207, Vancouver, Canada.

Greenberg, S., Fitzpatrick, G., Gutwin, C., and Kaplan, S. (2000). Adapting the locales framework for heuristic evaluation of groupware. *Australian Journal of Information Systems*, 7(2):102–108.

Greenberg, S., Gutwin, C., Roseman, M., and Cockburn, A. (1995). From awareness to TeamRooms, GroupWeb and TurboTurtle: Eight snapshots of recent work in the GroupLab project. Technical Report Research Report 95/580/32, Dept. of Computer Science, University of Calgary, Calgary, Alberta, Canada.

Greenhalgh, C. and Benford, S. (1995). Virtual reality tele-conferencing: Implementation and experience. In *Proceedings of the Fourth European Conference on Computer-Supported Cooperative Work*, pages 165–180, Stockholm, Sweden. Kluwer.

Grinter, R. (1997). From workplace to development: What have we learned so far and where do we go? In *Proceedings of GROUP97*, pages 231–240, Phoenix, AZ. ACM Press.

Grinter, R. E. (1995). Using a configuration management tool to coordinate software development. In *Proceedings ACM Conference on Organizational Computing Systems (COOCS'95)*, pages 168–177, Milpitas, CA.

Grinter, R. E. (1996). Supporting articulation work using software configuration management systems. *Computer Supported Cooperative Work: The Journal of Collaborative Computing*, 5:447–465.

Grudin, J. (1988). Why CSCW applications fail: Problems in the design and evaluation of organizational interfaces. In *Proceedings of the Conference on Computer-Supported Cooperative Work*, pages 85–93, Portland, Oregon. ACM Press.

Grudin, J. (1993). The CSCW forum. In Nunamaker, J. F. and Sprague, R. H., editors, *Proceedings of the 26th Hawaii International Conference on Systems Sciences*, volume IV, pages 51–58.

Grudin, J. (1994). Groupware and social dynamics: Eight challenges for developers. *Communications of the ACM*, 37(1):93–105.

Grudin, J. and Poltrock, S. (1993). Computer supported cooperative work and groupware. Tutorial Notes, Third European Conference on Computer Supported Cooperative Work, Milano, Italy.

Gruhn, V. and Jegelka, R. (1992). An evaluation of FUNSOFT nets. In Derniame, J. C., editor, *Software Process Technology: Second European Workshop*, Lecture Notes in Computer Science, Vol. 635, pages 196–214, Berlin. Springer-Verlag.

Gutwin, C. and Greenberg, S. (1996). Workspace awareness for groupware. In *Common Ground: CHI'96 Conference Companion*, pages 208–209, Vancouver, Canada.

Gutwin, C. and Greenberg, S. (1998). Design for individuals, design for groups: tradeoffs between power and workspace awareness. In *Proceedings of the ACM 1998 Conference on Computer Supported Cooperative Work*, pages 207–216. ACM Press.

Gutwin, C. and Greenberg, S. (2002). A descriptive framework of workspace awareness for real-time groupware. *Computer Supported Cooperative Work: The Journal of Collaborative Computing*, 11(3-4).

Gutwin, C., Greenberg, S., and Roseman, M. (1996a). Supporting awareness of others in groupware. In *Common Ground: CHI'96 Conference Companion*, page 205, Vancouver, Canada.

Gutwin, C., Greenberg, S., and Roseman, M. (1996b). Workspace awareness support with radar views. In *Common Ground: CHI'96 Conference Companion*, pages 210–211, Vancouver, Canada.

Haake, J. M. and Wilson, B. (1992). Supporting collaborative writing of hyperdocuments in SEPIA. In *Proceedings of the Conference on Computer-Supported Cooperative Work*, pages 138–146, Toronto, Canada. ACM Press.

Hagerstrand, T. (1975). Space, time and human conditions. In Karlqvist, A., Lundqvist, L., and Snickars, F., editors, *Dynamic Allocation of Urban Space*, pages 3–14. Saxon House, Farnborough.

Halverson, C. A. (1994). Distributed cognition as a theoretical framework for HCI: Don't throw the baby out with the bathwater - the importance of the cursor in air traffic control. Technical Report 9403, Department of Cognitive Science, University of California, San Diego, La Jolla, California.

Halverson, C. A. (2002). Activity theory and distributed cognition: Or what does cscw need to DO with theories? *Computer Supported Cooperative Work: The Journal of Collaborative Computing*, 11(1-2):243–267.

Hanseth, O. (1991). Integrating information systems: the importance of contexts. In R.K.Stamper, Kerola, R., Lee, R., and Lyytinen, K., editors, *Collaborative Work, Social Communications and Information Systems*, IFIP TC8, pages 133–156. Elsevier Science Publishers B.V.

Harper, R. H. R. (1992). Looking at ourselves: An examination of the social organisation of two research laboratories. In *Proceedings of the Conference on Computer-Supported Cooperative Work*, pages 330–337, Toronto, Canada. ACM Press.

Harrison, S. and Dourish, P. (1996). Re-place-ing space: The roles of place and space in collaborative systems. In *Proceedings of ACM 1996 Conference on Computer Supported Cooperative Work*, pages 67–76, Boston MA. ACM Press.

Heath, C. and Luff, P. (1992). Collaboration and control: Crisis management and multimedia technology in London Underground line control rooms. *Computer Supported Cooperative Work*, 1:69–94.

Heath, C. and Luff, P. (1993). Disembodied conduct: Communication through video in a multi-media office environment. In Baecker, R. M., editor, *Readings in Groupware and Computer-Supprted Cooperative Work*, pages 837–841. Morgan Kaufmann, San Mateo, CA.

Heath, C. and Luff, P. (1996a). Convergent activities: Line control and passenger information on the London Underground. In Engeström, Y. and Middleton, D., editors, *Cognition and Communication at Work*, chapter 5, pages 96–129. Cambridge University Press, Cambridge UK.

Heath, C. and Luff, P. (1996b). Documents and professional practice: 'bad' organisational reasons for 'good' clinical records. In *Proceedings of ACM 1996 Conference on Computer Supported Cooperative Work*, pages 354–363, Boston MA. ACM Press.

Heath, C., Luff, P., Kuzuoka, H., Yamazaki, K., and Oyama, S. (2001). Creating coherent environments for collaboration. In *Proceedings of the Seventh European Conference on Computer Supported Cooperative Work*, pages 119–138, Bonn, Germany. Kluwer Academic Publishers.

Heath, C., Luff, P., and Sellen, A. (1995). Reconsidering the virtual workplace: Flexible support for collaborative activity. In *Proceedings of the Fourth European Conference on Computer-Supported Cooperative Work*, pages 83–99, Stockholm, Sweden. Kluwer.

Heath, C., Svensson, M. S., Hindmarsh, J., Luff, P., and vom Lehn, D. (2002). Configuring awareness. *Computer Supported Cooperative Work: The Journal of Collaborative Computing*, 11(3-4):317–347.

Heeren, E. and Lewis, R. (1997). Selecting communication media for distributed communities. *Journal of Computer Assisted Learning*, 13:85–98.

Hillier, B. and Hanson, J. (1984). *The Social Logic of Space*. Cambridge University Press, Cambridge.

Hoffman, C., Kramer, B., and Dinler, B. (1992). Multiparadigm description of system development processes. In Derniame, J. C., editor, *Software Process Technology: Second European Workshop*, Lecture Notes in Computer Science, Vol. 635, pages 123–137, Berlin. Springer-Verlag.

Hollan, J. and Stornetta, S. (1992). Beyond being there. In *Proceedings of ACM CHI'92*, pages 119–125. ACM Press.

Hudson, S. E. and Smith, I. (1996). Techniques for addressing fundamental privacy and disruption tradeoffs in awareness support systems. In *Proceedings Conference on Computer Supported Cooperative Work CSCW96*, pages 248–257, Boston MA. ACM Press.

Hughes, J., King, V., Rodden, T., and Andersen, H. (1994). Moving out from the control room: Ethnography in system design. In *Proceedings of ACM Conference on Computer Supported Cooperative Work*, pages 429–439, Chapel Hill, North Carolina.

Hughes, J., O'Brien, J., Rodden, T., and Rouncefield, M. (2000). Ethnography, communication and support for design. In Heath, C. and Luff, P., editors, *Workplace Studies: Recovering*

Work Practice and Informing Systems Design, pages 187–214. Cambridge University Press, Cambridge.

Hughes, J., O'Brien, J., Rodden, T., Rouncefield, M., and Blythin, S. (1997). Designing with ethnography: A presentation framework for design. In *Proceedings Designing Interactive Systems (DIS 97)*, pages 147–158, Amsterdam, The Netherlands. ACM Press.

Hughes, J., Randall, D., and Shapiro, D. (1991). CSCW: Discipline or paradigm? In *Proceedings of the Second European Conference on Computer-Supported Cooperative Work*, pages 309–323, Dordrecht. Kluwer Academic Publishers.

Hughes, J. A., Sommerville, I., Bentley, R., and Randall, D. (1993a). Designing with ethnography: making work visible. *Interacting with Computers*, 5(2):239–253.

Hughes, P., Morris, M., and Plant, T. (1993b). Understanding and uncovering design issues in synchronous shared-window conferencing. *Interacting with Computers*, 5(1):115–130.

Hutchins, E. (1995). *Cognition in the Wild.* MIT Press, Cambridge, MA.

Ishii, H. (1990). TeamWorkStation: Towards a Seamless Shared Workspace. In *Proceedings of the Conference on Computer-Supported Cooperative Work*, pages 13–26, Los Angeles, CA. ACM Press.

Jirotka, M., Gilbert, N., and Luff, P. (1992). On the social organisation of organisations. *Computer Supported Cooperative Work*, 1:95–118.

Johansen, R. (1991). *Leading business teams: how teams can use technology and group process tools to enhance performance*. Addison-Wesley, Reading, MA.

Jørgensen, H. D. (2001). Interaction as a framework for flexible workflow modelling. In *Proceedings of the 2001 International ACM SIGGROUP Conference on Supporting Group Work*, pages 32–41. ACM Press.

Kaplan, S., Fitzpatrick, G., and Herring, C. (1998). Centers of collaborative work. In Darses, F. and Zarate, P., editors, *Proceedings COOP'98*, volume II, pages 89–92, Cannes, France. INRIA.

Kaplan, S. M. and Fitzpatrick, G. (1997). Designing support for remote intensive-care telehealth using the locales framework. In *Proceedings Designing Interactive Systems (DIS 97)*, pages 173–184, Amsterdam, The Netherlands. ACM Press.

Kaplan, S. M., Fitzpatrick, G., Mansfield, T., and Tolone, W. J. (1997). MUDdling through. In Nunamaker, J. F. and Sprague, R. H., editors, *Proceedings Thirtieth Annual Hawaii International Conference on System Sciences (HICSS30)*, volume II, pages 539–548, Los Alamitos, CA. IEEE Computer Society Press.

Kaplan, S. M., Tolone, W. J., Bogia, D. P., and Bignoli, C. (1992). Flexible, active support for collaborative work with ConversationBuilder. In *Proceedings of the Conference on Computer-Supported Cooperative Work*, pages 378–385, Toronto, Canada. ACM Press.

Kindberg, T. (1996). Mushroom: a framework for collaboration and interaction across the Internet. In *Proceedings of the ERCIM Workshop on CSCW and the Web*, Sankt Augustin, Germany.

Klein, M., Dellarocas, C., and Bernstein, A. (2000). Introduction to the special issue on adaptive workflow systems. *Computer Supported Cooperative Work: The Journal of Collaborative Computing*, 9(3-4):265–267.

Kraut, R. and Egido, C. (1988). Patterns of contact and communication in scientific research collaboration. In *Proceedings of 1988 Conference on Computer-Supported Cooperative Work*, pages 1–12, Portland, Oregon. ACM Press.

Kreifelts, T., Hinrichs, E., Klein, K., Seuffert, P., and Woetzel, G. (1991). Experiences with the DOMINO office procedure system. In *Proceedings of the Second European Conference on Computer-Supported Cooperative Work*, pages 117–130, Amsterdam, The Netherlands.

Kuhn, W. and Blumenthal, B. (1996). Spatial metaphors for user interfaces. CHI '96 Tutorial Notes No. 10, Vancouver, Canada.

Kuutti, K. (1991). Activity Theory and its application to information systems research and development. In Nissen, H., Klein, H., and Hirschheim, R., editors, *Information Systems Research: Contemporary Approaches and Emergent Traditions*, pages 529–549. Elsevier Science Publishers B.V., Amsterdam.

Kuutti, K. (1992). Identifying potential CSCW applications by means of activity theory concepts: A case example. In *Proceedings of the Conference on Computer-Supported Cooperative Work*, pages 233–240, Toronto, Canada. ACM Press.

Kuutti, K. (1995). Activity theory as a potential framework for human-computer interaction research. In Nardi, B. A., editor, *Context and Consciousness: Activity Theory and Human Computer Interaction*, chapter 2, pages 17–44. MIT Press, Cambridge, MA.

Kuutti, K. and Bannon, L. J. (1993). Searching for unity among diversity: Exploring the "interface" concept. In *Proceedings INTERCHI'93*, pages 263–268.

Kuutti, K. and Karasti, H. (1995). Supporting shared interpretation of a space of representations: A case of radiological conferences. In Cox, K., Marsh, J., and Anderson, B., editors, *First International Conference on Cognitive Technology*, pages 77–85, Hong Kong. City University of Hong Kong.

Lee, J. (1990). SIBYL: A tool for managing group decision rationale. In *Proceedings of the Conference on Computer-Supported Cooperative Work*, pages 79–92, Los Angeles, CA. ACM Press.

Leland, M. D. P., Fish, R. S., and Kraut, R. E. (1988). Collaborative document production using Quilt. In *Proceedings of the Conference on Computer-Supported Cooperative Work*, Portland, Oregon. ACM Press.

Leont'ev, A. N. (1974). The problem of activity in psychology. *Soviet Psychology*, 13(2):4–33.

Lonchamp, J. (1992). Supporting interaction activities of software processes. In Derniame, J. C., editor, *Software Process Technology: Second European Workshop*, Lecture Notes in Computer Science, Vol. 635, pages 34–54, Berlin. Springer-Verlag.

Luff, P., Heath, C., and Greatbatch, D. (1992). Tasks-in-interaction: paper and screen based documentation in collaborative activity. In *Proceedings of the Conference on Computer-Supported Cooperative Work*, pages 163–170, Toronto, Canada. ACM Press.

Luff, P., Hindmarsh, J., and Heath, C. (2000). *Workplace Studies: Recovering Work Practice and Informing Design*. Cambridge University Press.

Lynch, K. (1960). *The Image of the City*. MIT Press, Cambridge, MA.

Madsen, K. H. (1994). A guide to metaphorical design. *Communications of the ACM*, pages 57–62.

Malone, T. W., Grant, K. R., Lai, K., Rao, R., and Rosenblitt, D. A. (1989). The Information Lens: An intelligent system for information sharing and coordination. In Olson, M. H., editor, *Technological Support for Work Group Collaboration*, pages 65–88. Lawrence Erlbaum Associates, New Jersey.

Mansfield, T., Kaplan, S., Geraldine Fitzpatrick, T. P., Fitzpatrick, M., and Taylor, R. (1997). Evolving Orbit: A progress report on building locales. In *Proceedings of the ACM SIGGROUP Conference on Supporting Group Work (Group'97)*, pages 241–250, Phoenix, Arizona. ACM Press.

Mantei, M., Baecker, R. M., Sellen, A. J., Buxton, W. S., and Milligan, T. (1991). Experiences in the use of a media space. In *Proceedings Conference on Human Factors in Computing Systems CHI'91*, pages 203–208, New Orleans. ACM Press.

Martin, D., Rodden, T., Rouncefield, M., Sommerville, I., and Viller, S. (2001). Finding patterns in the fieldwork. In *Proceedings of the Seventh European Conference on Computer Supported Cooperative Work*, pages 39–58, Bonn, Germany. Kluwer Academic Publishers.

McDaniel, S. E. (1996). Providing awareness information to support transitions in remote computer-mediated collaboration. In *Common Ground: CHI'96 Conference Companion*, pages 57–58, Vancouver, Canada.

Medina-Mora, R., Winograd, T., Flores, R., and Flores, F. (1992). The action workflow approach to workflow management technology. In *Proceedings of the Conference on Computer-Supported Cooperative Work*, pages 281–288, Toronto, Canada. ACM Press.

Mi, P. and Scacchi, W. (1991). Modeling articulation work in software engineering processes. In Dowson, M., editor, *Proceedings First International Conference on the Software Process*, pages 188–201, California. IEEE Computer Society Press.

Millen, D. R. (2000). Rapid ethnography: time deepening strategies for HCI field research. In *Conference Proceedings on Designing Interactive Systems: processes, practices, methods, and techniques*, pages 280–286. ACM Press.

Mitchell, W. J. (1995). *City of Bits: Space, Place and the Infobahn*. MIT Press, Cambridge, MA.

Moran, T. P. and Anderson, R. J. (1990). The workaday world as a paradigm for CSCW design. In *Proceedings of the Conference on Computer-Supported Cooperative Work*, pages 381–393, Los Angeles, CA. ACM Press.

Nardi, B. A. (1993). *A Small Matter of Programming: Perspectives on end user computing*. MIT Press, Cambridge, MA.

Nardi, B. A., editor (1995a). *Context and Consciousness: Activity Theory and Human Computer Interaction*. MIT Press, Boston, MA.

Nardi, B. A. (1995b). Studying context: A comparison of activity theory, situated action models and distributed cognition. In Nardi, B., editor, *Context and Consciousness: Activity Theory and Human Computer Interaction*. MIT Press, Boston, MA.

Neuwirth, C., Kaufer, D., Chandhok, R., and Morris, J. (1990). Issues in the design of computer support for co-authoring and commenting. In *Proceedings of the Conference on Computer-Supported Cooperative Work*, Los Angeles, CA. ACM Press.

Nomura, T., Hayashi, K., Hazama, T., and Gudmundson, S. (1998). Interlocus: workspace configuration mechanisms for activity awareness. In *Proceedings of the ACM 1998 Conference on Computer Supported Cooperative Work*, pages 19–28. ACM Press.

Nuseibeh, B. and Easterbrook, S. (2000). Requirements engineering: A roadmap. In Finkelstein, A. C. W., editor, *The Future of Software Engineering (Companion volume to Proceedings ICSE 2000)*, pages 35–46, Limerick, Ireland. IEEE Computer Society Press.

Olson, J. S., Card, S. K., Landauer, T. K., Olson, G. M., Malone, T., and Leggett, J. (1993). Computer-supported co-operative work: research issues for the 90s. *Behaviour and Information Technology*, 12(2):115–129.

Olson, J. S., Olson, G. M., Storrosten, M., and Carter, M. (1992). How a Group-Editor changes the character of a design meeting as well as its outcome. In *Proceedings of the Conference on Computer-Supported Cooperative Work*, pages 91–98, Toronto, Canada. ACM Press.

Parsowith, S., Fitzpatrick, G., Kaplan, S., Segall, B., and Boot, J. (1998). Tickertape: Notification and communication in a single line. In *Proceedings 3rd Asia Pacific Computer Human Interaction (APCHI98)*, pages 139–144, Japan. IEEE.

Patterson, J. F., Day, M., and Kucan, J. (1996). Notification servers for synchronous groupware. In *Proceedings Conference on Computer Supported Cooperative Work CSCW96*, pages 122–129, Boston, MA. ACM Press.

Perin, C. (1991). Electronic social fields in bureaucracies. *Communications of the ACM*, 34(12):74–82.

Plowman, L., Rogers, Y., and Ramage, M. (1995). What are workplace studies for? In *Proceedings of the Fourth European Conference on Computer-Supported Cooperative Work*, pages 309–324, Stockholm, Sweden. Kluwer.

Preece, J., Rogers, Y., and Sharp, H. (2002). *Interaction Design: Beyond Human-Computer Interaction*. John Wiley and Sons.

Prinz, W. (1999). NESSIE: an awareness environment for cooperative settings. In *Proceedings 6th European Conference on Computer-Supported Cooperative Work (ECSCW'99)*, pages 391–410, Copenhagen. Kluwer Academic Publishers.

Pycock, J., Palfreyman, K., Allanson, J., and Button, G. (1998). Representing fieldwork and articulating requirements through VR. In *Proceedings of the ACM 1998 Conference on Computer Supported Cooperative Work*, pages 383–392. ACM Press.

Radjou, N. (1999). Collaboration beyond email. Technical report, The Forrester Report.

Ramduny, D., Dix, A., and Rodden, T. (1998). Exploring the design space for notification servers. In *Proceedings Conference on Computer Supported Cooperative Work (CSCW98)*, pages 227–235, Seattle, WA. ACM Press.

Reder, S. and Schwab, R. G. (1990). The temporal structure of cooperative activity. In *Proceedings of the Conference on Computer-Supported Cooperative Work*, pages 303–316, Los Angeles, CA.

Redmiles, D. (2002). Introduction to the special issue on activity theory and the practice of design. *Computer Supported Cooperative Work: The Journal of Collaborative Computing*, 11(1-2):1–11.

Rittel, H. W. J. and Webber, M. M. (1973). Dilemmas in a general theory of planning. *Policy Sciences*, 4:155–169.

Robertson, T. (1996). Embodied actions in time and place: The cooperative design of a multimedia, educational computer game. *Computer Supported Cooperative Work: The Journal of Collaborative Computing*, 5:341–367.

Robertson, T. (1997). Cooperative work and lived cognition: A taxonomy of embodied actions. In *Proceedings of the Fifth European Conference on Computer Supported Cooperative Work (ECSCW'97)*, pages 205–220, Lancaster, UK. Kluwer Academic Publishers.

Robertson, T. (2002). The public availability of actions and artefacts. *Computer Supported Cooperative Work: The Journal of Collaborative Computing*, 11(3-4):299–316.

Robinson, M. (1991). Double-level languages and co-operative working. *AI and Society*, 5:34–60.

Robinson, M. (1993a). Computer supported cooperative work: Cases and concepts. In Baecker, R. M., editor, *Readings in Groupware and Computer-Supported Cooperative Work*, pages 29–49. Morgan Kaufmann, San Mateo, CA.

Robinson, M. (1993b). Design for unanticipated use... In de Michelis, G., Simone, C., and Schmidt, K., editors, *Proceedings of the Third European Conference on Computer-Supported Cooperative Work*, pages 187–202, Milan, Italy.

Robinson, M. (1993c). Keyracks and computers: an introduction to "common artefact" in Computer Supported Cooperative Work (CSCW). *Wirtschaftsinformatik*, 35(2):157–166.

Rodden, T. (1991). A survey of CSCW systems. *Interacting with Computers*, 3(3):319–353.

Rodden, T. (1996). Populating the application: A model of awareness for cooperative applications. In *Proceedings ACM 1996 Conference on Computer Supported Cooperative Work*, pages 87–96, Chapel Hill, NC. ACM Press.

Rodden, T., Mariani, J. A., and Blair, G. (1992). Supporting cooperative applications. *Computer Supported Cooperative Work*, 1:41–67.

Rodden, T. and Schmidt, K. (1994). Putting it all together: Requirements for a CSCW platform. In Shapiro, D., Tauber, M., and Traunmüller, R., editors, *The Design of Computer-Supported Cooperative Work and Groupware Systems*. Elsevier Science, Amsterdam.

Rogers, Y. (1992). Ghosts in the network: Distributed troubleshooting in a shared working environment. In *Proceedings of the Conference on Computer-Supported Cooperative Work*, pages 346–355, Toronto, Canada. ACM Press.

Rogers, Y. (to appear 2004). The theory base of human computer interaction. In *Annual Review of Information Science and Technology ARIST*, volume 38. Information Today Inc.

Rogers, Y. and Ellis, J. (1994). Distributed cognition: an alternative framework for analysing and explaining collaborative working. *Journal of Information Technology*, 9:119–128.

Roseman, M. and Greenberg, S. (1996). TeamRooms: Network places for collaboration. In *Proceedings of ACM 1996 Conference on Computer Supported Cooperative Work*, pages 325–333, Boston MA. ACM Press.

Salvador, T. and Bly, S. (1997). Supporting the flow of information through constellations of interaction. In *Proceedings of the Fifth European Conference on Computer Supported Cooperative Work (ECSCW'97)*, pages 269–280, Lancaster. Kluwer Academic Publishers.

Sanderson, D. (1994). Mediated collaborative research: Claims, evidence, and a case study of a distributed science group. *Computer Supported Cooperative Work*, 2:41–65.

Sandor, O., Bogdan, C., and Bowers, J. (1997). Aether: An awareness engine for CSCW. In *Proceedings of the Fifth European Conference on Computer Supported Cooperative Work (ECSCW'97)*, pages 221–236, Lancaster. Kluwer Academic Publishers.

Sarin, S. K., Abbott, K. R., and McCarthy, D. R. (1992). A process model and system for supporting cooperative work. *SIGOIS Bulletin*, 12(2,3):213–224.

Schäl, T. (1996). *Workflow Management Systems for Process Organisations*. Number 1096 in Lecture notes in Computer Science. Springer-Verlag, Berlin.

Schmidt, K. (1991). Riding a tiger, or computer supported cooperative work. In *Proceedings of the Second European Conference on Computer-Supported Cooperative Work*, pages 1–16, Amsterdam, The Netherlands.

Schmidt, K. (2000). The critical role of workplace studies in CSCW. In Luff, P., Hindmarsh, J., and Heath, C., editors, *Workplace Studies: Recovering Work Practice and Informing Design*, chapter 6. Cambridge University Press.

Schmidt, K. and Bannon, L. (1992). Taking CSCW Seriously. *Computer Supported Cooperative Work*, 1:7–40.

Schmidt, K. and Simone, C. (1996). Coordination mechanisms: Towards a conceptual foundation of CSCW system design. *Computer Supported Cooperative Work: The Journal of Collaborative Computing*, 5(2-3):155–200.

Schneider, K. and Wagner, I. (1993). Constructing the 'Dossier Representatif': Computer-based information-sharing in French hospitals. *Computer Supported Cooperative Work*, 1(4):229–253.

Searle, J. R. (1969). *Speech Acts: An Essay in the Philosophy of Language*. Cambridge University Press, Cambridge, MA.

Segall, B. and Arnold, D. (1997). Elvin has left the building: A publish/subscribe notification service with quenching. In *Proceedings of Queensland AUUG Summer Technical Conference*, Brisbane, Australia. Available via http://www.dstc.edu.au/Elvin/doc/papers/auug97/AUUG97.html.

Shapiro, D. (1994). The limits of ethnography: Combining social sciences for CSCW. In *Proceedings of ACM Conference on Computer Supported Cooperative Work*, pages 417–439, Chapel Hill, NC. ACM Press.

Sharples, M. (1993). A study of breakdowns and repairs in a computer-mediated communication system. *Interacting with Computers*, 5(1):61–77.

Shepherd, A., Mayer, N., and Kuchinsky, A. (1990). Strudel - an extensible electronic conversation toolkit. In *Proceedings of the Conference on Computer-Supported Cooperative Work*, pages 93–104, Los Angeles, CA. ACM Press.

Shum, S. (1990). Real and virtual spaces: Mapping from spatial cognition to hypertext. *Hypermedia*, 2(2):133–158.

Simon, H. A. (1960). *The New Science of Management Decision*. Harper & Row, New York.

Simone, C. (1993). Integrating co-operative work supports from CHAOS perspective. *SIGOIS Bulletin*, 13(4):25.

Sohlenkamp, M. and Chwelos, G. (1994). Integrating communication, cooperation, and awareness: the DIVA virtual office environment. In *Proceedings ACM Conference on Computer Supported Cooperative Work*, pages 331–343, Chapel Hill, NC. ACM Press.

Sommerville, I. (1992). Human and social aspects in process modelling. In Derniame, J. C., editor, *Software Process Technology: Second European Workshop*, Lecture Notes in Computer Science, Vol. 635, page 33, Berlin. Springer-Verlag.

Spellam, P. J., Mosier, J. N., Deus, L. M., and Carlson, J. A. (1997). Collaborative virtual workspace. In *Proceedings of the ACM SIGGROUP Conference on Supporting Group Work (Group'97)*, pages 197–203, Phoenix, Arizona. ACM Press.

Star, S. (1991). The sociology of the invisible. In Maines, D. R., editor, *Social Organization and Social Processes: Essays in Honor of Anselm Strauss*, chapter 15, pages 265–283. Aldine De Gruyter, New York.

Star, S. L. (1989). The structure of ill-structured solutions: Boundary objects and heterogeneous distributed problem solving. In Gasser, L. and Huhns, M., editors, *Distributed Artificial Intelligence*, volume 2, pages 37–54. Pitman, London.

Strauss, A. (1961). *Images of the American City*. The Free Press of Glencoe, New York.

Strauss, A. (1978). A social world perspective. *Studies in Symbolic Interaction*, 1:119–128.

Strauss, A. (1988). The articulation of project work: An organizational process. *The Sociological Quarterly*, 29(2):163–178.

Strauss, A. (1993). *Continual Permutations of Action*. Aldine De Gruyter, New York.

Strauss, A., Fagerhaugh, S., Suczek, B., and Wiener, C. (1985). *Social Organization of Medical Work*. The University of Chicago Press, Chicago.

Strauss, A. L. (1987). *Qualitative Analysis for Social Scientists*. Cambridge University Press, Cambridge.

Suchman, L. (1994). Working relations of technology production and use. *Computer Supported Cooperative Work*, 2:21–39.

Suchman, L. (1996). Constituting shared workspaces. In Engeström, Y. and Middleton, D., editors, *Cognition and Communication at Work*, pages 35–60. Cambridge University Press, Cambridge.

Suchman, L. A. (1983). Office procedure as practical action: Models of work and system design. *ACM Transactions on Office Information Systems*, 1(4):320–328.

Suchman, L. A. (1987). *Plans and Situated Actions: The problem of human-machine communication*. Cambridge University Press.

Tolone, W. J. (1996). *Introspect: a Meta-level Specification Framework for Dynamic, Evolvable Collaboration Support*. PhD thesis, University of Illinois at Urbana-Champaign.

Tolone, W. J., Kaplan, S. M., and Fitzpatrick, G. (1995). Specifying dynamic support for collaborative work within wOrlds. In *Proceedings ACM Conference on Organizational Computing Systems (COOCS'95)*, pages 55–65, Milpitas, CA.

Trevor, J., Rodden, T., and Blair, G. (1993). COLA: A lightweight platform for CSCW. In *Proceedings of the Third European Conference on Computer-Supported Cooperative Work*, pages 15–30, Milan, Italy.

Truex III, D. P. (1991). Activity Theory and its relationship to ISD: organizational context and emergent behaviors. discussant's comments. In Nissen, H., Klein, H., and Hirschheim, R., editors, *Information Systems Research: Contemporary Approaches and Emergent Traditions*, pages 565–572. Elsevier Science Publishers B.V., Amsterdam.

Twidale, M., Rodden, T., and Sommerville, I. (1993). The designers' notepad: Supporting and understanding cooperative design. In *Proceedings of the Third European Conference on Computer Supported Cooperative Work*, pages 93–108, Milan, Italy. Kluwer Academic Publishers.

van der Aalst, W. M. P. and Berens, P. J. S. (2001). Beyond workflow management: product-driven case handling. In *Proceedings of the 2001 International ACM SIGGROUP Conference on Supporting Group Work*, pages 42–51. ACM Press.

Victor, F. and Sommer, E. (1991). Supporting the design of office procedures in the DOMINO system. In Bowers, J. M. and Benford, S. D., editors, *Studies in Computer Supported Cooperative Work: Theory, Practice and Design*, pages 119–130. North-Holland, Amsterdam.

Viller, S. and Sommerville, I. (1999). Coherence: an approach to representing ethnographic analyses in systems design. *Human-Computer Interaction*, 14(1-2):9–41.

Vygotsky, L. S. (1978). *Mind in Society*. Harvard University Press, Cambridge, MA.

Wastell, D. G. and White, P. (1993). Using process technology to support cooperative work: Prospects and design issues. In Daiper, D. and Sanger, C., editors, *CSCW in Practice: an Introduction and Case Studies*, chapter 8, pages 105–126. Springer-Verlag, London.

Wastell, D. G., White, P., and Kawalek, P. (1994). A methodology for business process redesign: experiences and issues. *Journal of Strategic Information Systems*, 3(1):23–40.

Whiting, R., Hayes, L., Fitzpatrick, G., Bryant, J., Bailey, G., Kennedy, L., and Hogg, P. (1999). TARDIS project report. In Walker, J., Whetton, S., Wise, M., and Stark, K., editors, *Proceedings HIC'99*, pages 357–359, Hobart, Australia. HISA.

Winograd, T. (1988). A language/action perspective on the design of cooperative work. *Human Computer Interaction*, 3(1):3–30.

Winograd, T. and Flores, F. (1986). *Understanding Computers and Cognition: A New Foundation for Design*. Addison Wesley, Reading.

Zager, D. (2002). Collaboration as an activity. *Computer Supported Cooperative Work: The Journal of Collaborative Computing*, 11(1-2):181–204.

Index

Abstraction
  analytic, 40
  in requirements engineering, 28
  generative, 40
  locale as shared, 91
  role of abstractions, 40–42, 217–221
  shared, 7, 151
Action-based systems, 30-32
Actions
  and interactions, 19, 52, 120
  in activity theory, 144
Activity Theory, 20–21, 144–145
  as theory in CSCW |217
Air traffic control study, 27
Airline operations room study, 84, 115
Algorithm, 28
Alpha World, 33, 83
Arenas, 114
Artefacts, 68, 129
  as mediating mechanisms, 138
  in activity theory, 20
  in distributed cognition, 22
  role of, 26
Articulation work, 25, 123
Awareness, 130
  core concept of, 26–27, 130
  event-based notification, 35, 194
  in space-based systems, 34
  mechanisms for, 134–138
  perception for, 131–134
  peripheral, 27
  provision of information for, 132–134
  technical support approaches, 34–35
  workspace, 35

Boundaries
  effect of, 94
  for room containment, 80–81
  peripheries as, 101
Boundary objects, 26, 112
Breakdowns
  locales framework analysis of, 207
  in system engineers study, 59–62, 69
  in telehealth study, 176
  trajectory, 129
Buildings
  Brand layers, 107

Centres
  individual as, 116
  locale as, 109
  principle of, 93–95
  representation in conditional matrix, 110–111
  social world purpose as, 100, 104
  versus boundaries, 80
Civic structure
  aspect description, 108–114
  in distributed research study, 164
  Orbit, 195
  in telehealth study, 179–181
Collaborative virtual environments, 33
COMIC project, 35, 83
Common artefact, 26, 118, 138
Computer Supported Cooperative Work
    See also CSCW
Concepts
  emergent from CSCW, 23–28
  making sense of for design, 43
  problems in use of, 219
  use of by practitioners, 219
Conditional matrix, 110–111, 179
Configuration management system, 17
  integration with tickertape, 197
  use by systems engineers, 73
Contextual Design, 146–147, 212
Control room study, 136
ConversationBuilder, 30, 37, 49, 78
Coordination mechanisms, 26, 118, 129, 138
CSCW
  definition of, 5

revised definition of, 6
systems design for, 29
CVS
See also Configuration management system

Designers NotePad, 38
Designing
CSCW approaches to, 28,
proposed framework use for, 149, 207
reflections on framework use, 208
social influences on, 37
Distributed cognition
as theory in CSCW, 217
overview of, 21–21
Distributed research study
collaboration features, 163-168
intro to internet exploration unit (IEU), 156–159
intro to Romany collaboration, 160–161

Elvin, 35, 194, 197–199
Embodied action
examples of, 136
taxonomy of, 136
Embodied interaction
foundational approach to, 216–217
Embodiment
physical
consequences of, 67–68, 135–137
virtual
in space-based systems, 34
consequences of lack of, 68–70
Ethnography
definition of, 16
rapid, 38
use of, 55, 155, 172
Ethnomethodology, 17, 144
Event notification systems
elvin, 195, 197–200
use of for awareness support 35, 195
Experience modelling, 39

Framework aspects
approach to use of, 148–150
overview of, 10, 92, 204
use of properties and dimensions, 97–98, 150
reflections on use, 169–170, 186–187, 205-211
use as heuristics, 151
Frameworks
mediating role for, 92–93, 215
relationship to theory, 205, 217–218

Goal
collective, 100, 219
in telehealth consultation, 175
Romany vs IEU, 163
Grounded Innovation Map, 40, 212, 215
Grounded theory
definition of, 16, 44
use of, 55, 156

Groupware
action-based systems, 30–32
CSCW systems, 5, 29
problems with, 31, 49
heuristics, 210
functional point systems, 29–30
Orbit, 189–196
space-based systems, 32–35
wOrlds, 51–53

Heuristics
groupware, 210–211
locales framework as, 92, 148

ICU
See also Telehealth study
IEU
See also Distributed research study
Individual view
aspect description, 115–120
in distributed research study, 165
in Orbit, 193–194
in systems engineers study, 65–66
in telehealth study, 178
view set, 116-118
Individuals-in-groups, 79, 115
Intensive Care Unit
description of, 172–174
See also telehealth study
Interactant
in theory of action, 19
in locales framework, 121, 122, 131
Interaction
co-located, 135
distributed, 135
See also action
Interaction trajectory
aspect description, 120–130
in distributed research study, 165–166
in telehealth study 177, 183-185
in theory of action, 19
Orbit, 195
routines, 19, 31, 128-129

Jupiter system, 33

Lancaster viewpoints, 39, 143
Language-action theory, 30, 49
Locale foundations
aspect description, 98–108
in distributed research study, 156–157, 158–159,
in Orbit, 191–193
in telehealth study, 175–176, 184
Locale
first definition of, 50–51,
framework definition of, 90
in system engineers study, 65
Locales framework
See also Framework aspects

Means
  definition of, 106–108
  in distributed research study, 158–159
Mechanisms of interaction
    See also Coordination mechanisms
Media and mechanisms, 85, 134–138
Media space, 33–34
  as place, 85
  evaluation of, 34
  reflections on use of, 83
  support for peripheral awareness, 27
Metaphor
  activity theory for design, 20
  for good design, 7
  of place, 84, 150
  of space, 81
    critique of, 79–84,
    systems based on, 32–33,
    worlds use of, 50
MIME Project, 39, 215
MUD/MOO
    See also Space-based systems
Mutuality
  aspect description, 130–139
  in distributed research study, 166–168
  in Orbit, 194–195
  in telehealth study, 178–179

Navigation, 34, 52, 112–114
NP-complete problems, 28

Office procedures study, 210
Orbit
  overview of, 189–196
  reflections on framework use, 200, 209
Ordit, 146–147

Patient record, 173
Patterns, 39, 212
Perception
  role of common 'stuff', 71, 80, 81, 130
  resources for, 132–138
    via tickertape, 199
  reversibility of, 71
  techno-centric approaches to, 131
    See also Awareness
    See also Mutuality
Peripheries
  as differentiated for social world, 101–102
  and centres, 93
Personas, 213
Perspective
  in civic structure, 108–109
  in social world, 64–66, 104
  of individual, 115
  principle of, 93–95
  trajectory, 121
Pervasive computing, 213
Phenomenology, 71, 216
Place
  from space to, 84–85
  locale as, 91
  versus room, 79–80
Presence
  in mutuality, 132
  in Orbit, 194
  physical, 67–68
  virtual, 68–70
Process support systems
    See also Action-based systems

Qualitative methods
  definition of, 44
  in CSCW, 16
  use of, 55, 155, 172
Quantitative methods
  definition of, 44

Reflective CSCW toolkits, 37
Requirements engineering, 29
Residual objects, 114
Resources
  definition of, 90
  in locale foundations, 106–107
Role
  in social worlds, 102
  use of for awareness, 138
Routine, 19, 31, 128, 210

Satisficing, 4, 13
Satisficing strategies, 71, 185
Scenario planning, 210
Shared abstraction
  locale as, 91
    reflections on use of, 211–214
    See also Abstraction
Site, 104–106
Site and means
  in distributed research study, 158–159, 166-168
  in locale foudnations, 104–108
  in systems engineers study, 50, 65
  in theory of action, 19, 50
  use of for locale, 90–91
    See also site
    See also means
Situated action, 17, 24
  goal of support for, 37
Social world
  in distributed research study, 156–157, 163–164
  in locales framework, 99–103
  in system engineers study, 64–66
  in telehealth study, 175–176, 183
  in theory of action, 19, 50
Socio-technical systems, 4
Soft Systems Methodology, 146–147
Space-based systems
  2-D, 32
  3-D, 33

awareness in, 34
embodiment in, 34
experiences with, 82–83
media space, 33–34
motivation for, 81
MUDS, 33
navigation, 34, 52
Space
critique of, 79–83
rationale for metaphor of, 81
physical
mutuality mechanisms, 135
workspace characteristics, 67–68
relationship to locale, 104–105
simulation approach, 81–82
virtual
mutuality mechanisms, 137
workspace characteristics, 68–71
Spatial model of interaction, 35
model of awareness, 137
Sue's screen workspace, 56, 63, 65, 80
Symbolic interaction, 18
System engineers study
breakdowns, 59, 69
CSG introduction, 55
elock group, 61–62, 65, 80
physical workspace, 67–68
scenario, 58, 64, 69
social world perspectives, 64–66
student computer labs, 60–61
virtual locale, 65–66
virtual workspace, 68–70

Tame problems, 28
algorithm as example of, 28
definition of, 4
software as, 23, 208
workflow models as, 30
Teamwave Workplace, 210
Technomethodology, 37
Telehealth study
consultation practices, 174, 183
Theory of action, 18, 50, 62, 151, 206
motivation for use of, 43, 90
Theory
common approaches in CSCW, 17–23
role in CSCW, 22, 217–218
Tickertape, 194, 197–199, 209
Tickertape, 197, 209
Time-space matrix, 24, 29
Travelling salesperson problem, 28

UML, 39
Understanding
communication of, 38
core concepts for, 23–28
methods for, 16–17, 38–39, 55, 146
proposed framework use for, 148–149, 205–206
reflections on framework use for, 168–170, 186–187, 206–207
technical influences on, 37–40,
theoretical approaches to, 17–23
Unit of analysis
activity theory, 20, 144
in distributed cognition system, 22
locale as, 9, 90, 211

Video-conferencing
in distributed research, 168
in telehealth study, 183, 186

Wicked problems, 41, 89, 147
definition of, 4
design paradox, 23
Workaday world, 81, 89, 98
definition of, 27
multiple locale views as, 118
Workflow management systems
See also Action-based systems
Workshops
use of framework in, 209, 212, 214
wOrlds
as basis for orbit, 189–190
mismatches with systems engineers, 78–79
motivation for, 49
room in, 51–52, 79
tour of, 51–53

MIX
Papier aus verantwortungsvollen Quellen
Paper from responsible sources
FSC® C105338
FSC
www.fsc.org

If you have any concerns about our products,
you can contact us on
ProductSafety@springernature.com

In case Publisher is established outside the EU,
the EU authorized representative is:
Springer Nature Customer Service Center GmbH
Europaplatz 3, 69115 Heidelberg, Germany

Printed by Libri Plureos GmbH
in Hamburg, Germany